POSITIVE CHRISTIANITY

IN THE THIRD REICH

Published by Sacra Press.

Cajus Fabricius, *Positive Christianity in the Third Reich: Including the 28 Theses of the German Christians and Miscellaneous Documents by Cajus Fabricius.*
The 28 Theses of the German Christians.
Translated by & used with permission from Corey J. Mahler
Walter Grundmann, *The 28 Theses of the Saxon*
© 2025 by Sacra Press

Sacra Press
www.sacrapress.com
contact@sacrapress.com or sacrapress@gmail.com

First edition.
Printed in the United States of America.

Go to www.sacrapress.com for more Reformed, right-wing, & classic books, to
become a subscriber and get perks, and to enjoy alternative Christian music of Psalms
& Saints.

Godspeed and goodwar.

POSITIVE CHRISTIANITY

IN THE THIRD REICH

BY

CAJUS FABRICIUS

INCLUDING
THE 28 THESES OF
THE GERMAN CHRISTIANS

AND
MISCELLANEOUS DOCUMENTS OF
CAJUS FABRICIUS

SACRA PRESS

SACRA AD GLORIAM DEI

CONTENTS

LETTER TO LAMMERS JUNE 23 1940

AFFIDAVIT JULY 16/17 1946

AFFIDAVIT JULY 18/22 1946

APPENDIX

THE 28 THESES OF THE GERMAN CHRISTIANS EXPLAINED
by Walter Grundmann

POSITIVE CHRISTIANITY

IN THE THIRD REICH

BY

CAJUS FABRICIUS

Originally published in Germany, 1937

FOREWORD

THERE IS MUCH MISCONCEPTION in the world today with respect to the position of Christianity in the Third Reich, opinion being rife that an anti-Christian attitude or paganism is at the moment predominant in Germany. These were the considerations which led me to issue an English edition of my book: "Positives Christentum im neuen Staat."

This book is in no way an official statement. The only official book on National Socialism is Adolf Hitler's "Mein Kampf." Official documents are also "The Programme of the National Socialistic Party" and the Laws of the State. I, for my part, have simply endeavored as a theologian to give in these pages a clear and scientific exposition of the substance of Christianity in its relations to the substance of National Socialism. The point of view, however, thus set forth in this little book is not only my own, but is shared by millions of German people who are real Christians and at the same time good National Socialists, unswervingly loyal to their Führer, Adolf Hitler.

The German edition of this book was published in 1935. Since then, the German situation, the fundamental principles of the National Socialistic State, and the attitude of the Fuhrer towards Christianity, have remained unchanged. A few days before writing these lines, the Führer in his speech to the Reichstag on 30th January said, that in all humility he thanked Almighty God for His grace manifested in the uprising of the German Volk. He said, too, in speaking of his personal experiences that he had had three unusual friends nearly all his life: in his youth, poverty; then, sorrow at the collapse of his People; and finally, anxiety for the Reich. This is the Führer's unchanged attitude, one conforming both to a Christian and a heroic figure.

Thus may this little book serve to spread the truth throughout the world. I hope that my attempt at its expression will be understood abroad, and I should be glad to receive any comments on what I have said from friends in other countries.

D. CAJUS FABRICIUS
30 Händel Allee, Berlin NW 87.
February 1937

INTRODUCTION

"WE DEMAND LIBERTY FOR all religious denominations in the State, so far as they are not a danger to it and do not militate against the morality and moral sense of the German race. The Party as such, stands for positive Christianity, but does not bind itself in the matter of creed to any particular confession. It combats the Jewish-materialist spirit within and without us, and is convinced that our nation can achieve permanent health from within only on the principle: The Common Interest Before Self-Interest."

Such is Point 24 of the Programme of the German National Socialistic Party. Since 1920, this has been the unchanged and unwavering guiding principle of the Movement with respect to its attitude towards religion, and, since 1933, the inviolable expression of what is to be as law to the whole German nation. Adolf Hitler, its Führer and Chancellor, has repeatedly affirmed this article, especially the main clause relating to Positive Christianity. This was particularly the case in the three notable speeches made by him in the year 1934, namely, on January 30th, August 17th, and 26th. On these three solemn occasions, the Führer stated in words that left no doubt as to their meaning, that National Socialism affirmed Positive Christianity.

Moreover, as a further explanation of his statement, Adolf Hitler declared that, by Positive Christianity, he meant the

Christianity of the two great Churches: the Evangelical and the Roman Catholic, both of which are represented in Germany. He also called upon these Christian Churches to do everything in their power to make the moral forces of the Gospel Message effectual influences in the life of the German nation. At the same time, however, he made it perfectly plain that he had nothing in common with "people in bear-skins," with those, namely, who, recalling the old Germanic tribes, would foist neo-pagan cult experiments upon the German *Volk*. On other occasions too, as for instance in his historically remarkable speech of May 21st, 1935, the Führer emphatically rejected the godlessness of Bolshevism, contrasting it with the fact that in National Socialistic Germany the Churches have not been turned into places of secular amusement. And even if the Führer does speak on occasions such as these of a new National Socialistic *Weltanschauung*, he means neither a new religion nor a new godlessness, but simply everything that is the result of national consciousness, of the ties of comradeship and of the heroic attitude of the National Socialistic German with respect to his mode of life, and his views of the world surrounding him. To these may be added everything needed for the reconstruction of man's inner life, and this includes, in no small degree, the forces of Positive Christianity.

Thus the fundamental lines to be followed are defined here clearly and simply. There remains, however, the task of tracing the programme of National Socialism with regard to religion m every possible direction, and with attention to the minutest details. Hitherto this has not been attempted in a manner sufficiently comprehensive and exhaustive. And yet, how vitally important it is to form a picture of the religion of the German *Volk* in all its details, and to consider the development of its religious forces in various directions.

And just in an era of new beginnings, such as we are now experiencing, it is indeed doubly important for religious principles to be worked out on a perfectly clear basis, and in every possible direction. For during times such as these, when the inner life of a nation is in the process of being revolutionized, how easy it is for a certain confusion of mind to arise, whereby many a trend of thought has come to the fore that had once already existed, only, however, to fall into oblivion where it has remained until now, when the auspicious moment for its reappearance and the realization of its aims would appear to have arrived. Efforts of this kind are remarkably prevalent at the present time, and, in consequence, a certain religious unrest has seized hold of our *Volk*, most disturbing to the peaceful reconstruction of our new *Reich*, leading as it does men's minds astray, and so placing difficulties in the path of national unification.

Since this is the situation in which our spiritual life finds itself today, it is all the more necessary to state with simple directness the real attitude adopted by National Socialism towards religion, and to consider it in detail from every point of view. An exposition such as this, however, can only be undertaken by an expert, that is to say by one who is an authority on the subject, and as a researcher has devoted himself to the work of investigating the Christian religion—in short, a theologian, and at the same time a convinced National Socialist.

It was the need for such a treatise that brought me to the fore. I am conscious of a sense of responsibility to God and to my own conscience, both in my capacity as theological expert on confessional questions, and as an Evangelical Christian, I felt it incumbent on me to proclaim the truth in all publicity. As an official of the State and as a political leader within the Party I am bound by a two-fold oath to the Führer of my *Volk*. But my religious and political duties do not clash, nor do they necessitate any inward struggle, but rather the one supplements the other, and both stand together in complete harmony. Indeed, they do even more than this: in my own life and thought, Christianity and National Socialism are closely knit together. And just because I am a Christian and a theologian, I felt compelled to put on the "brown shirt." Just because my inmost being is filled with the most sacred feeling of responsibility, I have felt for years past a sense of duty towards my *Volk* in its time of distress. For this reason therefore, my path had perforce to lead me into the movement which has been called upon these days to rescue my *Volk* from need. My life during the past decisive years has been mapped out accordingly.

Conscious of my responsibility as a Christian and as a Professor of Theology in the early days when National Socialism was struggling to assert itself, I became one of the founders and pioneers of the Students' Labourservice Corps. Community life, such as I experienced in labourcamps with my students and unemployed Youth of all classes, made me one of Adolf Hitler's most loyal supporters. Not primarily through hearing speeches, or reading books and newspapers was I won for the National Socialistic cause, but rather through my experience as an independent leader of the labour camp with all the heavy responsibilities connected with this task that also included strenuous physical work. Thus, I was formed into a National Socialist in the smithy of life, having become one of the great comradeship not only with all my heart and mind, but with flesh and blood as well.

My own personal attitude, therefore, gives me every right, indeed, makes it my duty to publish an expert opinion on the principles of National Socialism with respect to religion. As an expert I shall adhere strictly to facts, having no intention of obtruding any personal theories or pet ideas that might tend to divert attention from the main line of thought. Rather shall I show with unwavering consistency how the attitude of National Socialism to the Christian religion, as evidenced in the Party Programme and in the Führer's own words, has been determined both by the substance of the Christian religion and by the substance of National Socialism. But while keeping my own personal opinions in the background, I shall, on the other hand, also refrain from bringing forward the philosophical ideas or fantastic utterances of other writers, who may perhaps have grasped only a part or even nothing at all of the meaning of Christianity or National Socialism, and are thus guilty of a certain dilletantism particularly dangerous in matters of such serious import. And least of all am I inclined to make use of the views on *Weltanschauung*, laid down by these writers, who, half converted to National Socialism as they may be, are still partly in the toils of the prejudices of the liberalistic and marxistic era, being caught up, so to say, in the spirit of those epochs, which, known as the ages of Reason, Romanticism, and Technics, placed their mark on European thought from the 18th to the beginning of the 20th century.

Both forces, however, Christianity as well as National Socialism, will be dealt with by me as present realities, more with respect to what they are today, than with respect to their historical development and growth. For in this case we are not primarily interested in what has been and now is no more, but we wish to view the present and from it cast a glance into the future. We do not wish to travel far afield but prefer to consider what is alive today and close at hand.

This little book was written with the general purpose of assisting in the work of reconstruction, and of promoting peace and unanimity. My exposition has perhaps its combative side, too, but that is simply in order to clear up misunderstandings and smooth away difficulties. Where I am polemical, it is absolutely impersonal, least of all would I attack fellow Christians and National Socialistic comrades. I fight against thoughts only, but here, too, not against systems of thought expounded in literary work of one kind or another, but I attack those ideas that are so as to say in the air and make their influence more or less strongly felt, or give hints of it only in existing trends of thought.

Such is the thought underlying my treatment of the question of Positive Christianity as the foundation of National Socialism. It has been found advisable to divide the exposition itself into two main parts. The first subject of investigation to be dealt with concerns the National Socialistic policy with respect to Religion. Conclusions will thereby be drawn from the Party Programme applicable to the general attitude of the Party and the State towards Church life. In a second exposition, the inner associations will be treated of, and it will be shown how the spiritual forces of Christianity must needs have a great influence in the life of the newly awakened German *Volk*.

PART ONE:

THE RELIGIOUS POLICY
OF NATIONAL SOCIALISM

T O FORESTALL ALL MISCONCEPTIONS we must show what religious policy would contradict the very essence of National Socialism before we judge of what is meant by the affirmation of Christianity in National Socialism.

I: WHAT WE REJECT

1. Liberalism

The whole attitude of National Socialism shows a striking difference on comparison with all that is to be included in the name of Liberalism. Every singling out of human individuals, every separation of interests, confusion of opinions, every irregular appearance of selfish interests, everything that calls forth and emphasizes differences between individuals and between various groups, is repellent to the spirit of National Socialism, since it disturbs the unity of the *Volk*, breaks up the team spirit and menaces the powerful solidarity of the nation.

And least of all would it be compatible with National Socialism were a form of religious Liberalism to find a place in Germany, that is to say, the springing up of several hundreds or thousands of religious societies all at liberty to represent not only the old traditional teachings but also strange and questionable doctrines, and to abuse and accuse one another of heresy. A religious Liberalism of this kind would be far more dangerous than Liberalism in secular affairs, because Religion always lays claim to the whole individual, and shuts off the individual person and individual groups from the world outside far more completely than do secular interests.

For this reason therefore, the religious policy of National Socialism is absolutely apposed to the principle "pronouncing Religion to be a private affair," laid down by the Social Democrats, and which was derived from liberalistic ideas, in the hope of dealing a blow at the power of Religion by breaking up the Churches into private societies. In National Socialistic Germany, Religion is not a private matter at all, it concerns the whole *Volk*. True, one can ascribe the religious policy of National Socialism to the utterance of Frederick the Great: "Here, each must be saved after his own fashion"—but these words spoken by the great king, and which were to become proverbial, referred only to the peaceful intercourse between the Evangelical and Roman Catholic Christians in his country, and must not be understood to mean an unbridled Liberalism.

But again, it must not be argued here, that the Party Programme itself allows liberty to all religious beliefs. Religious liberty there most certainly is in the National Socialistic State. This does not mean, however, that a wild growth of private religious opinions and a breaking up of the Churches into groups is desirable. What is implied is simply this: no one is forced in the

Third *Reich* to adopt any form of Religion. And again, no one is to be compelled by the State to join any one of the great Churches, or to withdraw from it. Finally, it implies that within a religious body, the many individuals who go to form it are not to be confined within the narrow limits of some form of belief. On the contrary: as everywhere in the newly awakened German *Volk* powers are allowed free play, those of creative personalities in particular being permitted to develop freely and vigorously, so within the great Churches as in every religious community, the characteristic features of personal piety will not be suppressed, but will be given every opportunity for vigorous development, in so far as they do not sow the seeds of discord, or cause confusion of mind and so prove a menace to the spirit of unanimity prevailing in the *Volk*.

But the anti-liberalistic attitude of National Socialism in matters pertaining to Religion has another aspect. The Liberal Era had a favourite scheme and sought to realize it in various ways: it was "Separation of Church and State." This catch-word was not only based on the idea of the individual and private nature of Religion, but also on the view that a distinct line must be drawn between Religion and secular culture. This universal letting loose of individual interests resulted in a splitting up of culture in its various domains, and a limited, one-sided devotion of individuals and groups of individuals to special cultural spheres. Indeed, these divisions in cultural life even led individuals in their philosophy of life to specialize in one particular domain of culture, whereby all other spheres were either rejected or were looked upon as of no importance. Thus there arose the practical materialism or utilitarianism of Marx and his followers, which only acknowledged technico-economical culture as of any value; there were others, art-lovers to whom only the world of beauty meant anything at all, and who, engrossed by it, had lost all understanding for other things; there were men of science and circles of intelligentsia who only appreciated intellect, despising everything else; there were humane moralists, in whose eyes the highest value of all was the moral or right relationship between man and man, and who were only slightly interested, or not at all, in the other spheres of life.

This condition of separate and limited standpoints must also include the principle: "Separation of Church and State." For this phrase may be so interpreted as to mean that occupation with things temporal is to be separated from occupation with things spiritual, because it is thought that the bulk of mankind is engrossed with temporal things and does not concern itself with what is sacred. And if one goes on to presuppose that the State is without Religion, that is to say, it concerns itself chiefly with secular interests, the principle may be inferred: "Separation of Church and State."

This principle, however, is totally opposed to the nature of National Socialism. The whole meaning of the new life in Germany as revealed in National Socialism is man's desire to leave behind him the gulfs and schisms in cultural spheres, all the specialization, mutual distrust, suspicion, and hostility, and to form instead an organic, living, co-ordinated culture, which, notwithstanding its manifoldness, is yet permeated with the one spirit common to all. The various spheres of culture must naturally be differentiated. We are fully aware that the physical useful in technico-economical culture is different from the aesthetic-beautiful, and again, that the investigation of truth is a thing by itself, just as is care for the community of mankind, [and] also that Religion as the surrender to the superhuman life of the Godhead differentiates itself from all connections and activities which bind us to human and temporal things. But at the same time, we know that the differentiation between the spheres of life must on no account mean a severance or schism, but that they have their common roots and foundations in human nature, and in the nature of things, and are further united and interwoven by countless reciprocal effects. And the National Socialistic State is no "pagan" holding aloof from the Church as if from the sphere of what is sacred. On the contrary, the State is the lawful organization of the living *Volk*, of the same *Volk* that possesses the whole of temporal culture, and with it, Religion. In the *Volk* too, the organization of the State must naturally be in living, reciprocal connection with the organizations of all the other spheres of culture, including the Church.

From the standpoint of National Socialism, therefore, it is impossible to assert that the new movement has nothing to do with Religion owing to its political character, and that the State must stand aloof, not concerning itself with ecclesiastical matters, just as the Church keeps aloof from State affairs. A religious policy with this view as its basic principle would remind one of the French Revolution in the 18th century, but certainly not of the National Uprising in Germany in the year 1933.

A policy of aloofness and alienation with regard to the relations between Church and State would indeed be most disastrous. It would open up a fatal chasm between churchfolk and the worldly-minded, and cause a front to be formed at least as dangerous, if not more so than the former gulf between the bourgeois and the proletariat. And, moreover, in a Church obscured from the light of publicity, dark places would be created, where, under the protecting mantle of sacred things, revolutionary elements could foregather and threaten the German *Volk* and all that it holds sacred with dissolution and destruction.

2. Attacks on Christianity

More alien to the essence of National Socialism than the
separation of Church and State is any attack on Christianity.
Antagonism to the Christian Religion is much more compatible
with the spirit of Jewish materialism rejected by the Party
Programme, and closely corresponds to the spirit of Bolshevism,
the deadly foe of National Socialism. If as in Marxism, material
pleasures and manual labour are to be regarded as the highest
values, and time-honoured institutions are to be trampled under
foot, while spiritual values are held to be merely illusive
phantoms, and it is considered unworthy for any human being to
believe in a higher life, then, it must naturally follow that
Churches are blown up, priests deprived of their rights or even
murdered, the propagation of religious beliefs forbidden, and all
suspected of piety subjected to suffering. National Socialism, on
the other hand, as a Movement emanating from within and
testifying at every turn how great is the power of the spirit,
perpetually striving to awaken man's noblest instincts, summoning
him to obedience, to respect, to self-abnegation and to sacrifice,
would contradict itself, nay more, it would destroy itself, were it in
any way to promote anti-Christian activities, or to tolerate such
machinations even in their very beginnings. Marxism coined the
phrase that Socialism is as much opposed to Christianity as fire is
to water, and it may here be said of National Socialism; its
relationship to anti-Christian activities is as that of fire to water.

And if there should still be a few individuals in Germany today,
who, with regard to this point, prefer to swim in the old channel of
the last era, scoffing at priests and devout people after the manner
of Marxist free-thinkers, looking askance at anyone professing to

be a Christian, even preventing him perhaps from attending public worship, and looking upon the clergy of a Christian Church as second-rate citizens, then it is a sign that such people have not yet grasped the significance of the new era and are rather to be considered as a grave menace to the peace and inner strength of the German *Volk*.

But in passing another misconception must be removed. This refers to the relationship between Christianity and Judaism. Long before the rise of National Socialism there were certain national, literary circles amongst the *Intelligentsia* of the upper middle classes of pre-war days, who, for the sake of their German nationality, believed it necessary to reject Christianity as being historically connected with Judaism. On the appearance of National Socialism and its attacks on the Jewish supremacy in our *Volk*, these *Intelligentsia* thought the moment had arrived for a similar attack on Christianity. This point of view is definitely rejected by the clause referred to in the Party Programme, and it is unnecessary to examine it further here. Besides it is clear that the spirit of the Christian Faith has nothing to do with the Judaism we National Socialists are combating. Our attacks are directed against the present-day Judaism, the ally of the powers of destruction, which, in all secrecy, through the agency of banks, *bourses*, and press seeks to rule the world. We oppose the mixture of our race with that of the Jews. Moreover, we have liberated our *Volk* from the dominating power of Judaism, and are constantly on the defensive against all attempts to renew this supremacy. But nothing is further from our intention than to confuse the spirit of this kind of Judaism with the Christian Religion, and to attack the Christian Faith as "Jewish." Such an act would be in absolute contradiction both to the essence of Christianity and to the spirit and Programme of Nation Socialism.

3. Substitutes for Religion

National Socialism has as little desire to found a new religion as it has to attack Christianity. Attempts of this kind must rather be considered a menace to the unity of the *Volk* demanded by National Socialism. It is already an historical disaster that the German *Volk* is fated to have not only one but two great Christian bodies, the Evangelical and Roman Catholic Churches. Wise statesmanship of the highest order, and a personal desire for peace, is constantly demanded in order to preserve the inner solidarity of the *Volk* under such conditions. But how increasingly great is the difficulty when a third religion confronts the two great Christian Churches, and in opposing them claims the right of calling itself the one and only future religion of the German *Volk*. The difficulty however, becomes a very grave danger when the exponents of such a new religion declare their ideas to be the philosophy of life in actual agreement with the spirit of the German race and with National Socialism.

If we investigate the substance of the new religion that would appear to be offered to the German People as a substitute for Christianity, we are filled with a deep and genuine dismay. First of all, we get the impression that it is not the case of one religion but of a great many, and men of learning as well as various writers dispute as to which of their systems is to become the true spiritual food of the German *Volk*. It is to be expected, however, that these learned men and writers will continue to disagree as they have hitherto been doing, and so we have a picture that is both bewildering and disintegrated, and is likely to remain so. Thus there is danger of not only a third but of a fourth, fifth, and even more cults being founded, each of which lays claim to be the only true religion of the *Volk*.

Neither are the doctrines expounded in these new religions at all promising. Some are simply echoes of Christianity, others and to a greater extent, are reminders of the philosophy of the rationalists with their glorification of humanity and reason, or of Nietzsche's naturalism with his deification of those who are in communion with Nature and are critical of culture. Sometimes, too, there is a revival of Indian ideas of self-redemption. All these beliefs, however, are but pale wraiths lacking the force, the depth, and the richness originally peculiar to those thoughts and systems. Neither is surrender to what is supernatural and superhuman the predominant feature of the new cults; rather do we find a glorification of Nature and of man in particular, who is held to be sufficient unto himself and capable of attaining perfection by himself.

The basic principle of these new cults is accordingly the same as in the case of the older movements of free-thought and free religious beliefs of the last epoch. The only difference is that these same ideas which were considered applicable to mankind in general are now spoken of as being essentially Germanic.

All such aims are contradictory to National Socialism.

The Führer, with the exemplary modesty characteristic of his whole being, decisively forbids any honour to be paid to him which is fitting for God alone, and all genuine National Socialists follow his example. When the Führer states on occasion that he "has faith" in the German *Volk*, and when we National Socialists profess "our faith" in the Führer, that does not mean the conception of a new religion; it is simply a confession of trust and confidence between man and man, and is included in our trust in

God, but is by no means that trust in the Divine Power itself. We are well aware, and the Führer himself has made frequent mention of it, too, that we are only instruments in the hand of Divine Providence, however great that human endeavour may be which has been so effectual in the great turn of history we are now experiencing, and which is still effectual. And we likewise refuse to deify those earthly forces which laid the foundation of the German uprising and are still basic principles. Race, blood, soil, freedom, honour are to us high values, and it is of lasting worth that National Socialism has so firmly impressed the supremacy and importance of these forces and virtues upon an uprooted mankind and a sick *Volk*.

We will not and dare not relax our enthusiasm for those sublime things. But we know that such things, sublime and glorious as they may be, are yet of this earth and are human, so that, although we may consider them as willed and created by God, we must not look upon them as supreme divinities themselves.

These facts require constant reiteration in the full light of publicity, not only for the sake of the matter itself, but also because we know that in other countries the enemies of new Germany are busily engaged in spreading slanderous reports as to how Germany is in the thralldom of paganism, and that Christians are being persecuted by the State for their Faith's sake. News of this alarming description are not only reported by Christians, but are also propagated by Jews and pagans; and the Foreign Press, if at all hostile to Germany, wallows in such reports and gives them full publicity, particularly in those papers that in past years completely ignored ecclesiastical questions. These slanders are published with the intention of prejudicing Christians of every other land against Germany so that they may close their ranks and form as solid a front as possible against our *Volk*.

We must defend ourselves against such defamations. Today, the German People amongst the nations of the earth is the strongest bulwark against all the powers of darkness threatening the overthrow of Christian culture. Indeed we may say: the powers of dissolution and disintegration, that with sinister and diabolical strength are striving for mastery in the world today, are nowhere so effectually repulsed as in National Socialistic Germany. For this reason all foreign nations who fight us as being non-Christian in their eyes, find themselves in very tortuous and most dangerous paths, and, in so far as they are Christians themselves, combat, in their appalling delusion, those very things for which they would stake their lives.

In view of this situation predominant in the world at present, it is doubly important for us to defend National Socialism unceasingly and untiringly against the defamatory reports that it favours paganism, be it openly or secretly, and desires on the strength of its authority to introduce a substitute for the Christian religion.

II: WHAT WE AFFIRM

1. Positive Christianity

ABANDONING NEGATIVES, LET US now ask the question: what is the religion upon which the new life in Germany is to be constructed in accordance with the basic principles of National Socialism? What is the strong, life-giving spiritual food upon which the soul of the newly awakened *Volk* is to feed? The answer is: Positive Christianity.

But what is Positive Christianity? It means, at any rate, the religion that has grown and become as one with the spirit of the German nation throughout the history of centuries. The utterances of the Führer have made this perfectly clear, and undoubtedly it is in accordance with the essence of National Socialism. For everywhere this Movement forms connections with all the noblest powers it discovers and knows to be national in the German spirit. Thus it is perfectly natural that the new Movement should seek contact with the religion so intimately woven by countless living associations into the history of our *Volk* both in past history and the present day.

"Positive" means here as everywhere "the real thing," but in the case of a spiritual power like religion, it means what is a historical reality. A special meaning, however, within this general interpretation may be given to the word "positive," and with it to the term "Positive Christianity." The "real thing" may be understood as something opposed to what is artificial, supposed, or pretended. Thus a difference has been made between the positive, historical religion and a rational, philosophical trend of thought.

Taken in this sense, to profess "Positive Christianity" would be to reject all systems of freethought and free religion together with all would-be rationalistic interpretations of Christianity. Again, "Positive Christianity" may be taken to mean what is universally known as "practical Christianity," which is a Christianity not exhausting itself in expressing convictions of faith, but one active in loving one's neighbour. But the sense of the word "positive" must not be strained too much in interpreting "Positive Christianity." A political Party Programme, like that of the National Socialists, has most certainly not taken upon itself the task of pronouncing a limited and special type of Christianity to be its religion. Moreover, the Programme itself adds that it "does not bind itself in the matter of creed to any particular confession." Hence, generally speaking, it is obvious that nothing else except the historical and real Christian Religion is meant, which, as the living religion of the *Volk*, cannot be confined within a narrow scheme, but encloses within itself individual opinions and points of view in abundance.

2. Two Great Churches

In Germany, however, while considering the situation of Christianity, we are confronted with an important fact of which we have already made brief mention, but must necessarily spend a moment or so in its further consideration, because it would appear to place special difficulties in the way of National Socialism. It is the duality of the great Churches. Some two thirds of the German nation belong to the Evangelical Church, and about one third to the Roman Catholic Church. But National Socialism wishes to consolidate the nation in all its parts into one strong inner unity. How is this to be accomplished when in its inner life, that is, in religion, the nation is divided into two great communities, one of which is the largest organization in the country next to the Reich itself, and the other forms an organization that is mainly represented in other countries?

The answer to this is as follows: National Socialism has not the intention of forcing every German to become Evangelical, nor to insist on his conversion to Roman Catholicism: neither does it intend by the authority of the State to establish one Church representing a mixture of both creeds. All such measures would be in sharp opposition to the recognized basic principle of confessional liberty, were attempts to be made to violate the consciences of many millions of people. Besides, all National Socialists, who are at all conscious of their responsibility, know enough of history and human nature to see that any attempts of this kind would lead to stubborn opposition. Rather must the differences between the great Churches be left as noble rivalry in the spiritual arena.

How the destinies of the two great Churches will be further shaped in the coming decades and centuries is not for the State nor for the Party as such to determine. It must be left to the great Guide of History to develop the inner life of our *Volk* in this respect according to His will, and never must pressure of any kind whatsoever be practiced by the State or by the Party; reckoning as they do with facts they must simply tolerate the co-existence of two great Churches in Germany. At the same time, however, they must so exercise their influence that the duality of the Churches should not be prejudicial to the inner peace of the nation. Let there be liberty of religious discussion, but at the same time care must be taken to see that freedom is united with love and dignity, to the avoidance of malice, slander, and suspicion, and that even the most important debates be carried on as between experts and in a brotherly spirit.

The difficulty presented by confessional duality cannot be avoided by simply declaring that both State and Party ought officially to disregard the fact of confessional diversity. A standpoint such as this would be absolutely opposed to the essence of National Socialism. Indeed, it would be exactly the point of view adopted by Liberalism already rejected by us as being anti-National Socialistic, and which we must always continue to reject. No real German, be he an Evangelical or a Roman Catholic Christian, would ever think for a moment of giving up or of denying his Christian sentiments; and no one may demand of him anything approaching the nature of such a step. Least of all would National Socialism tolerate such unreasonable requests so contrary to its nature, and desiring as it does the whole personality and not a character so pieced together that it can be divided at will. Further, it desires an organically uniform culture, and not what would appear externally a collection of cultural domains, each capable, as it were, of being enclosed within walls and of locking itself behind barred doors.

The path of National Socialism leads in the opposite direction. In every domain of German life, multiform characteristics of individuals, the diversity of groups, and the plurality of spiritual trends of thought are duly appreciated; but everything is brought from out the spheres of secrecy, treachery, malice, and contradiction to the full light of day and brotherly understanding.

And so in the German nation today and in all National Socialistic associations, the difference between Evangelical and Roman Catholic Christians may not be hidden or suppressed, and no one may cast suspicion on, or refuse to recognise another because he professes a different creed, or prefers another form of religious practice or methods of Church organization. This very difference ought to make him all the more respected and appreciated as a German and a Christian brother.

Much might be said in this connection about the substance of the two great types of Christianity and their attitude towards National Socialism, which, owing to their diversity of character, is obviously not quite the same. But this is not the place for me to deal with the differences existing between Evangelical and Roman Catholic Christians, since the task I have set myself here is the exposition of the basic principles of National Socialism with respect to Christianity as expressed in its spirit and in its Party Programme. For the rest, I am writing now as an Evangelical theologian heedless of confessional strife, and leave it to Roman Catholic theologians to do the same. I am, however, convinced that the survey of the principles of Christianity which I as an Evangelical theologian have set forth in these pages will be approved by very many Roman Catholic Christians, dealing as it does with fundamental truths, that, in spite of differences, are affirmed by countless Roman Catholic Christians.

3. The German Evangelical Church

The attention of Party and State is naturally directed in a high degree to the Evangelical Church, comprising as it does more than 40 millions of German citizens in the Reich itself; and, beyond the frontiers where it forms the soul of Germans living abroad in all parts of the world, it numbers at least another 10 millions. This Church deserves the name of Church of the German *Volk* more than any other religious community. Outwardly, it is one and the same with the great bulk of the People, and not only this, its inner life is most intimately bound up with the inner life of the German nation. This Church, therefore, is one of the great living facts confronting every National Socialist at all conscious of his responsibility and who considers in all seriousness the present and future position of his *Volk*.

In this great Evangelical Church, there is a certain multiformity of opinions and trends of thought. Here are to be found Christians of a more conservative turn of mind and others who hold more progressive views; there are Pietists who devote themselves more than others to the practice of piety; others, again, there are whose devoutness is most closely linked with secular life, either as workers serving their fellows in the social sphere or else by connecting their faith chiefly with the questions of intellectual life; and again, amongst these are to be found those who "rationalistically" trust to human understanding for their conception of God, and others who "dialectically" emphasize the separation of the Divine from the human, as the infinite from the finite. These diversities of opinion, however, amongst those holding Evangelical views, are of considerably less importance than the gulf between Protestant and Roman Catholic Christianity. Neither has their duration been that of centuries as in the case of the separation of the two great Churches, but they come and go with decades and generations. Incidentally, a multiformity of views is consistent with the essence of a truly great and living National Church.

Another important point is that in Germany such differences of opinion have hardly ever been known to lead to final disintegration and to the formation of Free Churches, unless foreign influences have made themselves felt, as has already happened to a very small extent. The feeling of unity in the German Evangelical Churches has always been exceedingly strong, notwithstanding the change of views, so that a splitting up of the Churches as in England, for instance, has never taken place here. This kind of German Evangelical Church will probably continue to be preserved in future. For just at the very moment when everywhere in Germany, as elsewhere in the world, the urge for unity is apparent, and great efforts are being made towards the reunion of separated Churches, it would indeed be an unusual condition of things were a cleavage worthy of particular remark to occur within the Evangelical Church of Germany. The unrest which befell the Evangelical Church in 1933, having already been noticeable in the preceding year, cannot allow the Government and Party to adopt a policy of aloofness. Rather is it necessary for responsible, political authorities to investigate with particular care the question of this unrest and its accompanying symptoms. Close co-operation with the Church Administration and with theological experts is imperative in order to make the position perfectly clear and restore peace. For the new unrest was not merely caused by an inner ecclesiastical theological dispute, but it was due in no small measure to the national resurgence. True, it was not [the] result of a proper understanding of National Socialism, but was caused by certain misconceptions and a vagueness, which, in conjunction with the political revolution, arose in the spiritual life of the German people.

One important cause, perhaps indeed the most important cause of the recent quarrels, is to be found in the fact that certain writers and their followers, all supporters of free thought, created the impression that National Socialism is necessarily connected with a new pagan creed that was to replace the Christian religion. This immediately brought the Opposition Party within the Church to the fore. This party, however, in the course of events did not only militate against the pagans but against the German Christians who affirmed both Christianity and National Socialism. Opposition was then extended against the Reich Church Government, because it was thought that the German Christian and the Reich Church Government were making common cause with National Socialism that was supposed to be "pagan" at heart. A second cause of the conflict was to be found in the Church Constitution. A most thorough reconstruction of the Constitution of the German Evangelical Church on the lines of the "Reichs-Reform" had been undertaken because it was believed, and correctly, too, that, normally speaking, each Church is organized in accordance with the existing social order of a people. The Opposition Party within the Church, however, were unwilling to renounce the existing forms which after the Revolution of 1918 had been constructed as emergency constitutions, and were partly adaptations of old Church Administrations under former ruling princes of the German States, and were partly derived from the democratic system of the Weimar Reich Constitution.

A third important cause was that certain political elements critical of National Socialism attached themselves to the Church Opposition Party, hoping thereby to prevent the inner consolidation of the German *Volk* by making use of the disturbances within the Church. In consideration of the close connection of the tension within the Church with the political reconstruction of the *Volk*, the Reichs Government is naturally unable to hold aloof from Church affairs.

Rather is it a more rational proceeding on the part of State and Party to eliminate all possibilities of conflict with the Evangelical Church. The appointment of a Ministry for Church Affairs in the summer of 1935 was a propitious beginning, and it is to be expected that the activities of this Ministry and the efforts of all concerned will be effective in finally restoring confidential relations which are an essential preliminary to the promotion of the nation's inner unity.

III: WHAT WE STAND FOR

1. The Recognition of Christianity by the Party

L ET US NOW CONSIDER more closely the relations between National Socialism and the Christian Religion.

It is taken for granted in National Socialistic Germany, the internal peace of which has always been the Führer's chief care, that the Christian religion professed by the overwhelming majority of the nation should be regarded with the utmost reverence. This would also be the case even if a ruler were a free-thinker or if the sentiments of his entourage were professedly anti-Christian. Again, it would be extremely unwise on the part of men holding high offices in State and Party if they permitted anything, however trivial, that would promulgate the idea that they wished to interfere with the Christian Faith and the furtherance of Christian life.

A deep respect for and recognition of the Christian religion on the part of the State and the Party have important consequences for the position of the Church within the nation. The Church is to be unconditionally allowed all the privileges becoming to its dignity and which can be claimed by any statutory corporation. It is granted entire liberty to preach the Gospel with all the means at its disposal, and to preserve and promote Christian life. It is the duty of the guardians of public peace to protect Church Services and all Church institutions with the utmost rigour against defamation and ridicule—in fact, to repulse every act of violence directed against the Church and its representatives.

2. The Christian Standpoint of the Party

We have, however, in the course of these remarks, only reached the threshold of what is to be said concerning the relations between Christianity and National Socialism. For the Christian religion is not merely regarded with outward respect by the National Socialists or considered from a distance as something great and sacred it may be, to other and narrower circles, but for themselves as something negligible or useless. Neither is the Christian religion looked upon as something that merely adorns life, or enhances the beauty of some earthly experience in moments of uplift; nor is it only some sphere of life visited perfunctorily when occasion demands, in order to do for the sake of appearances what to others is a sacred and solemn act. No, "the Party as such stands for positive Christianity" is the pronouncement of the Party Programme, and that means vastly more than mere respect and regard, more than mere toleration of what now exists once and for all, and which must be preserved as one of the old traditions of the People.

Generally speaking, we mean by "standpoint" the foundation supporting us, that which gives us a hold and security. We should hover in the air and plunge into the abyss if we were without a firm standpoint. Now, if the Party as such takes Positive Christianity as its standpoint, it means that the National Socialistic Movement finds its hold, its support, in Christianity, and that, without this solid foundation, National Socialism would hover in the air and plunge into the abyss.

Important too, and the best possible explanation in this connection, is the statement in the Programme that the German nation can achieve permanent health "from within." That is to say: Positive Christianity is the innermost life, the spirit, the soul of the National Socialistic German People, or in other words. National Socialism itself has its roots deep in the Christian spirit; it is a Movement determined by Christianity.

This does not mean, however, that National Socialism itself is actually a religious Movement. National Socialism as such is nothing else but the vigorous drawing together of a People menaced by danger and destruction into one great bond of inner unity. It is substantially more national in character, being a reversal of the relations existing between men within the nation, hence, an event that is realized in the domain of social culture. National Socialism as such, is therefore not a religious reformation, but is nevertheless an upheaval in a Christian People, and so the tumult in the minds of men brought about by the awakening to a new conception of national life, penetrates the innermost spheres of life even into religion itself, and consequently a Christian awakening through the national uprising would appear a perfectly natural thing. And moreover, the rich fullness of the Divine Spirit would bestow new gifts and endow the national regeneration with the final qualities of strength and depth.

And so when in the Party Programme Positive Christianity is spoken of as being the essential standpoint of the Party as such, if permanent health is to be achieved from within, and when the Führer appeals to the Christian Churches to make their moral influence an effectual force in the nation, this is sure proof that doors are not closed to Christianity in Germany, but that instead they are opened wide to allow the stream of the Holy Spirit to flow into the lives of the People and transform barren soil into a fruitful garden of God. The German *Volk* is ready to be sanctified, its soul, weary and parched in the age of materialistic barrenness and Marxian agitation, longs for the noblest of spiritual food, tarries and waits for those who have authority to preach the Gospel Message to give them this food, in the hope, too, that all personal forces will be active in promoting the regeneration of the spirit of the People from within. This, and this alone, is the real meaning of the clause pronouncing Positive Christianity to be the standpoint of the Party.

But another more weighty question arises—for us the core of the whole matter: wherein does the inner connection consist between the Christian religion and the National Socialistic view of life or *Weltanschauung*? It is not sufficient for us to know, that, according to Point 24 of the Party Programme, both belong together; nor is it enough to find that the Christian religion forms the kernel of National Socialistic views of life or *Weltanschauung*. Rather must we investigate the nature of those forces, which, emanating from the spirit of Christianity, permeate the whole life of the People. Inversely, it must be determined in how far the forces proceeding from free-thought are inadequate or detrimental to the life of the *Volk*. And above all, we must keep in view in how far Christian forces are conducive to success in the present heroic fight of the German *Volk* for life and honour, and to what extent pagan forces are a hindrance. But this makes a new and thorough investigation necessary.

PART TWO:

THE CHRISTIAN FOUNDATIONS
OF NATIONAL SOCIALISM

H E WHO LIVES ON the heights of human life reaches up to the superhuman and so possesses real religion. For religion is surrender to the supernatural. But he who lives in the plains of human life is remote from the superhuman, and consequently has no real religion, or, if he declares what is purely human to be the supreme Being, then his is a false religion, and he himself practices idolatry.

A true leader of the People, one occupying the highest position of all and at any moment prepared to pronounce momentous decisions undertaking thereby responsibility for millions of his followers, knows he is united with the superhuman, and bends his will to God. And a People that has experienced a change of fate, having awakened from weakness, sickness, and feverish dreams to new health and strength, experiences in its resurgence not only the highest of human things, but it feels the power of the superhuman. And also each single insignificant human being carrying within him what is noble in man, rises in some great decisive crisis of his life above the merely human, and in touching thus the fringe of the superhuman becomes reverent and devout. But human worms crawling along the ground know nothing except what is human and less than human, and do not rise to what is truly divine, but are sufficient unto themselves and even confuse themselves with what is divine.

Because of this, it is a matter of course that the Führer, Adolf Hitler, occupying the high position he does, feels and has expressed in many a notable speech, that he is under the providence of Almighty God, and is responsible to the great Guide of the destinies of nations. Neither are we surprised when he sometimes closes an address with a prayer; once he even concluded a great speech on May 1st 1933 with the words: "We will not leave thee except thou bless us." And again, it is a matter of course that National Socialism is, on the whole, to those who gaze into its depths, the experience of some immense change of destiny bestowed by God. Here we have proof of the indissoluble connection between the development of the power of our national uprising and a deep, reverent submission to God.

National Socialistic piety does not consist in man's deification of himself, or in his creation of new, imaginary idols—in a really great epoch such aberrations make no appeal to men's minds— rather does he look to the Lord of the world and to the God of all nations of the earth whom his forefathers have already served in the usages of congregational life as well as in the forms of religion and divine worship, all of which from time immemorial have been bound up in the inner life of the German People, that is to say, in the forms of the Christian religion. Consequently here then is to be found the necessary inner connection between the Christian religion and the National Socialistic attitude.

It is therefore agreed that, generally speaking, the National Socialistic spirit is closely connected with the powers of the

Christian life. But what is applicable in general is no less true of the individual aspects and motives of the Christian life.

And now we shall try to visualize those living forces in detail. We shall therefore treat of God's children and kinship with God, and dominion over the world; love for one's neighbour; sin; redemption and the Redeemer. We shall realize how the different powers of the Christian spirit find their fulfillment in the life of the German People, and in the heroic struggle of the moment in particular. At the same time, however, we shall keep in view those attempts at religion offered to the German People today under the name of Neo-Paganism, and we shall ask ourselves if they possess any value as sources of health and strength for a nation fighting for its very existence.

I: KINSHIP WITH GOD

1. Kinship with God and Dominion Over the World

ALL CHRISTIANS UNITE IN the use of the Lord's Prayer addressing God as children do their Father. The more genuine their Christianity is, the more do they feel that what they pray is the truth. All real Christians submit to the Lord of the world and to the God of all the nations of the earth, just as children are submissive to their father. They experience in their child-like surrender how the superhuman Spirit descends and receives them into His divine life so that they are filled with His Spirit.

The state of being God's children comprises many special motives. In it, the Christian life is child-like joy, sublime felicity, of the peace of God and a happy refuge for the human mind in the Divine Spirit. And this in its turn results in the child-like surrender of the human will in voluntary obedience to the Divine Will, a striving in the same direction as God is working out His purpose, the desire to perform what is divine, to be perfect as the Father is perfect. This gives rise to a child-like trust in God, to the conviction that the Father in the world surrounding us directs everything in accordance with His divine will, just as He directs the happenings of our own lives that even the sufferings and unpleasantness of which the world is full, are there for the purpose of serving the honour of God. This frame of mind, however, is accompanied by a child-like humility, that is to say, life in unison with the Father is lived within the narrow compass of the world, and the restriction of the world with all its hazards and uncertainties, difficulties and obscurations, is recognized as such, and is affirmed as the framework, as the husk, as the shape in which God realizes the salvation of His children. All these—felicity, obedience, trust, humility—when organically forged together in one uniform experience, make up the substance of this kinship with God.

In this child-like surrender to the Lord of the world, man, from a height which he otherwise would never have reached, experiences an inner release. The great security of the human spirit enfolded in the superhuman, Divine Spirit allows the sons of men to participate in the exaltation of God beyond the narrowness of the world. In the midst of this world man has inwardly gained superiority over the world, nothing that is of this earth has power to enslave him, and he lives exalted above all things.

But in the Christian religion this does not mean fleeing the world or denying it. Closeness to God is not experienced remote from the world and away from things connected with the world. From the height to which man has ascended as a child of God, he influences the bustle and hurry of the world. He regards all his worldly goods as divine gifts. He lives and works in this world to the honour of God, and to him service in the world is divine service. True, divine service in the narrowest sense of the word is, and remains the direct surrender of the soul to the divine reality of life. But divine service in the widest sense of the word is activity in all the spheres of this earthly life, service in human society, search for truth, cultivation of the beautiful, and all physical work.

With the domination of the Christian personality over the world there is a further connection, namely this, that in a life consciously placed under the direction of the Divine Spirit, every value and every activity is arranged in its proper order. When man submits unconditionally to the rule of the superhuman Spirit, then the consequences for his whole life, including all worldly connections, are that the spirit controls the flesh in everything. The values determining human life from the sacred through the good, the true, and the beautiful, down to the useful, appear to grade themselves naturally in that the inner life unconditionally takes the highest place, the sensual the lowest, and that everywhere the sensual is kept in control by the spirit and reduced to its right measure. This attitude preserves man forthwith from every kind of excess in the sensual life, indeed, from every "revaluation of all values" whereby the Christian grading of values professed by National Socialism is reversed. In this sense, our Programme declares: "We combat the Jewish materialistic spirit within and without us." Corresponding to this is the well-known principle: "To abolish the thraldom of interest" included in another part of the Programme. This demand fits perfectly into the grading of values which conforms to the Christian attitude of mind. Indeed, we are reminded of the words of the New Testament: "Ye cannot serve God and mammon," which, applied to the situation under discussion means: the domination of the goods of this world, including money and borrowed capital, ceases for those who are impelled by the Divine Spirit, and consequently look upon material life not as the highest but as the lowest sphere of life.

Free-thinkers and the advocates of free-religious movements, however, who look upon the individual, or the community, mankind or the People, as the Supreme Being, and in deifying these refuse to recognize surrender to a superhuman Spirit, possess no ultimate standard for the grading of values. Thus great divergency is noticeable in the philosophical systems and trends of thought from the 18th to the 20th century in their determining of what is the highest value. Humanitarians there are who would glorify the social life of mankind as such— intelligentsia, who consider thought to be the culmination of human life—aesthetes, who regard art as the sublime in life,—and there are also very doubtful revaluations such as the practical materialism of the Marxians or the naturalism of Nietzsche, all being philosophies of life that may be either included in the "Jewish-materialistic spirit" rejected by our Programme, or else are dangerously near to it. For the more mankind and the physical phenomena of Nature surrounding us are regarded as divine, the more quickly does the spirit of naturalism and materialism gain ground, and the more rapidly does the importance of spiritual values vanish, and the sensual spreads like rank growth and the animal in man clamours for its rights. In other words: the deification of mankind quickly degenerates into a deification of subhuman nature as has been proved by numerous instances where Marxism holds sway, but it is also to be found in other trends of thought as well.

A word now remains to be said concerning Christian character in relation to the heroism demanded in Germany of every loyal German in these days of national resurgence.

The standpoint [or foundation] to be expressed is perfectly clear. The knowledge of having dominion over the world which is part of the Christian Faith, creates strong characters that cannot be shaken. It gives men a feeling of great stability in the vicissitudes of life, a steady purpose in all the activities of this world, an unconditional reliability and fidelity in all the changes of time, an untiring diligence in everything that has to be accomplished.

When the nucleus of a nation is composed of men of this stamp, or when a spirit such as this dominates a people, a wonderful source of strength thus exists for them. For men of this kind guarantee invincible calm, endurance, equability, and steadfastness of soul in the spirit of the nation. This spirit can, moreover, preserve a nation from inner disintegration and dissolution, and can guide it from an era of destruction into an age of reconstruction, of unity and solidarity. Consequently, the permanent recovery of our German *Volk* also comes "from within," that is to say, from the sources of holy life dwelling in the depths of the soul by virtue of kinship with God. And precisely in the heroic fight to be won before our *Volk* can hope to recover from its collapse, there can be no better source of strength than the life-giving streams that flow from the depths of the Godhead into the soul of the nation open to receive them. For the consciousness of having dominion over the world gives God's children strength to overcome all difficulties, to become indomitable fighters, to ward off every danger in a cheerful spirit, to break down all obstacles boldly and courageously, and form a brave knighthood scorning death and the devil.

There are, however, free-thinkers and supporters of free religions, including the representatives of a new religion that claims to conform to German type, who now come forward and preach a philosophy at variance with what has just been said about the relations between Christian sentiments and human development of strength. In such circles whether they represent liberal or social views, or uphold national or international sentiments, the conviction is widespread that, to men, man is the supreme being, and besides him only Nature exists. And it is irrational to believe in the superhuman, living God just as it is irrational in daily life to put one's trust in the supreme power of a divine being. A religion such as Christians profess, with its teaching on humility, makes man delight in slavery of mind, makes him cowardly and obsequious, and prevents the manly development of his powers. As a contrast to this they call upon man to develop by himself and boldly defy all such powers from above that seek to subdue him, and, in accordance with one's private sentiments, this standpoint is proclaimed as a form of godlessness, or as a new substitute for religion, according as there is a lack of religious feeling or an enthusiastic reverence for man and Nature.

As we have already shown, man can develop his human powers more easily when they are rooted in the superhuman and he is thus accustomed to deal with things of this life from above as it were, and not from below. And when, in Christian Faith, humility finds a place which is the affirmation of the limits of human nature, this does not mean it is a contrast to heroism. Rather does it belong to the substance of the really true, heroic spirit. For the real hero who has to assert himself in danger and distress with all the high values he defends, knows better than anyone else the limitations of his powers. The profound thoughts contained in the stories of Achilles' heel and Siegfried's vulnerable spot express this unequivocally. And the qualities of the real hero must include modesty, one of the most important of all the virtues. Judged by moral standards, the man who praises his own heroic deeds is not highly respected. Rather is it a proof of noblest heroism when he refrains from mentioning his victorious deeds, or at the most speaks of them in all modesty as but the fulfillment of his duty. Well may the real hero bend his will to God who is the source of his strength and sets the limits to his actions. In this way, it is impossible to look upon humility as an obstacle to heroic sentiments.

2. God and Volk

We must now investigate the question as to how the Christian's belief in God harmonizes with belief in the German *Volk*, one of the basic principles of the National resurgence. There are certain people, those to whom the Führer alludes as "men in bear-skins," who would appear desirous of establishing a new Germanic "Folk-religion." Our standpoint with regard to this matter is as follows: since in religion man rises to the superhuman, which means he advances beyond human limitations and communes with the Power recognized by him to be the Ruler of the world, so is the horizon of the world which man conceives in experiencing God of great vastness at every stage of religion. It is always identical with the end of the world known to him. Is his clan his world? Then the spirits of his clan are to him supreme beings. Are the bounds of the world to him the boundaries of his *Volk*? Then the deities or the one deity of his *Volk* are to him absolutely the supreme godhead. Should his vision extend beyond the boundaries of his own nation to the nations surrounding his, even to the nations of the earth, then the many deities of the other nations form together the conception of the divine, or the one godhead ruling over all is worshiped as the supreme being. Should religion, however, notwithstanding the widened horizon, confine itself to a limited sphere on earth, it is but a survival of past ages, or, if such limits are artificially constructed it is a reversion to an ancient stage in the history of mankind, having nothing to do with a higher culture or even with higher religion. Religions of this kind found on paper, may well serve to elevate the mind in small literary circles, but in the spiritual life of a great nation they are but curious phenomena, and one cannot expect them to become a source of strength for a whole Nation, least of all for one that would work its way up from the depths of bitter need to a new life. We National Socialists assuredly think with reverence of the religion of our forefathers. We reject, however, all attempts to resuscitate the dim shapes of pre-historic days, or to create a new "folk-religion" by adopting a modern deification of man and Nature, and limiting it to our own *Volk* and land. For we take our stand with our Führer upon the basis of Positive Christianity.

Christianity is a world-religion. It comprises and unites many peoples. It is predominant among the Indo-Germanic peoples of the earth, who, by reason of their culture and their politics, rule the greater part of the world. The God Whom Christians worship is the God of the whole world and the God of all nations. But amongst the various nations in the world the Christian religion, which in the Gospel is represented as one only, has to a certain extent mingled with the characters of nations, and consequently, without any artificial means, but solely through the growth of history, has absorbed in many inward and outward things the spirit of the people that adopted it—Greek, Roman, German and English—and confronts us now, a unity in multiformity and a multiformity in unity.[1] And so the German spirit has become fused with the spirit of the Christian religion at various stages,

---

1   For details respecting the various kinds of Confessions vid. my other publications: Ecumenical Handbook of the Churches of Christ (English translation Berlin. Evnng. Pressverband fiir Deutschland, 1927); Corpus Confessionum (Berlin, Walter de Gruyter & Co., 1928 IT.); Types of Religion (Article in the Dictionary: Religion in History and the Present Day. Vol. IV (Religion II) Tubingen. J. C. B. Mohr, 1930)

such as in the German mysticism of mediaeval days, then again in Luther and the Reformation, as well as in religious and secular movements of more modern times—all this in its rich fullness of historical happenings but which we may not follow up here in detail since we are not discussing past history but are dealing with the living present. One fact, however, stands out clearly: we as Germans of German type are at the same time Christians, and as Christians are at the same time Germans of German type. Hence, to us, Christianity means no eradication of folk-characteristics but rather an experiencing of the supreme Divine Power behind the outward wrappings that go to make up our racial characteristics.

Accordingly, therefore, our *Volk*, too, has a place in our Christian Faith. To us God is no dim conception indifferent to things of the world and its multiplicity, but the Father reveals Himself to His children through the Holy Ghost, who dwells in them in bountiful fullness of life. We belong to Him and see the world in Him and Him in the world. We believe that Nature and the nations of the world are His creation and under His fatherly care. This is the essence of our trust in God, and consequently a most important factor in the lives of the children of God. In the Divine ordering of the world, however, everything in Nature, the smallest as well as the largest, all living things, every individual, every nation has its place and its meaning in all the characteristics peculiar to its being and vitality, which precludes any obliteration or denial of distinguishing features.

But within this world our German *Volk* is a part of the Aryan race; German blood courses through our veins, and we live on German soil. We love this *Volk* with all the surrender we are capable of, and we love precisely this people of ours today, raised as it has been from out the depths of direst need by an overwhelming act of Divine Providence. And in this great happening, we look upon the fact that the Führer, Adolf Hitler, has been given to us as a very special mark of God's mercy towards us. We shall never be weary of thanking God for this special ordering of our history in the great happenings of the world.

But as National Socialists who take their stand upon the basis of Positive Christianity, we do not intend for a moment to deify the Führer, the *Volk*, the Race, Blood, or Soil. When the expression "eternal" Germany is occasionally used, no idolatry is implied. For "eternal" in the language of the *Volk*, particularly in expressing enthusiasm, simply means "an indefinite time." Thus no one practices idolatry in calling something "eternal." Or is it idolatry when two lovers make vows of eternal fidelity, or if two countries on the signing of a treaty shall henceforth remain "undivided for ever," or if the mathematician reckons with the number "infinite?" Neither is it idolatry to speak of "sacred" Germany. For to Christians living in the Holy Spirit of kinship with God, it is assuredly an indisputable truth that everything that is under the protection of God and blessed by Him is accordingly sacred. In the New Testament, the body is spoken of as the temple of the Holy Ghost and is therefore sacred. Luther also declared that secular work performed by believers to the glory of God, even if only the most ordinary and simplest of household duties, is sacred work.

As a Christian people, we Germans have also learned in child-like trust to place everything under God's Providence. We are even told in Luther's Catechism to take clothes and shoes, food and drink, house and homestead, wife and child, fields, cattle and all our goods straight from the Father's hand as gifts. For this reason we take it for granted that our *Volk* and country are guided and governed by Divine Providence. And when today, our country has been visibly blessed by God, it is quite natural for Christian

Germans to speak of "sacred Germany" without entertaining idolatrous thoughts of any kind whatsoever. There are. it is true, as remarked before, a few isolated groups of anti- Christian free-thinkers and supporters of free religions who may use similar expressions in an idolatrous sense. They must not. however, be included amongst those who understand the full meaning of National Socialism, but are to be classed with those upon whom we have frequently passed judgment as being advocates of free-thought and free-religion.

As we now in all reverence consider our *Volk* to be under God's protection, but only as one nation amongst many, and under the protection of God who rules all nations and the whole world, the question in concluding arises as to whether this Faith does not weaken our strength for our earthly tasks, and the development of our *Volk* in particular. The answer is that the strength of a nation is strengthened most of all when its soul constantly ascends to the exalted heights of the Godhead, far beyond itself, above all nations and all things to where God is, and on its returning from this flight it descends to the world, to the nations and to itself imbued with new strength and with new love.

Assuredly it is fitting for a nation to remember itself, its dignity and honour. But this national attitude draws its final support and inner strength again and again from the depths of the truly Divine. A super-national religion, therefore, cannot be considered as weakening but must rather be regarded as the source of a nation's strength. A significant historical instance of this may be given here. Simultaneously with England's development into the greatest Empire of the world a great religious revival developed about the middle of the 18th century when tremendous national strength was displayed. This movement, started by the Methodists, was not actuated by national motives but was purely super-national having only one aim in view: that of spreading "holiness over the land," or in other words to instill godly strength into men's minds. This powerful religious movement was no obstacle to England's national development of strength; on the contrary, it has been said that, with a piety making men calm and strong, Methodism preserved the English people from the disorders of a Revolution similar to that connected with the Free-thought Movement in France. Thus the German Volk, in so far as it is Christian, will not weaken the strength of the Third Reich, but the more Christian it is, the more will it in its earnest piety form the noblest and most vigorous kernel of the nation, when in years to come Germany will have to maintain her position, not like England it is true, by developing into a WorldReich, but in strengthening the place she has won in the council of the nations.

II: LOVE FOR ONE'S NEIGHBOUR

1. Love, Justice, Honour

OUT OF KINSHIP WITH God arises love for one's neighbour. The children of the Father are united in brotherly love in one great, holy family. The one Holy Spirit, streaming from the superhuman life of the Godhead into their hearts, creates a common spirit of unity and makes them one, so that finally the many are as of one heart and one soul. Thus love for one's neighbour is an indispensable feature of the real Christian mind. In dominion over the world, which, as was said before, is the immediate effect of kinship with God, love for one's neighbour comes first as the greatest of all virtues. In it, the working of the Divine Spirit is made manifest in secular life.

On asking ourselves the question: What is love for ones neighbour? we shall find that in substance it is the community-spirit, the devotion of the one to the other and to society. In this way are united sympathy, friendliness, warm-heartedness, and deep joy in sharing life in common. In this connection, too, we find a feeling of spontaneous goodwill—the urge of inner conviction without any outward pressure of the ego—, towards the common spirit and fellow-creatures for the promotion of the welfare of the community and all within it. And to this must be added the trust one has in the other, and which the individual has in the community, and the community in the individual. This creates the firm conviction of being able to hold fast together at all costs, even if the one knows but little about the others. And then there is fidelity, which through all the changes of time binds the one closely to the other. This universal conception of love for one's neighbour assumes at the same time the character of service in the Christian community, as we are told in the New Testament: he will be the chief who is servant to all. Hence, all these forged together—sympathy, good-will, trust, service—form the substance of love for one's neighbour.

This however, does not exhaust itself in merely adopting a friendly frame of mind; it expresses itself in kind words, and above all in helpful acts. But neither is help only extended to the inner life; it comprises everything that is human; most particularly, however, is it directed to the physical needs of those bound by the ties of brotherhood. Ever since Early Christian days, it has been customary amongst Christians to regard it as a sacred duty, indeed, as a service to God, to feed the hungry, give drink to the thirsty, to clothe the naked, to visit the sick, to go to the prisoners, to shelter the stranger.

As the queen of all virtues which go to form the life of a community, love for one's neighbour holds a higher place than the two other basic principles which together with it make the foundations of human society, namely, honour and justice. Honour, wherein is expressed the importance of the individual in his individuality for society, and justice, wherein is emphasized the equality of all individuals in the community-spirit, are assumed beforehand and recognized to be elementary principles in Christian community-life. But both are surpassed by the love that encircles the individually different, as well as the universally similar, and which gives the individual his honour and all the others justice, but which at the same time is higher than honour and justice. For to take honour for himself isolates the individual and makes him harsh towards the community-spirit. Justice taken by itself despises the individual and absorbs him in the common spirit. But love sets the individual within his proper limits by taking his place and serving the community with his own special powers, and gives the principle of justice, too, a subordinate position by not merely acting on the principle of requital—"an eye for an eye, a tooth for a tooth," and in repaying good with good and evil with evil—but it bestows the good from its divine heights without expecting anything in return, forgiving even the evil it has suffered in order that injustice may not disturb or even destroy brotherly unity.

National Socialism, a movement in substance and name with its center of gravity in society, finds itself precisely at this point in close contact with the Christian religion. Not only may we speak of an inner connection, there is more than that; for in this sphere, National Socialism actually coincides with Christianity. It is itself practical Christianity, a national realization of love for one's neighbour: "The common interest before self interest," as it is called in Point 24 of the Party Programme; and in the speeches of the Führer and his coadjutors, as well as in the innumerable pronouncements of the Party, not only do these words echo forth, but there is a call for devotion to the national community, for comradeship, for sacrifice, for trust and fidelity, and, above all, for service. Expressions such as these are not vain words; they are backed by deeds and by deeds of a greatness never before experienced in such a manner in the history of nations, or indeed in the history of brotherly love. The National Socialistic Movement has succeeded in restoring to order and discipline a People standing on the brink of universal deterioration and divided into hostile classes by a wild and lawless propaganda of hate. It has transformed, moreover, deep-seated distrust into unconditional trust, infidelity into fidelity, discord into concord, strife into peace—and after an era in which each wished to be master and assert his own rights. And more, National Socialism has once again made service, obedience, and submission honourable things. In effecting this, legal measures have been extensively employed and appeal made to the honour of the whole *Volk* without, however, detracting in any way from the devoted surrender of the individual to the whole as a ruling power.

Thus Christianity and National Socialism are one and the same in love for one's neighbour, in that they are insolubly united for all time and can never be parted. The Christian Message, as the Führer has expressly stated, has the special task of making the Churches use their moral powers to influence the *Volk*, which means that from the Gospel Message there springs the delicate and spiritual growth of brotherly love, namely, the life of kinship with God, and spreads all its spiritual riches over the life of the *Volk*. National Socialism again, as a folk-movement has the task of making this inner growth a vigorous influence in the life of the nation.

Of a character different to that of Christian love which is realized in National Socialism are various theories and practices that have come down to us from the Ages of Reason, Romanticism, and Technics, also such that emphasize their wish to be "Germanic" and offer their theories to the German *Volk* as something of particular value. There are, it is true, among modern theoreticians and practicians of social life, particularly some years ago, those who recommend Christian love for one's neighbour as the greatest of all virtues for curing the ills of society. But since the liberalism of the Age of Reason, repeated objections have been raised against the love for one's neighbour. "Free" modern man thinks that the service and devotion which Christian love entails —similar to humility in piety—is something degrading, undignified, insulting, something injurious to man's pride and reducing him to the status of a slave. And to strengthen the argument, reference is preferably made to the well-known words of the Sermon on the Mount, according to which he who is smitten on the one cheek ought to turn the other also.

Marxism is enthusiastic in denouncing Christian love as "slavish happiness" and preaches hatred of the capitalistic class, because it robs the proletarian of his honour and freedom. Similarly, too, some of those proclaiming national honour and liberty may occasionally be heard opposing the misunderstood love for one s neighbour. But such a comparison does not conform to our Christian and at the same time National Socialistic point of view. Most assuredly are liberty and honour high values in our eyes, and it is our firm conviction that a People in days of degradation and oppression must never tire of fighting for its honour and liberty, just as it is a duty to challenge any interference with honour and freedom in the life of every free and honourable person. But we know, on the other hand, that service and devotion to the community do not exclude liberty and honour, but include them; and we know, too, the meaning of the words, "whosoever smiteth thee on the right cheek, turn to him the other also." According to the context of the Sermon on the Mount, it simply means that the love which gives and forgives, not the justice which repays, is the mainstay of moral life. For this love, as the Sermon on the Mount shows, is no "slavish happiness but is a victorious virtue dominating the world. For it belongs to the perfection which makes the children of God like their Father, the Lord of the world, Who maketh His sun to rise on the evil and on the good, and sendeth rain on the just and on the unjust. That through forgiving love the children of God do not degrade themselves, but are raised instead to God on high, is seen in the prayer uttered by all Christians: "Forgive us our trespasses as we forgive them that trespass against us."

2. Help in Word and Deed

Thus is love for one's neighbour in its full extent common to both Christianity and National Socialism. This also applies to the method by which brotherly love is realized in order to promote peace inwardly amongst men, and externally to further their welfare by alleviating distress. After the first impression, it is true, there would appear to be a wide gulf between Christians and National Socialists in the method of loving one's neighbour. Generally speaking, we are wont to find Christian love working very quietly with tenderness and the use of spiritual means. National Socialism on the other hand, has been most vigorous in order to reconstruct the unity of the nation. Where necessary, it used its fists against Communism in the streets. After the Party came into power, strict laws forbade the continuance of all political parties that had formerly caused disruption and hatred in the People. This, however, is only an apparent contrast to the usual Christian method. Even Christian love must, where necessary, employ vigorous methods when it comes into contact with dissolute elements and criminals, and must needs make use of severe discipline as soon as gentler methods fail. National Socialism found itself in the same position when attempting to help the German People. It was confronted with the most appalling degradation and dissolution, and had perforce to resort to very strong measures in order to snatch the whole of the great nation from the very brink of an abyss, and set about constructing its internal peace. But at the same time National Socialism applied more gentle and more spiritual methods to win compatriots for the new community of the *Volk*. In stimulating speeches and writings, indeed, it might be said by political preaching on a large scale, the Führer was able in the early days of his campaign to win German hearts for the future comradeship, and his influence was of that deep and spiritual nature only possible in a Christian sermon on brotherly love. Then, too, on the assumption of power, when it meant shouldering responsibility for the whole nation, the same noble means were employed to alleviate the distress that prevailed everywhere. With a care only to be found in Christian philanthropy, ways and means have been found to relieve the want and suffering of all the poor and needy. A gigantic programme of methods for creating employment was drawn up, and already millions have been rescued from the misery of unemployment. And even more has been accomplished, particularly in winter, when provision is made for all those suffering from hunger and from cold, and in a manner conforming absolutely to Christian methods. National Socialism has continued the work begun before its assumption of power, by the Christian Churches in conjunction with secular societies, but with far greater success than could possibly have been achieved by anyone in the years of internal discord in the nation. The method employed in this work of relief is, as the Führer has expressly put it, that of voluntary giving. This corresponds to the ancient and well-tried custom of appealing for contributions and of receiving ready offerings.

Totally opposed to this Christian and National Socialistic method of proffering relief is Marxism, both in theory and practice. It directs men to start with their own interests and claim privileges from the community. It indignantly rejects all giving and receiving as something derogatory both to the giver and recipient. The Marxian idea of people's welfare corresponds more or less to the institutions of today—taxation and State insurance. These institutions, which we, too, make use of, are doubtless most important factors, placing as they do people's welfare on an assured material basis. Since, however, their functions are merely mechanical and purely financial, both Christianity and National Socialism do not consider them the sole means or noblest form of eradicating social evils, but give them a secondary place. The voluntary surrender of the personality to the whole and the unselfish sharing of one's own possessions with the needy are for us today as in the past the noblest form of showing love for one's neighbour.

3. Family, Nation, Mankind

The question now remains to be answered respecting the attitude of Christianity and National Socialism towards the various social circles which have arisen in the human race, and are due partly to its nature and partly to its historical development. Such communities formed by man are to be found in plenty and either include or intersect each other. Three of these are of fundamental importance, namely, the family, the nation, and mankind.

At this point, there would appear to be an important difference between the attitude of Christianity and that of National Socialism, so that the question might well be asked whether a certain amount of opposition might not even exist between them, or, at any rate if it is at all possible at this important point to speak of Christianity as the basis of National Socialism. The difference which appears to be here might be expressed somewhat as follows:

the Christian standpoint is international, that of National Socialism national.

This manner of contrasting the two, however, is based on a serious confusion of ideas. Assuredly there is an inter-nationalism and a nationalism sharply opposed to each other. Philosophy has long put forward the indistinct conception of mind in which not only all the differences between human individuals disappear, but also the differences between communities. This idea about mind, which has developed new power since the Age of Reason, and has formed since the Age of Technics a substantial foundation through world-intercourse, dominates Marxism and is the aim of Bolshevism whose wish is the dissolution of the family and the nations through a world-revolution in which mankind in general shall flourish. On the other hand, there is a view of Nationalism narrow in its outlook, not so prevalent in Germany as in other lands. Men holding this point of view consider their own nation to be the best amongst the nations of the earth, and with smiling superiority look down on all others. It even happens that a nation regards itself as the chosen people called upon to rule the others, or to be the most important in this world. A sharp distinction, therefore, must be made between these two very limited points of view and Christianity and National Socialism.

The situation is rather this: from what we have already discussed, it is obvious that neither the Christian religion nor National Socialism exists on mere conceptions or is governed by one-sided theories. Rather do both rely upon the living fullness of reality. For this reason, both respect the graded circles in the life of the human community with all their multiformity. And moreover, brotherly love does in no way abolish any one of these social circles, but expands rather within all the spheres of human community-life, and, indeed, a special power of love makes itself so strongly felt therein, that it not only brings into harmony the wishes of individuals, but also the opposing claims of the various social circles.

This may be observed most clearly in the Christian and National Socialistic views on and treatment of the family. If the Christian point of view were strictly international, it would perforce deny and forbid the family as being a barrier to universal human contacts. National Socialism, too, would have to attempt to abolish family life, were it to affirm the standpoint of a limited view of Nationalism. For it would in that case look upon family life as a hindrance to national unity. Neither is correct. In reality, the sanctity of marriage and family life has always been preached in Christian religion, and it is precisely the Christian Message that has in this very point had an extraordinarily powerful influence on the moral education of the nations. National Socialism follows the same path in its message. And since the assumption of power, new work has been done in this direction which must certainly be called practical Christianity. In the preceding years there had been a serious increase in the country of shattered marriages and ruined family lives. National Socialism, however, now makes vigorous and successful efforts to enable marriages to take place, notwithstanding the outward poverty that still exists, and strives to build up large families as living cells of the organism of the *Volk*.

And just as the family would never be abolished for the sake of other social circles, so would Christianity never deny the *Volk* for the sake of mankind, nor would National Socialism deny mankind for the sake of the *Volk*. In the days of the Early Christians, as has been proved by the New Testament, the national circumstances of the age were not overlooked or even rejected, but were recognized as permanent, and Christians were exhorted to submit to civil authority. To this very day, the principle is to be found in the

Christian Confessions of Faith, that, for Christians in civil life, the laws of State are authoritative. And the practice of Christian brotherly love, that on principle is bound to no particular social circle, has naturally not been chiefly international in its activities, but has concerned itself more especially with those living beside us, that is to say with the members of the family and our fellow countrymen.

National Socialism, for its part, does not think for one moment of denying the existence of mankind in general for the sake of its own nation, or to accord to other nations a lesser right to exist than it itself possesses. True, a conception of mankind is rejected in which national differences are no longer definable, and most of all are rejected the international machinations of those elements without home or country who make it their business to disintegrate nations in order to prepare the way for the world-revolution. In the same way, every kind of world-policy is rejected that does not do justice to the characteristics and the sound life-interests of individual nations. But a peaceful building up of international relations is being striven after so as to promote peace, and allow great nations to exchange their best goods both spiritual and material, without any traces of jealousy. This would be in perfect and complete harmony with the idea of Christian love, indeed the world peace which the Christian Churches are striving after will perhaps be furthered more by the world-policy of our Führer, Adolf Hitler, than has hitherto been done by the numerous international conferences held in the name of mankind.

III: REDEMPTION

THAT LIFE IN ALL its fullness and depth, which Christians as God's children carry within them and continually strive to make more perfect and complete, exists in them through Christ, the Son of God. Real Christians have become such through the real Christ. Without Him, they simply would not exist. Hence the reality of Christ is the indispensable pre-supposition for the Christian life, and everything we have hitherto dealt with was, without making mention of His name, a description of the reality of Christ. We must now treat of this point in more detail. It is, however, neither possible nor permissible to do so here, in the exhaustive manner of a detailed doctrinal system, and we must perforce confine ourselves to the few important points concerned with our special inquiry into the relationship between Christianity and National Socialism. In the following exposition, therefore, I must leave some important points untouched which personally, are close to my heart. The main consideration at the moment is to give a simple and clear outline intelligible to all, including those who are not yet capable of grasping the subtle distinctions in Christian life and thought.

The fact that the reality of life in the relationship of God as a Father to His children rests on the reality of Christ, is explained as follows in the Christian Faith: Man as a creature born into the world is not already a child of God in the full sense of the word; he can only become one by undergoing re-creation or re-generation, while in his natural state he is full of faults and failings, or, as we say, he is sinful. Re-generation or re-creation, however, takes place through God's operative power particularly in His educating mankind in history, and the individual in the course of his life. In the midst of this divine operative power, however, stands Jesus Christ, the Redeemer. Thus the closer consideration of redemption through Christ may best be divided into a threefold inquiry. We must think of in turn, the fact of sin, regeneration, and finally of Jesus Christ Himself, and in each case ask ourselves the question: what does this mean to National Socialism?

1. Sin and the National Corruption

When seriously-minded people hold fast to a high standard of life, every deviation from the path leading towards the goal they are striving to reach, creates in them a feeling of acute tension. The more such people gaze with clear vision at the reality surrounding them and at the true state of their interior lives, the more plainly do they see how far they fall short of perfection, and so they feel their own shortcomings all the more keenly as being the opposite to all they ought and desire to be.

Thus do all earnest Christians, whose relationship to God is that of children to a Father and who have gained a victory over the world, feel that something is lacking in their lives in as much as they are not perfect children of God and have not yet overcome the world. And the more serious they are, and the more calmly they consider their real estate, the more convinced are they of their sinfulness, which means living at enmity with God and in subjection to the world. They may, perhaps, have something in their hearts that is of the peace of God, of voluntary obedience to

God, and of humility, in short, of thoughts inherent in all those, who, in very truth are God's children. But at the same time, they experience again and again unrest and conflict in their own hearts, are resentful and disobedient to the Divine Will, discouraged, too, and desperate even, and arrogantly claim the right to be masters of their own lives. But when the children of God have gained a victory over the world evidenced by their vigorously emphasizing and appreciating all that is sacred and good, as well as all the other inestimable values in this life, they will, on the other hand, always feel the most keen distress, and regard as sinful all attempts to give preference to what is sacrilegious, evil, and mean.

And, if of the temporal virtues, the generous and forgiving love for one's neighbour prevails, and ungrudging lovingkindness, as evidenced in confidence and service, takes a foremost place, then hatred in all its various forms and effects, discord and envy, distrust and arrogance will be looked upon as sin. All this is clearly realized by Christian minds as the bare truth, no attempts being made to hide or excuse anything either in regard to one's self or to anyone else. It may, therefore, be universally said: the higher a man's aspirations are, the more seriously does he regard sin, and the greater and more momentous does its magnitude appear in his eyes. Conversely, the less noble his point of view, the more lightly does he look upon sin, and is all the more readily prepared to minimize its importance, or even perhaps to deny it altogether.

The extreme seriousness with which the question of sin is met, has always been a special characteristic of the Christian mind, more particularly in Christian Germany. Never has one of the great Churches taught that everything man does is sin. Such a view is only entertained by a few pessimistic philosophers and theologians. Rather do the Churches emphasize that, in spite of sin, the creative goodness of nature has not disappeared. But the consciousness of existing sin plays an important part in the depths of the interior life, and in the popular sermon. Indeed, many congregations feel a sense of well-being in hearing the preacher continually rouse men's consciousness by references to sin, shaking them out of the lethargy of their souls.

The very opposite is the view of the free-thinkers and adherents of free religions, both national and international. Ever since the Age of Liberalism there has prevailed amongst philosophers and the intellectual movements following in their train, the universal conviction that good predominates in human nature, and that man must certainly be able to attain perfection by himself, were he not prevented from doing so either by others or by unfavourable conditions in his environment. Severe criticism is therefore meted out to those clergy who preach on sin and repentance in the Churches, and a demand is made rather to help men by continually emphasizing the good that is in them, and for the rest to create more favourable surroundings.

Many theories and practical experiments based on this shallow optimism have marked the work of the last few centuries. The biggest attempt of all is Marxism, the results of which system may be studied in Russia today, where the would-be "good" nature of Youth, freed from all family ties, riots at will in every conceivable kind of excess and crime. Germany, too, was not spared similar experiments, if only to a small extent, particularly, for instance, after November 1918, when the Marxists opened the prisons, broke the canes in the schools, turned the reformatories into holiday-homes, and reaped thereby an increase in dissolution and crime.

Where now does National Socialism stand? The answer is perfectly obvious. It is not on the side of free-thinkers and their school, but it supports Christianity. Even in the early days of the

National Socialistic struggle for existence, it called with unerring truth, the good good, evil evil, the noble noble and what is mean, mean.

And now that the reins of power have passed into the hands of the National Socialistic Movement, this moral attitude has been emphasized and upheld afresh in the words and deeds of the Party, as well as in the decrees and acts of the State. Once again, Youth has been brought under control, a vigorous war is being waged against evil, crime receives its just punishment, and sentences are once more executed in the manner justifying their purpose.

Since the Party affirms this moral attitude, it is but reasonable that the National Socialistic State welcomes the Church as its ally, just because the latter severely condemns sin and keeps the conscience of the nation alive to its danger. The Church has a very special mission in regard to the moral training of the nation, namely, to stir up the hearts of men to their inmost depths, and to bring to light with absolute directness the most subtle and most secret faults, and by this means [to] carefully instruct men as to what is good and what is evil.

Thus does the Church perform its stupendous task of safeguarding the souls of men by forestalling evil. Many a man has been deterred from committing crime and from suffering punishment at the hands of the State.

Conversely, it is but right, for the National Socialistic Movement and the State it affirms, to turn against all religions that menace this strictly moral attitude. Point 24 of our Party Programme is invincible on this point. It refuses liberty of religious practice to all religious denominations which militate against the morality of the Germanic race. These include not only such religions wherein gross crimes and blasphemy occur, ritual murder and religious unchastity, but also the expressly rejected spirit of Jewish materialism, and all the closely allied "reversals of values" that call good evil and evil good, and are especially dangerous when they recommend themselves to the Third Reich as new religions desirous of serving the German *Volk*.

Particular emphasis must again be laid on the fact that the conception of the seriousness of sin common to National Socialism and the Christian religion alike and forming a tie between them, is by no means contradictory to the heroic character which we assume or at least hope every German to have in the struggle for liberty today. A philosophy little suited to the heroic spirit is the shallow optimism found in free-thinkers. This has not grown out of the heroic battle of life, but has had its being in the quiet rooms of learned men, and is suited to contented, comfortable citizens who perform their daily round of duties, and move along in the old rut without any great exertion on their part. The heroic man, on the other hand, who has to dare something and fight hard, risking his very life for great things, plunging boldly again and again into dangerous uncertainties, knows full well what is meant by imperfection, error, and wickedness. It is no mere pet theme of poets when they make their tragic heroes sinful; life itself has taught them that it must be so. For it is just when on the heights in heroic life that backslidings occur, but again the consciousness of imperfection in this case forms a foundation on which heroism may be built. The deeds of almost superhuman heroism performed by the sons of our *Volk* as soldiers on the battlefield may be largely accounted for by the fact that at the beginning of their military training these same soldiers were told day after day, in the most emphatic manner possible, how inferior, inadequate, and faulty their efforts were. Here again, at this most important point, the Christian spirit and National

Socialism are united against pagan free-thought. This also applies in no less degree to the views on the growth of the new man.

2. Regeneration and National Uprising

According to Christian conviction the higher life takes possession of man through the tremendous educative power of the Divine Spirit operating within us, and which must be considered as a new creation that reaches its culminating point in what is known as regeneration, because it forms the beginning of our relationship to God as Father, just as physical birth has made us human children. This regeneration has been experienced by countless Christians and by whole Christian nations. It has taken place as one great event or as a gradual growth in the lives of individuals, and has also swept over nations, either in one great awakening, or has come to them and remained as perpetual inspiration. The meaning is always the same — the old man dies and the new man comes to life, or as Luther has put it in his well-known catechism: "that the old Adam is to be drowned with all his sins and evil lusts, and that the new man should come forth who shall live in the presence of God in righteousness and purity for ever", that is to say, he is snatched from a life in which hostility to God and subservience to the world predominate, to a life in which we stand as children of God and victors over the world.

In this upward growth of the new life however, filled as it is with a bountiful plenitude of single experiences, two things stand out in sharp prominence; the experience of the Divine forgiveness of sins and the attainment of strength to overcome sin. The repentant sinner is received into the House of God the Father just as he is, burdened with all his sins without having to climb step by step, the weary path of gradual release from sin. This is forgiveness of sins. But here where his soul breathes the Divine essence he feels the impulse to begin a new life in the strength of God. This leads to a steadily increasing progressiveness in overcoming sin. Everywhere in the great Christian Churches, and in the smallest of Christian communities where the Gospel Message is rightly understood, those two things are taught and experienced. It shows a misunderstanding of the Christian religion when the assertion is made that Christian salvation ends with the knowledge that sins are forgiven whereby man still remains on the same level of proneness to miserable sin. There may be it is true, many a superficial Christian whose interior life is dull and who is content with a casual cognizance of the Divine forgiveness o(sin. Christians of this type are still half outside, but not within the Father's House. And still less does Christian salvation end with man's believing himself able to fight against sin, and having no need for the forgiveness of sin. There are assuredly seriously minded Christians honestly struggling to live a sinless life. But these lack insight into their human weakness. Both are essential, life in the fellowship of the Father, and the working of the power of God within us form the perfect being of the new man.

Those supporters of free-thought and free religions who preach the natural goodness of man know no regeneration. In their opinion, man was perfect from the very beginning, and in such a measure that there is no need to speak of an inward conversion, or even of a new creation. True, a higher life is dimly imagined at this point, but in so far as it is striven after, it does not occur in the experience of an overwhelming regeneration, but in a process of "self-perfection," that is to say, in a gradual uplifting by means of one's natural strength, whereby the petty weaknesses and mistakes noticeable to one's self at times, disappear and are ousted by more valuable achievements.

The National Socialistic Programme, however, mentions in our Point 24 the "permanent health of our nation from within." It presupposes a spiritual and moral sickness of the *Volk* that requires treatment, and thinks of inner forces which will make this healing effectual. And so it was never thought that the German nation could never be self-perfecting when the Programme was issued in 1920. The actual experiences in the history of the period between 1920 and 1933 far exceeded in their catastrophical character the slight references to sickness and permanent health in the Party Programme. The sick *Volk* became a *Volk* doomed to die, and the Movement, too, realized in the national uprising, did not develop smoothly and quickly in spite of the enormous expenditure of energy, but was sorely tried and disciplined by the great Guide of human history, and had perforce to endure on its weary way disappointments and reversals of fortune, even imprisonment, bloodshed, and death. And even after assuming power, the Movement had to fight against misunderstanding and obstinacy, and years will have to elapse before the difficult task of enlightening the nation is accomplished, [before] hostile elements [are] subordinated and all misunderstandings respecting the basic principles of National Socialism, including all religious errors, swept away.

This, however, is not the self-perfection of a healthy race, but rather its rescue from perilous danger, necessitating painful operations and bitter remedies. It is a new creation, a regeneration. Here again, we find National Socialism in these—its experiences and in its manner of experiencing them—standing side by side with Christianity against the advocates of free-thought. True, the uprising of the German *Volk* is not a religious revival but a national and moral regeneration. All Christian Germans, however, endowed with clear vision and living in this great era see in the regeneration of the *Volk* a new creative act of God's that stirs up their hearts to the very depths. And it may be that the national awakening will lead to a real religious awakening as has already been the case so many times in history when political revolutions have been accompanied by earnest religious revivals. Perhaps we, too, may now experience an awakening to a new holiness of life.

3. The Redeemer and the Führer

The growth of new life that rises from the Christian attitude of mind, is, like the whole of life in its relationship to God, made real through the life of Jesus Christ alone. If Jesus had not come into the world as the Christ, that is to say as One anointed with the Spirit of God, then we should not exist as Christians, that is, as those anointed with the Spirit of God. Our regeneration and new creation take place only through the strength of Jesus Christ. Death and resurrection of our inner life is death and resurrection with Jesus Christ. And the reality of our new life does not merely rest upon the fact that a general Christ principle or a Divine redeeming Power exists in the world, but only because Jesus appeared as Man amongst men in human abasement, and, within the narrow limits of this earthly life made real the fullness of the Divine life—[thus] are we participators in the Divine Spirit and are thus able to call God our Father in this Spirit. It is true that Christendom is not of opinion there is no other Divine revelation except through Jesus Christ. On the contrary, we know that God's hand is to be traced in history and in Nature. We are convinced, however, that the revelation of God was made complete in Jesus

Christ, and that from Him, for the first time, full light was shed upon the meaning of history, nature, and one's own life.

It is not our task in these pages to solve the mystery of the person of Christ, nor to enlarge on the profound thoughts concerning Him that have occupied men's minds for nearly two thousand years. We simply wish to show that everything we have already said respecting kinship with God, dominion over the world, loving one's neighbour, forgiveness of sin, and overcoming sin is but a cursory description of the fullness of life emanating from Jesus Christ, from Him Who by His work, teaching, death, and resurrection was at the same time for us, in us, and over us, and will be so to all eternity.

Free-thinkers and the supporters of free religions object to the Christian's belief in Christ. They do so because it is in no way compatible with their mode of thought that the power of God could possibly be revealed in one human individual. To them, the Divine is generally some indistinct conception of "being," or of Nature or of mankind, and they fail to understand the creative power of that which happens only once and as such is incomprehensible. It is most difficult to convince them that a Redeemer lived in all humility on earth, suffering even on the Cross and dying there. At the most, they can conceive the Divine as glorified and exalted, but not in the poverty, narrowness, and distress of earthly life. And when free-thinkers emphasize the goodness, the perfection and godliness of the natural powers of man, it appears to them a contradiction of terms to speak of a Redeemer Who came to save sinners and gave His life for them.

Again, in this important point, National Socialists, as is compatible with their whole attitude of mind, are on the side of Christianity and not of free-thought. For like Christians they have not gained their views of life from any systems of philosophy, but from the stern realities of life. One fact in this struggle for existence has become to them an overpowering reality: the Führer. In him, they have experienced the incontestable fact that all great happenings in history do not originate in the universal but in the particular, not in crowds but in some great personality. In him, too, they have experienced that great historical deeds are not only planned in the magnificence of royal palaces, or at the official boards of parliaments and ministries, or even in the buildings of large banking houses, but may have their source in one simple life that started in modest circumstances, having to struggle onward through poverty and privation, and, after much hard fighting, finally reaches the height, and even on the height thinks only of self-denial and sacrifice.

But never do National Socialists think of confusing the Führer with the Redeemer. Our Führer himself would utterly condemn the mere suggestion of any such idea. The political Führer, who sets his people free, is not the Saviour of the world Who calls them to repentance. But in the fact that something stupendously great has manifested itself in a single personality, in circumstances which might appear to be akin, Christians ought all the more readily grasp the fact of the Führer, and National Socialists more easily that of the Redeemer; where both Christianity and National Socialism unite, perfect harmony must necessarily exist.

But there is more. Inner connections also exist. The Führer himself belongs to those who fulfill the will of God and realize the life of Christ in this life in an extraordinary degree. The Führer in uniting the nation and helping it to rise from the laxity and neglect into which it had fallen, to a sense of moral discipline, fulfills the law of Christ respecting love in a way few mortals could ever hope to emulate. By defending with a strong hand the spiritual heritage of the German nation against the powers of darkness, he also protects our most sacred possession, the Gospel, guaranteeing, moreover, the further spread of its power. And when he himself, in the strength of his trust in God, places the destiny of the whole nation in the hands of the Father, he manifests the Spirit which through the coming of Christ has become a living power in the world.

CONCLUSION

T HE RESULTS OF OUR investigations have produced conclusions so simple and clear that they might well be spoken of as a matter of course. This must also be said of the religious policy of the Third Reich. But it is extremely difficult to put what is taken for granted into practice. For nowhere is our German nation so difficult to govern as in the domain of spiritual things and especially with respect to religion. Here individual opinions abound and assert themselves to such an extent that unanimity can only be achieved with very real difficulty. Moreover, the changing influences that marked the last epochs of intellectual life, could not fail to create a feeling of bewilderment in men's minds, which of necessity placed great obstacles in the way of all attempts to enlighten and unite those at variance with each other.

And yet the solution of the religious question is of paramount importance today; indeed, it is perhaps the most urgent and imperative of all questions. At a time when as now the firm spiritual foundations are being laid for life in a great nation, order must be created in the innermost sphere of all.

But the energy and great wisdom of our Führer will assuredly find the proper way out of all difficulties, and we, as Christian National Socialists, firmly believe that the Guide of the history of nations will direct this most sacred cause of the German People to a glorious end.

GERMAN CHRISTIANS IN THE STRUGGLE FOR THE GOSPEL

by
D. Cajus Fabricius

Professor of Theology at the University of Berlin

Originally published in Berlin, 1934

Introduction

The German Volk is united, but German Christianity is not yet. There is peace in the German Reich, but not yet in the German Evangelical Reich Church. The National Socialists have succeeded in uniting the German Christians. In the state, all political parties have disappeared. In the church, the old parties are indeed broken, but there is a threat that a partisan mentality will spread here, bearing all the ugly traits of past church-political struggles. There is a danger in the fact that the old German affliction, fraternal strife, which has fortunately been overcome in political life, is now celebrating its most horrific orgies in the church—precisely where one would first seek a place of peace and where, from the outset, the unity of the Volk should receive its innermost strength.

However, we must not lose courage simply because the current ecclesiastical situation does not yet correspond to the political one. It is a law of great historical development that the organizations of ecclesiastical life only gradually reshape themselves according to political transformations. This adaptation sometimes progresses extremely slowly. For example, it is well known that after Bismarck's founding of the Reich, it took more than half a century for the German evangelical regional churches to merge into church unions. Therefore, we must not become impatient if today the ecclesiastical events follow the political ones with a delay of several months.

And in our present situation, it must be noted that ecclesiastical matters have developed at an unusually rapid pace. The stormy progression, in which the political events of the year

1933 followed one another, has, to a certain degree, also transferred to church life, and remarkable achievements have already been made in the Evangelical Church. Hardly half a year after the beginning of Adolf Hitler's chancellorship, the constitution of the German Evangelical Church was already completed, its establishment having been ideologically prepared and actively implemented by the German Christians. At the same time, through the German Christians, a firm relationship of trust between the National Socialist movement and Evangelical Christianity was established, so that the Führer himself expressed his goodwill towards the German Christians at a decisive moment.

The German Christians now set about tackling their essential and at the same time their greatest and most difficult task: to permeate the German Volk, which had been spiritually corrupted by Marxist propaganda and shallow civilization but has now been awakened to new life through National Socialism, with a great national mission, inwardly infused with the spirit of the Gospel.

From various sides, theologians of opposing directions played into the hands of the German Christians—Sadducees on the one side, Pharisaic scribes on the other—and each of these groups claimed the entire church for itself, believed it could win over the masses of the Volk, and sought to take church leadership into its own hands.

This necessitates theological engagement. The German Christians do not seek scholarly disputes. They have only one great goal in mind: to bring the Gospel to the National Socialist German Volk, and they wish not only to teach the good news but also to live it. They want the entire Volk to live in the spirit of Jesus Christ, for sinners to be inwardly transformed by the power of the Crucified and become children of God, who rejoice in the forgiveness of sins from the Father and thereby gain inner peace, strength for brotherly love, and a life of joyful connection to the world. The German Christians, therefore, have nothing to offer the contending parties other than the simple Gospel. However, they must express the Gospel theologically in their struggle. Just as the Master Himself, in conversations with His theological opponents, had to give theological form to His joyful message—now to one side, now to the other—so too must His followers use theological expressions in order to assert themselves in the battle of opinions.

Our next task, therefore, is to clear the way with the weapons of reason so that the power of the living Gospel may then be able to exert its influence all the more freely within the German Volk. The following explanations are also intended to serve as a weapon in this defensive struggle.

I: Parties and Worldviews
in the Light of the Gospel

1. *The Grouping of the Parties and Their Predecessors*

The current parties in the Evangelical Church of Germany exhibit a striking resemblance to the political constellations as they took shape in 1932. This clearly demonstrates the law of historical development, which we initially considered—that ecclesiastical events represent a subsequent repetition of political processes.

In 1932, aside from the Catholic Center Party, there existed, on one side, the National Socialist German Workers' Party, along with the Stahlhelm and the German Nationalists, and on the other side, the Communists and Social Democrats. Today, German Christians find themselves between, on one side, the concealed community of Professor Karl Barth in Bonn and the church party associated with it, which calls itself "young" and "reformation-oriented" and has received strong new impulses from Professor Barth, and on the other, the externally acting "Faith Movement of the German National Church," which was founded in Berlin by Dr. Krause.

Both sides have made advances that temporarily threw the internal life of the church into great turmoil. On November 13, 1933, Dr. Krause, then still a district leader of the German Christians, abused a large assembly to present his earlier German-Irish views and misused National Socialist assembly discipline to create the impression that his opinion was the conviction of the

German Christians. He spoke of a "scapegoat and inferiority theology of the Rabbi Paul," demanded the abolition of the Old Testament, and disguised religion as faith in God within one's conscience, as love for one's neighbor, and as heroic piety. Although Dr. Krause had to immediately separate from the German Christians, and although the Reich Bishop soon condemned his teachings as heresy, an equally embarrassing advance now came from the other side. A so-called Emergency Pastors' League of a young reformist orientation, which had been active for some time, called on its members to read a pulpit announcement during worship services on the first Sundays of 1934, in which a utilitarian government theology was denounced for justifying paganism and heresy. As part of this announcement, a decree from the Reich Bishop was to be read, which specifically condemned the misuse of worship services for church-political purposes. Only a portion of the emergency pastors followed their leaders' call. The others were perhaps ashamed to read this sorrowful document. However, some at least stated that they wished to demonstrate their disobedience in a consecrated place.

It is not our task to judge these two fateful advances. We leave the judgment to the heavenly Judge. However, with God's help, we must work to quickly heal the wounds that have been torn open in this struggle. And we seek to do this by uncovering the deeper causes from which this conflict arises. The understanding of these connections will serve to soothe passions and calm agitated minds.

2. The Ideological Foundations of the Parties

As often happens in Germany, this dispute of opinions is ultimately not about church politics but about worldview questions. On the surface, it may seem as though both attacks truly meant what they were aimed at: the leadership of the Reich Church and the German Christians, who support the church leadership. In reality, however, neither is actually the target. In actual fact, neither the Reich Church nor the German Christians are being hit; they both want nothing more than to preach the Gospel to the German Volk. In fact, the thrust and counter-thrust are reciprocal. To name names, it is Barth against Krause and Krause against Barth. It is ultimately not about names and individuals, but rather about philosophical and theological systems associated with these names and individuals.

What lies in the background, broadly speaking, is on the one hand a philosophy of self-deification of man, and on the other hand a philosophy of divine fate; here, talk of the power and glory of man, there, talk of the powerlessness and insignificance of man; on one side, action and progress, on the other, submission and stagnation.

The German-believers (Deutschgläubigen) or German-churchers (Deutschkirchlichen), or whatever else they may call themselves—partly pagan, partly Christian, partly semi-Christian —thus the type that emerged in the Krauseputsch,[2] stands in the philosophical tradition of the 18th and even more so the 19th century. It is based on the worldview of the comfortable pre-war era, in which humanity was convinced that through the forces of its good nature and through its resources in culture, through technology and economy, through art and science as well as through social institutions, it could complete itself, eliminate chance, master the external world—in short: shape its own happiness and perfection. And when this worldview took on a religious character, it was filled with the conviction that man could redeem himself, that he could be his own savior, indeed, that humanity itself was the true deity. Under the influence of Kant's

---

2   ["Putsch" is a German word meaning coup or insurrection, typically referring to an attempted but unsuccessful overthrow of an established order —here led by the previously mentioned Dr. Krause.—Editor]

moral philosophy, but also under the impact of Ludwig Feuerbach, this worldview spread throughout the 19th century. It became the philosophy of Marxism, but also of Reform Judaism and of the societies for ethical culture that were popular among Jews.

In the 20th century, this mindset, under the influence of Nietzsche but also as a result of an overall heightened naturalism, took on a certain turn toward the naturalistic. And insofar as völkisch movements emerged and aligned themselves with this worldview, the ethnic or even racial foundations of humanity were emphasized as essential to its perfection. However, the fundamental view remains the same: that man is his own savior. Only now, instead of general humanity, race or Volk takes its place, and the deification of humanity now transforms into the deification of race or Volk.

Even in the present, these connections can be clearly observed. There are free-religious groups that yesterday called themselves "proletarian" and today call themselves "German" or "Aryan," yet they continue to practice the same cult of man as before, only under a different label. It also appears that numerous former communists will align themselves with the German-believers, as they still hope to achieve something for their old goals even under the changed circumstances.

This had to be said to understand one of the two contending parties. And now, the other side.

The immense catastrophe of the World War and the turmoil of the postwar period has profoundly shaken humanity's self-confidence in its own strength and cultural institutions. The cultural complacency and self-deification of the liberal era, no matter under what headings it presents itself, has since then appeared to anyone who looks openly at the present and future as an outdated worldview and way of life. Humanity has painfully experienced its own limitations. It has learned that there are forces in reality that it does not master, but that instead master it. It has gained an understanding that in the world, one must at every step reckon with what is called "fate."

This postwar spirit has found expression in Germany in very striking literary works. In philosophical historiography, Oswald Spengler's *The Decline of the West* was epoch-making, portraying the development of humanity as a fateful blossoming and decline of cultures. In philosophically inclined theology, this worldview found various expressions. The most striking among them was the theology of Professor Karl Barth, who, in an extraordinarily intellectual manner, articulated the ideas that God is not a mere opinion and that man is not God, that time and eternity, heaven and earth, church and world must be separated, and that the Gospel must also be viewed from this perspective.

This "dialectical theology," as it is commonly called, has lasting value insofar as it earnestly reminds Christianity of the limits of humanity, and insofar as it specifically supplements and corrects the theology of the past era, in which the divine was often excessively intertwined with the human. It is a theology of timeless significance, insofar as it represents nothing more than a critical commentary on the text of all theological systems. In this sense, it will leave an indelible mark on the spirit of future generations, just as the terrible distress of the postwar period will imprint upon human thought for a long time the realization that man is, in truth, not the sole master of his own fate.

But this position of dialectical theology has not remained merely a critical commentary on the text of theology. Among its adherents, it has increasingly become the very text of theology itself. This happens to varying degrees—more so with some, less with others. However, the more its characteristic features are worked out, the more it develops into a rigid, narrowly confined philosophical doctrine, specifically, a philosophy of human limitation. One now hears more about the remoteness of God than about closeness to God, more about God's judgment than about His grace, more about human distress than about redemption, more about limitation than about the divine power and wisdom of the Cross of Christ, more about the fear of God than about the blessedness of the children of God, more about hope than about fulfillment, more about the distress and insignificance of humanity in this world than about the life tasks that God sets, more about the separation between the Church and the worldly life of the Volk than about their inner connectedness.

This association reminds some more of the messages of doom proclaimed by certain prophets of Israel and John the Baptist rather than the message of comfort brought by Jesus. For in the Gospel, all these emphases are exactly the opposite of how they appear here. The Gospel precisely shows how one moves from separation from God to God, from judgment to grace, from sin to redemption, from slavish fear to the freedom and joy of the children of God, from hope to fulfillment—how all of this is ordered according to the living Christ, how through the spirit of Jesus Christ new people are created who live their entire lives in this world for the glory of God. And a Church that corresponds to the Gospel stands in the midst of the world and among the Volk, just as He did, who sat at the table with the blind and sinners.

Surely, the preachers of dialectical theology stand closer in spirit to the Gospel than their words suggest. But especially to the outside world and especially in church politics, where they appear as guardians of the true faith, they actually proclaim in biblical terms a philosophy of human nothingness, and they cast their critical question marks behind all the work and daring of energetic men who have grasped the meaning of the great new age and are convinced that the time of misery is over for the popular church as well as for the people and that a new day of courageous action has come.

Karl Barth originally did not want to be a church politician. He wished to pursue his theology with his students, far from the world, and if the times became too oppressive for him, to withdraw with a secret congregation into catacombs. Perhaps the building of catacombs has already begun. But apart from that, he has—surely against his own will—become the father of a fanatical church-political party. These were theologians who, around March 21, 1933, recognized the arrival of the new era and soon after constituted themselves as the "young reformational movement." They were originally close to the German Christians, as they, like them, recognized the necessity that in the new era, a new, vigorous action of the church was required. However, they were rejected along with the German Christians by Barth, who suggested that all "movements" originate from the devil. But from the outset, they used dialectical concepts, emphasized in particular the boundary between church and world, and became more and more those who stood on the sidelines, criticizing and rebuking—and, not infrequently using the dialectical method—identifying among the German Christians heresies that were sometimes real, sometimes apparent, and sometimes nonexistent.

These are the ideological backgrounds and interconnections that one must understand in order to comprehend the parties that currently disturb the life of the Evangelical Church in Germany.

The German Christians belong to none of the contending factions. They do not want parties at all, but rather a united Evangelical Church in a unified National Socialist Germany. And they desire nothing other than to proclaim the unadulterated, unabridged, pure Gospel to the German Volk in this church.

In this, their position aligns with that of National Socialism. For National Socialism, as its program immutably proclaims, stands on the foundation of positive Christianity. And this is not mere rhetoric but corresponds to the essence of the matter. National Socialism is neither a philosophy of human self-deification nor a philosophy of divine fate, but rather a people's movement (Volksbewegung), whose Führer is anchored in God and knows that a Volk can only draw its ultimate strength from genuine and profound piety. Certainly, National Socialism has achieved victory through an immense human exertion, and thus one can understand, though not entirely justify, that some National Socialists feel compelled to adhere to the liberalistic self-redemption religion adorned with völkisch or racial markers. However, deeper-thinking National Socialists, foremost among them the Führer, also recognize the other side of life. They have learned the limits of humanity sufficiently in the school of war and the hardship of the post-war period, thereby acquiring a hardened realism that accounts for all the finitudes of human life and channels all grand aspirations into proper, pragmatic courses. And the Führer knows, just as his best comrades-in-arms do, where his ultimate source of strength lies, and therefore, he is tireless in speaking of fate, providence, and Almighty God. Yet, this does not hinder him but rather drives him to fulfill new moral deeds and give new laws to the life of the entire Volk.

So much had to be said about the ecclesiastical situation and the position of the German Christians in general. Now I come to the details.

II: Individual Questions of Faith and Life in the Light of the Gospel

When I now speak of details, this does not mean that I intend to present the Gospel in all its aspects in the following. Even less do I intend to provide a complete "Dogmatics of the German Christians." Nor do I intend to formulate future doctrines. Rather, I am determined to express the living as living, regardless of whether all my readers find this mode of expression appropriate or not. I also wish to speak only of what currently moves minds. If I further refer to my themes as "questions," this does not mean that the matters discussed here are questionable within the Gospel or doubted by the German Christians. These matters are only disputed among the warring factions, ultimately between the philosophy of human self-deification and the philosophy of divine fate, which mistakenly attack the German Christians but in reality fight each other.

I therefore ask that all inquisitors and heresy judges forgive me if my mode of expression does not fully conform to their habits at times. Likewise, however, all heretics must accept that here an attempt is made to express the pure Gospel, which the German Christians seek to proclaim to the German Volk.

In this spirit, we now wish to speak of heroic piety and neighborly love, of God within and outside us, of sin and the cross, of Volk and church.

1. Heroic Piety

The German Volk is today full of heroic spirit. A league of heroic men has, through valiant struggle, achieved that our Volk rises to freedom after long disgrace. All National Socialists are attuned to struggle and victory.

It is therefore self-evident that the Christian piety of the German Volk also takes on heroic traits. We are convinced of fighting and winning through God's strength. And in this, not only are the victory and honor of our Volk in the council of nations a sacred concern for us, but we also wish that within our own Volk, the cause of God may triumph over the powers of darkness. That is why we see ourselves as one with the heroic spirit of Luther and recognize ourselves as followers of Jesus, who, through the Spirit of God, subdued demons, who with the word of truth fought against error and lies, and who, through the power of his life, conquered death.

And because the age of collapse, —[because the age] of cowardly submission and appeasement politics is over, [therefore] a piety that exhausts itself in resignation, that speaks more of human nothingness than of the power and blessedness of faith, is alien to us.

But our piety is not exhausted in heroism, in fighting and overcoming the world, nor do we idolize ourselves because we are fighters, nor do we idolize a person simply because he is heroic. Even Jesus Christ, the Son of God, is not our Lord and Savior simply because he was heroic. We know that the religion of hero worship corresponds to a primitive age, where men were just awakening from savagery and where the great among them conquered the opposing powers through strength and skill.

But for us as Christians, struggle is not the dominant part or even the entirety of our lives. It is only the outward aspect, the way in which we confront the opposing forces in the world. Our true life, that for which we fight, lies in the innermost depths of our souls, in realms where we find peace and profound communion with God.

2. Neighborly Love

Today, we experience in our German Volk an order and discipline, a camaraderie and obedience, a sense of belonging and a unity that repeatedly fills us with astonishment and admiration. Especially in our Volk, which for millennia suffered from internal division and whose masses were further incited to mutual hatred and mistrust through conversion, we now observe with ever-growing joy how people from different classes and tribes, educational backgrounds, and levels of wealth are powerfully united. We also see how even those who initially resisted are gradually becoming accustomed to the principle and reality that the common good takes precedence over self-interest. And we listen with the deepest agreement as the Führer of our Volk simultaneously extends an offer of peace to the entire world, and we hold the hope that in the not-too-distant future, brotherly respect and decent sentiment will prevail in the interactions between the nations of the earth—especially if the other nations also succeed in banishing the forces of dissolution within their own ranks and in shaping their lives with discipline and harmony.

In this great event, we as Christians perceive an tremendous wonder of God, which fills us with the deepest gratitude. We see in it an undertaking of organized neighborly love, the like of which has never been realized on such a scale in the history of the Christian religion. And we wholeheartedly and with joyful enthusiasm place ourselves in the service of this cause, working in our own way in smaller and larger circles to ensure that not only external discipline but also the fullest inner unity is established everywhere.

On the other hand, we look with deepest regret and greatest concern upon those who still do not understand the meaning of God's actions in our time. Hopefully, there are no longer any theologians today who believe they must conclude from their theology of fate that the Church should not concern itself with the social needs of the Volk because it is merely an institution for proclaiming the Word. However, as is unfortunately all too obvious, there are still Christians and theologians today who disturb the inner peace of the Church and violate brotherly love by slandering Christian brothers for alleged heresies. There may even be Christians who do not fight against this but allow it to happen—that foolish agitational articles from Germany are spread in the foreign press, thereby endangering world peace and the peaceful flourishing of the Christian churches by denigrating the reputation of the German Volk, which today represents the strongest bulwark against the anti-Christian power of Communism. These misguided brothers are not yet on our side, for they have not yet understood in what forms Christian love must manifest itself today.

However, we also do not want to be confused with the preachers of human self-redemption, who regard charity as the essential content of religion—formerly in the form of humanity or the solidarity of all mankind, today in the sense of the völkisch or racial community. Charity is certainly a noble thing and of immeasurable blessing for the nations of the earth. But it is not an absolute power that exists in itself; rather, it springs from the depths of the Godhead, and wherever there are Christians who have faith in God, they know in faith that love is only truly genuine and profound when it comes from faith.

Now our gaze shall turn to the depths of the Godhead and of faith.

3. God in Us and Outside of Us

The innermost and ultimate question at stake in the dispute of opinions is whether God is in us or outside of us. As we have noted, this was the underlying issue behind the formation of church parties, and it now concerns us again as we seek an expression of what is essential in the Gospel.

The Christian religion is neither to be equated with human self-redemption nor with the experience of a divine fate, and Christian piety is neither the proud self-awareness of being one with divinity nor the servile submission to a foreign lord. Rather, the Christian religion is the possession of divine fullness of life, which is incomparably broader and richer than either of the two opposing worldviews.

Our Christian faith is an innermost being-grasped by God, who is our Father and at the same time the Lord of Heaven and Earth. In this inner being-grasped, we are children of God. We have the peace of God in our hearts through the Holy Spirit, we place our will in obedience to the will of God in this spirit, and we look with trust upon the ways of God in this world. From this arises a joyful worship in our worldly life and a courageous overcoming of opposing forces. But at the same time, we are certain that our life unfolds within very specific boundaries set by God as fate, and we humbly acknowledge that God, as the Lord of the world, shapes our life as it pleases Him, and that He gives direction to all our striving and working in accordance with His mysterious counsel.

But let us now ask more precisely: How does the Christian religion relate to the two opposing standpoints? The answer is: It encompasses both—the divinity as well as the devotion to God, but in such a way that divinity is the essential, the core, the truly sustaining element, whereas devotion to God is the ever-resonating accompaniment, the outward-facing side of our inner life. This is why the Christian message is called the good news—because it is precisely the blessed security in the Father's love, and not the trembling submission under the lord of the world, that is predominant; because Christians have not received a spirit of fear and servitude, but rather the spirit of joy, peace, and divine sonship.

From here, a perspective now opens up on the conditions among races and the religions of humanity, and it is necessary to briefly address this, as racial matters today stand at the forefront of public discussion.

The Gospel applies to all peoples and races, and over the course of millennia, people from all nations and races have come to the Gospel. But it is beyond doubt and is, in fact, a great, irrefutable historical fact that the Christian world religion has thus far become predominantly the religion of the Aryan peoples of the West. On the other hand, it is indisputable that the Christian religion has been rejected by the overwhelming majority of the Jewish people, as well as by the Semites in general. The entire New Testament bears unanimous testimony to the unbelief of the Jews, and up to this day, only a very small portion of the Jewish population, in Germany as elsewhere, has embraced the Gospel. This evidently stems from the fact that Aryans, by their general natural disposition and religious sentiment, are more inclined toward the Gospel than the Semites. The Aryans, in their religion, display a yearning for deification, an energetic striving toward divine perfection, a will to become one with the deity and thereby be liberated from the world and all its constraints. In India, which has the longest and richest religious development of this kind, these characteristics have been worked out in particularly radical form. The Semites, however, especially in Judaism and Islam, have developed their piety in a different direction. They have a tendency toward submission, surrendering themselves as servants to the divine Lord, finding their perfection precisely in the sense of their own insignificance. It is evidently due to this differing nature of the races that the Gospel has been predominantly embraced by Aryans but hardly at all by Semites. Certainly, both races find something in the Gospel that resonates with their deepest longing and search. But what is dominant in the Gospel, as we have seen, is the divinity that the Aryan man in particular seeks, whereas the humble submission merely echoes along, aligning with the Semitic nature.

From this consideration, an important conclusion arises for our present situation. We do not have the task today of shaping the Gospel for the Aryan race or even abolishing it, as if it were an imposed Semitic religious form that is inherently foreign to us. Rather, Christianity is the world religion, given to us by God, in which we, like all Aryan peoples of the West, have been rooted for centuries with our innermost being and whose fullness of life we continually experience in new awakenings. However, we must ensure that the Gospel is in no way bent toward Judeo-Christianity or even Judaism, meaning that it must not be transformed from a religion of freedom and sonship into a religion of fear and servitude.

From this follows the self-evident position of all Christians regarding the Old Testament. I cannot deal with this matter in detail here, as my topic is the Gospel and not the Old Testament. However, one fundamental point must be stated: the position of a Christian towards the Old Testament can and must be no different from that which our Lord and Master himself took. Whoever knows the Gospels knows what this means, and whoever does not yet know them should read them! We understand the Old Testament as Jesus understood it; we abolish what he abolished, and we keep what he kept. What in it corresponds to the Gospel, we uphold. But we firmly reject, in the name of Jesus, the Judeo-Christian presumption of equating the Old Testament with the New.

4. Cross and Sin

When we have spoken of God in us and outside us, and of the blessedness and humility of the children of God, the content of the Gospel is still not exhausted. It is an essential part of the Christian faith that we come into sonship through the power of the Crucified One, out of sin.

On this point, the dispute between the opposing factions has flared up particularly fiercely. The proponents of human self-redemption praise the goodness of human nature and therefore speak contemptuously of the "scapegoat and inferiority theology of Rabbi Paul." Conversely, those who emphasize the limits of humanity speak of the power of human sin to such an extent that redemption is pushed into the distant future. And when they speak of the crucified Redeemer, they like to emphasize again the strangeness and repulsiveness—the "offense of the Cross."

Both parties distance themselves from the Gospel to the extent that their proclamation diverges in these two directions. The Gospel does not align with an idealized image of human goodness that does not exist; rather, it takes man in his full reality, just as he appears in the mirror of Christian perfection—that is, as one who is not what he should be, but is full of sin. And thus, redemption is not self-fulfillment, but rather it comes from the life force of the Redeemer, from whose fullness Christians at all times receive grace upon grace. The fullness of life in Christ, from which salvation comes, extends far beyond what is revealed in his death on the cross. Yet, even the event of the crucifixion itself contains a fullness of life, which has been repeatedly emphasized throughout Christian history. What is essential about the cross, however, is that it is a stumbling block. And it is particularly a stumbling block for the Jews, who are lost. To those who are saved, it is divine power and divine wisdom. In it, Christianity sees the atonement, in which God presents himself to mankind, where he places the Crucified as atonement so that mankind, once and for all, is no longer in need of an expiatory sacrifice. Beyond this, however, the cross is, for Christianity, the mysterious expression of the fact that man, who is full of the living Christ, dies to sin with him and rises to a new sanctified life.

We must once again look beyond races and religions, especially since in the dispute between the parties, the racial aspect seems to be decisive here. The rhetoric of the "scapegoat and theology of inferiority of Rabbi Paul" must be abandoned once and for all. Atonement and scapegoats were not unique to the Semites but existed in all religions that recognized guilt and sin, and especially in the law of the ancient Germans, there is much mention of compensation paid for transgressions. And regarding what is called the "feeling of inferiority" by Paul, there is a serious misunderstanding. The feeling of sin, which refers to the awareness of one's own imperfection before God and the conviction that one is far from being what one should be, is found nowhere as prominently as among the Aryan peoples, among whom the Jews have brought about the most radical pessimism. It corresponds to the high-reaching spirit and the longing for deification in the Aryan man that he experiences his distance from divinity as most painful.

Thus, it is once again quite understandable that the Christian religion was rejected by the masses of the Jews but was accepted by the Aryan peoples of the West. And we do not allow the Gospel to be viewed with suspicion as if it were a Jewish message that does not correspond to our kind.

5. Volk and Church

If I still speak of Volk and Church, I do so only incidentally. For the question of how the peoples' church (Volkskirche) is structured in a country is not a question of the Gospel, but rather a question of church practice and church law. However, if I nevertheless say something about Volk and Church, it is because this question is particularly emphasized by the opposing parties and treated as if it were among the most fundamental matters of faith.

From the perspective of the Gospel, only one thing needs to be said regarding the question of "Volk and Church": the people's church (Volkskirche) must be structured in such a way that the Gospel can spread freely to all members of the Volk. This was also the way of Jesus. He was the Holy One of God, but he did not withdraw from the Volk into secluded sanctuaries to proclaim an elaborate doctrine to an isolated "church people." His powerful preaching resounded not only in the synagogues, but also on the mountains of the land, on the shores of the sea, in houses, and in the public squares of villages and cities. And he did not speak only for the edification of believing Jews, but sat at the table with tax collectors and sinners and invited all the Volk from the streets and highways to himself. This must also be the practice of the church within our Volk.

The opposing parties hold different views. Some rail against the "clergy," desiring a purely lay church and seeking the sacred exclusively in the worldly life of the Volk. Others anxiously separate the church from the world and the worldly Volk; they constantly fear that the church might become overly entangled with the world. They particularly believe they must shield their youth and elders in their church associations from any contact with secular organizations, as if these were pure heathenism and only in those lay true Christianity.

The path of the German Christians must be different—it must be the path of Jesus. We must proclaim the Gospel on the streets and in the houses, in the public squares and on the mountains. Above all, we must go into the great National Socialist organizations of the Volk, both those of the youth and those of the adults. There, as we know, millions of fervent hearts await us—everywhere that souls have awakened and yearn for nourishment for their innermost lives. We want to win them over and welcome them with open arms into the great evangelical church of the German Volk.

However, one condition must be met today: the German Volk, as it exists today, must have absolute trust in its church. The Volk, having freed itself after years of unspeakable hardship from the dominance of foreign spirits and foreign races, must not harbor the suspicion that this spirit and these people will once again take hold of its church. If this were to happen, then the doors that are currently open to the Gospel within the Volk would once again be shut. Therefore, for the sake of the Gospel, church laws must be in force—laws that, while not themselves the Gospel and thus not contradicting it, nonetheless help ensure that the Gospel can unfold its unbroken power within the Volk.

Conclusion

At the end of our reflection, our gaze turns toward the future. As German Christians, we live more in the future with our thoughts than in the present. We are responsible for the proclamation of the Gospel among the German Volk. The way must be cleared for this in the future.

The present still places difficult obstacles in our way. There are still church parties in the non-partisan Reich. The German Christians are not a party. But alongside them stand parties that bitterly oppose one another. We have seen enough of them in our discussion. But what is to become of the future?

In the Reich, not only have the old political parties disappeared, but anyone who attempts to form new political parties in the future will be severely punished. They will be regarded as traitors to the country. Such laws are not possible within the Church. However, as Christians, we are obligated to take to heart what the State upholds—the unconditional duty of unity—upon our conscience, and to work with all our strength to ensure that the rising partisanship is overcome by the compelling power of the Gospel, so that the spirit of love and discipline conquers all the loveless and undisciplined.

GERMANY AND THE RELIGIOUS WORLD SITUATION

EXPLANATIONS AND PROPOSALS

by

D. Cajus Fabricius

Originally published 1937
By Herman Püschel, Dresden

Preface

The problems addressed in the following pages are so extensive that they extend not only into the entirety of theology but also into numerous adjacent fields. Therefore, they can only be treated comprehensively in very large works. However, these problems have gained such current and public significance in the present situation that they must also be discussed briefly and concisely for immediate use.

At the same time, these problems are being applied to Germany today to such an extent that it is necessary to clearly outline the German perspective.

This will be attempted in the following presentation, first by outlining a picture of the situation and then by addressing in brief theses the questions that currently concern people. What I say about this, I do not say officially—neither on behalf of the German Reich nor on behalf of the German Evangelical Church. It is an attempt by a Christian theologian, albeit as a theologian who has thoroughly reflected on the addressed problems. The present situation had to be taken into account, so I hope that I can be understood both domestically and abroad.

Regarding the questions that have not yet been addressed here, I would like to refer to some of my other publications: *Positive Christianity in the New State* (published by H. Pülschel, Dresden); *Ecumenical Handbook of Christian Churches* (Evangelical Press Association, Berlin-Steglitz); *Corpus Confessionum* (W. de Gruyter, Berlin).

I would be particularly grateful if my readers would let me know how they judge the matters discussed in these pages.

Berlin NW 87, Händel-Allee 30, in July 1937.

Cajus Fabricius.

I: The World Situation and Its Problems

1. Crisis Sentiment in the Churches of the West

In recent times, Christian thinkers in the West have claimed that the present moment represents a severe crisis, a tremendous challenge to the Christian churches. They point out that in several countries of Europe, such as Russia, Italy, and Germany, the "totalitarian state" has emerged, demanding absolute authority. This claim was particularly emphasized during the preparations for the major world conferences of 1937 in Oxford and Edinburgh. It was pointed out that in Germany, as in Italy and Russia, the total state is being "deified" and "worshiped" and that this modern idolatry stands in stark opposition to the worship of the living God revealed to the world in Christ.

In doing so, the Christians of the Western churches often focus specifically on Germany. With its strongly pronounced authoritarian claims, Germany is seen as the country in which evangelical churches are struggling under an oppressive burden. The claim is that evangelical Christianity in Germany is now under a challenge comparable to that which the Christians of Fascist Italy faced, where the state itself attempted to take control of the church. People have referred to Germany as the land of the Reformation and emphasized that it has become a land under threat, a battlefield where the fate of evangelical life is being decided anew after centuries of struggle. It has been said that evangelical Germany today represents an experiment to determine whether the Christian gospel and the total state can coexist. The situation is compared to the struggles in totalitarian Italy or Bolshevist Russia, and its significance is emphasized as not merely national but global—affecting the faith of 650 million Christians worldwide to fight against the onslaught of political anti-Christianity.

Under the influence of the current situation, Christian issues have been discussed in international church movements for several years. Accordingly, themes have been established for the world conferences. At the Oxford Conference on "Practical Christianity," the general theme was: "Church, People, and State." At the World Conference on "Faith and Church Constitution" in Edinburgh, time was devoted to themes that appeared to be problems of the present but are closely connected to timeless questions, which, however, gain particular significance in this crisis—namely, grace and the church, the spiritual office, the Word of God, and sacraments.

2. German Assessment of the World Situation

For us Germans, it seems necessary to address the current situation and its challenges with an open word in order to eliminate misunderstandings and simultaneously promote peaceful cooperation between peoples and foster friendly relations between the churches.

We Christians in Germany agree with Christians in the Western world that the high spiritual culture emanating from the Gospel, and its power within humanity, is now engaged in a life-and-death struggle against mighty enemies. These enemies can generally be summed up as the attitudes described in the Western world as "secularism," which refers to a tendency among large segments of the population to entirely abandon the spiritual and eternal values of Christian culture and focus solely on material goods and the care of earthly life. The struggle against the living God and disregard for Him as the highest authority, as well as the notion that all human endeavors should be limited to achieving material success and enjoying the goods of this earthly life, characterize this secularism. It expresses itself exclusively in the profane realms of life, such as technical and economic fields, art and science, or in the care of human communities, but lacks a holy life of the spirit.

We Germans, however, further believe that within this general secularism, the greatest threat to the Christian way of life today does not come from the state or a new god but rather from the power that our Lord and Master has already identified and fought as the true adversary in every time and place: Mammon, which has always been perceived by Christians as the most dangerous enemy. Mammon represents enslavement to material goods, the elevation of temporal life as the highest value, and, above all, service to money—that is, to power—with the hope of using it to gain and possess the whole world and its glory.

In its most dangerous form, Mammon dominates the modern world and seeks to take possession of all its treasures. It has found its worst expression in Russian Bolshevism. This ideology is inspired by the economic theories of the Jew Karl Marx, which form the foundation of practical materialism. According to this worldview, physical life, sensory pleasure, and physical labor are the highest goals of human existence. In this theory and practice, the state plays an important role. It is no longer the highest being, but merely the preeminent tool for ensuring complete secular production. In this system, atheistic Bolshevism desires to establish itself as the worldwide power that eliminates all religion.

Bolshevism has become an extraordinarily dangerous enemy of Christianity in all its forms. It fights against the church, as evidenced by the fact that over 40,000 priests have already fallen victim to its wrath. It is also a mortal enemy of all nationalist movements and opposes any organization of human life rooted in traditional values. The brutal suppression of religion and culture in the Soviet Union is clear proof of this.

However, we must state that the danger of secularism does not exist only in Bolshevism. It also lurks in the form of capitalist materialism, which, while presenting itself differently, is no less deadly to the Christian faith. Both forces—Bolshevism and unrestrained capitalism—share a common goal: the complete destruction of the Christian worldview. This realization demands vigilance, ensuring that attention is not diverted to the so-called German danger at the expense of addressing this genuine and pressing threat.

But even in the West, the spirit of Mammon can be found. It prevails under the name "Utilitarianism" everywhere that material gain, business, capital, or the profit of an individual person or nation is regarded as the highest good. Even here, the state is occasionally seen as Mammon's most important helper, assuming that the state's task is to regulate life primarily so that its citizens, at home and abroad, can conduct business as effectively as possible.

Apart from these types of Eastern and Western materialism, the service of Mammon can be felt throughout the world today. There exists a world power of money that seeks to ensnare people with demonic force. This power, however, is connected to international Jewry, which, through capital, holds a significant share in the mammonistic world domination.

3. The National Uprising of the German People

Germany, too, was long ruled by the power of international Mammonism. Through its national uprising, it has freed itself from this domination. "Breaking the bondage of interest" and fighting against "Jewish materialism" are central points of the National Socialist program and the practical policies of the Third Reich. In this way, the German people have broken the chains that today still subjugate a large part of humanity, and by struggling and prevailing, they have rejected the most brutal challenge that confronts Christian humanity today. This is the fundamental fact that must be considered first when speaking of idolatry in modern humanity and the challenges faced by the Christian nations of the present.

What has happened in Germany was not the creation of an absolute state, which is now worshiped as a new god after the sanctuaries of Mammon have been shattered. It is nothing more than this: a Christian nation, after years of oppression and exploitation by foreign powers, has liberated itself.

From the moral neglect of a decayed house, the German nation has risen to discipline and order, has united after a long period of political division into a forceful unity, and, after an era of Christianity, has regained its honor among the nations of the world. In this, nothing extraordinary has occurred—only what has long been a given among other Christian nations, and these nations should therefore have no concerns about Germany.

However, we evangelical Germans view this national revival as an immense act of God upon our people and as a particularly gracious provision of divine providence. But even this does not mean the idolization of our own people or state, which other Christian nations might see as a challenge. It does not even mean that we claim any special favor for our people in the divine world order. In this regard, we are far behind some Americans who refer to their country as "God's land." Equally distant are we from the viewpoint of some Englishmen who believe their nation to be the chosen people of God and that the promise of world dominion for the people of Israel has been fulfilled in the British Empire.

For our part, we do not regard such beliefs as a threat to Christianity, but rather as a peculiarity. All the more, we may expect that our Christian joy at the renewal of our people and the gratitude we humbly offer to God together with our Führer, Adolf Hitler, will not be seen by other Christian nations as a challenge, nor even as a peculiarity, but rather as something self-evident.

4. Neo-Paganism

There are indeed certain movements in Germany today, of which one might even say with some satisfaction that they are "expanding the people." These are those associations that are called "free-thinking humanists" or "neo-pagans," and they typically refer to themselves as "German believers." The members of these associations, among whom are many former Marxists, largely adhere to the tradition of foreign thinkers who, in earlier times, influenced German philosophy. Among them, one often references the legacy of Ludwig Feuerbach, who was influenced by French skepticism and proclaimed a "religion of humanity," as well as Ernst Haeckel, who, following the Englishman Charles Darwin and the Jew Baruch Spinoza, taught a naturalistic "monism." Lastly, there were the influences of Friedrich Nietzsche, who, building on Darwin's theory of evolution, developed a naturalistic philosophy of the "Übermensch" (superman).

The members of these associations not only emphasize that their views represent a "German" faith but also profess allegiance to National Socialism. They form a counterweight to the so-called "religious socialists," who regard Marxism as a kind of religion.

We observe these associations in Germany with great attention. Their books and publications have caused some concern because they frequently claim not only to be good National Socialists but even to be the true representatives of National Socialism. They are also responsible for misleading Christians in other countries, giving them the false impression that neo-paganism is widespread in Germany and may even be the secret religion of the National Socialist Party and the state.

This assumption has primarily led to the belief that Germany worships the "total state" as a god. In reality, however, none of these associations are official. They are also so fragmented and small, and receive so little support from the major Christian churches, that they cannot in any way be considered representative of our nation as a whole or even a significant part of the German Volk.

5. The Christian Character of National Socialism

The German Volk, in its overwhelming majority, is and remains a Christian Volk. More than 40 million belong to the German Evangelical Church, and more than 20 million to the Roman Catholic Church.

The Christian religion as the religion of the German Volk is not only a fact but is also guaranteed through the program of the National Socialist Party, which declares that "the Party as such represents the standpoint of a positive Christianity." The Party, therefore, does not take the position of neo-paganism but instead assumes that Christianity is the German Volksreligion (national religion).

From all this, we are convinced that the strengthening of the German Volk does not present a challenge to the Christian nations and churches. On the contrary: by casting off Mammonism and fighting the true enemy of Christianity—Bolshevism—the experienced Christian German Volk is performing a Christian service, which other nations must recognize and through which they must become Germany's allies if they wish to act in accordance with Christian principles.

However, since we have noticed that certain misunderstandings in world public opinion regarding the actual situation of our nation have caused concern among Christian churches abroad, we are prepared to exchange thoughts in friendship with our Christian friends around the world regarding the issues that concern them—Church, Volk, and State; Church, Word, and Grace.

II: Church, Volk, and State

1. The Christian Understanding of Man, History, and Community

God created the world and, within it, mankind. Through His Spirit, He continuously creates anew and sustains what has been created, both in the world and in man. God created the diversity of mankind in such a way that people are not entirely equal to one another but instead distinguish themselves as individuals and, in tribes, nations (Völker), and races, represent distinct types and develop characteristic traits—yet in a way that personal interaction among all people in humanity remains possible. Man is destined by God to elevate himself beyond mere natural existence, to attain salvation, and to fulfill his duties in this world to the glory of God.

Therefore, according to the Christian view, man is neither created by the Devil, nor does sin exist entirely apart from God,[3] nor is he himself God, inventing the concept of the Creator from his own imagination.

God reveals Himself to man through His Spirit in the history of both the individual and the nations. The perfect revelation of God in Jesus Christ also reveals the meaning of history. It teaches that the emerging nations, guided by God, serve the greater good. The manner in which God, in history, actually realizes His purposes

---

3   [It seems Fabricius is emphasizing that sin is not an autonomous force or power beyond God's reach or divine sovereignty.—Editor]

among the nations and individuals remains shrouded in mystery. However, within the framework of this mystery, man repeatedly recognizes the workings of divine providence—namely, where the Volk and individuals experience particularly exalted moments of existence.

Thus, history is neither entirely meaningless nor merely the result of human sin, nor is its meaning entirely comprehensible in every respect.

The human communities, with their laws in all their diversity, are orders of God, arranged in such a way that smaller communities do not dissolve the larger ones but are integrated into them. In the community, which is spiritually animated, the unity of the divine spirit is revealed.

The communities and their laws are neither absolute nor unconditionally willed by God; rather, they are disturbed by sin and thus imperfect, yet they are not mere arbitrary human constructs either, nor are they direct representations of the divine.

2. The Church as a Community

The Christian Church is the community of all believers on earth who are united in the foundations of faith and bound together through love.

The shared foundation of faith in the Christian Church is the power of the living God, which has found its expression in the Gospel.

The Gospel is the joyful message that God is our Father and we are His children. This awareness deepens our inner peace and trust in the merciful love of God, renews in us the love for our brethren, and gives us strength for all righteous work. We receive all these gifts through the power of Jesus Christ, who raises us through grace from mere community to communion with the Father.

The Church is not a human institution but was founded by Christ and is guided by the divine Spirit. However, as a community, it also partakes in all human and worldly affairs.

The Church, as a human community, does not exist apart from the broader human community but rather participates in the diversity and transformation of human societal forms.

It is interwoven, one after another and alongside one another, with the forms of family, tribe, Volk, empire, religious, national, and international associations. It is sometimes inclined toward consolidating unity, at other times drawn into division and conspiracy, into friendships or secret alliances. It also partakes in all processes of renewal and tensions in social life, whether individualistic or collectivist, whether revolutionary-driven or static-conservative.

It contains within itself all forms of governance found in human communities. It has officials, authorities, tribunals, representatives, and laws. It is governed democratically, aristocratically, constitutionally, monarchically, or in an absolutist manner.

All these forms do not essentially differ from their corresponding secular counterparts. They are not naturally consecrated, meaning, they possess no sacred content but rather a worldly function. However, a sacred aspect is sometimes attributed to the form itself, often leading to the form being perceived as sacred and thus receiving a special dignity that grants it a higher status. Conversely, the social form may also be seen as merely an external framework for a particular community.

The social structures within which the Church finds itself at any given time generally mirror the secular environment in which the Church exists. This is governed by a principle in which Church institutions adjust to worldly social forms. At the same time, however, the sacred nature of the Church also contributes to stability. Secular communities, in contrast, tend to change their forms more frequently than ecclesiastical communities do.

3. The Volk

Among the human communities with which the Christian Church interacts and by which it is shaped, the nations have always held, and still today hold, a particularly prominent position.

We call nations the highest human communities within humanity.

The unity of a nation is maintained by a whole range of circumstantial factors. These include natural, partly spiritual, and partly historical elements, such as blood inheritance, common residence, language, shared cultural development, religion, historical destiny, and above all, an inherent sense of belonging. The stronger these bonds, the greater the unity and cohesion of the nation.

In the largest Christian nations, which today dominate life on earth, these prerequisites exist to varying degrees.

Yet despite all this, a strong national self-awareness prevails in all these Christian nations. This is not diminished by the Christian character of these nations but, on the contrary, is often deeply interwoven with their Christianity.

In this respect, the German Volk occupies a special position among Christian nations. Unique only is the fact that the German has retained a sense of belonging to his smaller nation within the greater national whole. A sense of national unity exists among the German Volk, yet at the same time, a deep sense of connection to local and regional communities is preserved.

Even after the experience of the last war, the German did not separate himself from his regional identity. Rather, he continued to affirm the significance of this unity within the greater whole.

As a result, the German Volk stands among the Christian nations as an example of how national identity does not necessarily mean isolation or estrangement from others but can develop as a self-contained national consciousness. This does not place the German Volk in opposition to the broader unity of Christian nations but instead affirms an organic sense of Christian brotherly love that goes beyond mere political or economic interests.

4. Church and Volk

Given the high significance that nations hold as the highest form of human community within mankind, and based on the fact that churches are generally integrated into worldly community structures, it is self-evident that the Christian Church on earth organizes itself within national churches.

This structuring of the Church according to nations does not necessarily mean a decline of the Church. There are even groups of independent national churches in which strong bonds of unity are maintained. This is the case, for example, with the Reformed Churches of the East and the Lutheran churches of the North.

The national community of Christians is sometimes even regarded as highly beneficial. This is demonstrated by the efforts to unite not only similar but also differing groups within certain national church communities. The Federal Council of Christian Churches in America, the Association of Free Churches in England, the Swiss Evangelical Church Federation, and other similar organizations that have been successfully established show this with unmistakable clarity.

There are even efforts to establish uniform national churches that are not only united under a common church government but also share a unified doctrine and form of worship. Such efforts, however, have so far faced considerable difficulties. A historical example is Great Britain in the 17th century, where the attempt to unify the various Christian churches under an episcopal or

Presbyterian system led to bitter conflicts and ultimately resulted in bloody civil wars.

In Germany, church unification efforts have been observed for quite some time. In 1922, the 28 regional churches, which at that time still largely retained the political structures of earlier times, joined together to form the German Evangelical Church Federation. Later, the Herrnhuters and some Reformed congregations also joined. Additionally, four groups of free churches united to form the Association of Free Churches.

In 1933, after the national uprising, the formation of the German Evangelical Church was proclaimed, aiming to bring about a unified national church while still allowing the traditions of individual regional churches and distinct religious orders and practices to remain untouched.

Conceptual confusion prevails today in Germany, where the nation has been unified into a powerful entity, regarding ideas that call for a similarly uniform national church. These ideas resemble those that sought to establish a national church in England during the 17th century. It is too early to assess how such efforts will develop, but one can already discern two tendencies:

1. A purely German national church, encompassing the entire Volk and absorbing all Evangelical and former Roman Catholic Germans into itself. The result would be that Roman Catholic Christians, to the extent that they remain strictly bound to Rome, would be excluded from this church. The recognition of existing confessions is intended, their organization, their constitution, their doctrine, and their worship service to be restructured in favor of the other. However, the widespread belief remains that a shared Christian foundation exists in both major churches. Despite their confessional differences, this gives Christians in Germany a sense of community, and the sectarian conflicts of previous centuries have faded into the background. Realistically, as we see in National Socialist Germany, we must work toward resolving this issue first. Beyond this, achieving unification is just

as impossible in Germany as it is in all other countries where Evangelical and Roman Catholic Christians live side by side.

2. Of particular note is the effort of Old Catholics to establish a Catholic German national church. Over time, this may achieve a certain degree of success. It is conceivable that many dissatisfied Roman Catholics, who cannot bring themselves to take the step toward the Evangelical Church but are nonetheless repelled by the Roman system of their Church, may align themselves with the Old Catholic movement. There is little information available about these movements, and they seem to take a friendly stance toward the Evangelical Church, though they will never fully merge with it.

3. Nor is it possible to establish a Christian national church that is neither Evangelical nor Catholic. From experiences of this kind, we are well aware of historical events in the secular world, and their success can only be measured over a long period. Much is being done—the "One Christ" and "Together in Christ" brotherhoods emphasize the goal of unity, but they have merely abstracted reality and, in doing so, have neither diminished nor destroyed the love of the Christian denominations. However, it may still be possible to establish a national church in Germany in which Evangelical and Roman Catholic Christians who are not bound to Rome come together. Yet such a church would not be a German national church but rather a newly established church existing alongside the two major existing churches.

4. Likewise, only a very small sect would emerge if a group of neo-pagans were to take leadership in founding a German national church. No Christians would follow them, only small groups of the internally divided "German believers," and it would result in a formation similar to the free church congregations that developed out of the national church movements of the German Catholics around the middle of the last century. These groups led a meager shadow existence until they ultimately dissolved largely into Marxist free-thought movements.

5. Race

Races are physical and spiritual modifications of humanity. They are generally broader in scope than nations. They represent characteristic types that clearly distinguish themselves from one another, yet they can also intermingle and merge into each other.

The spiritual characteristics of a race manifest in history with varying degrees of intensity. Their emergence is determined not only by natural circumstances but also by specific historical destinies that races experience throughout history.

Because of the broad nature of races, the race problem becomes a pressing issue for individual nations only under particular historical circumstances. This occurs primarily in times of significant movement and transformation, when new oppositions arise and the question of the dominance of one race over another comes into focus.

Among the great Christian nations, the race problem has become particularly prominent in North America in recent decades, in its conflicts with people of color and with Judaism. In Germany, racial questions have remained a persistent issue due to its confrontation with Judaism.

While in Germany this is not a matter of biological racial differences but rather a theological and sociological problem, it is nevertheless noteworthy that certain Jewish circles, which religiously still belong to Judaism, are particularly engaged in political activity. Rather, the Jewish question in Germany has fundamentally been addressed from a moral standpoint.

As early as the 19th century, the Evangelical theologian and clergyman Adolf Stoecker recognized the moral danger associated with the increasing power of Judaism. He regarded as threatening Judaism's predominant interest in money and business, meaning the spirit of Mammon, which had become a defining trait of Judaism.

At the same time, National Socialism's position toward Judaism was also taken from a moral perspective. Adolf Hitler and many others observed, in the period following World War I, that not only were leading positions in the German government occupied by Jews, but that Jews were also increasingly spreading into the leading circles of German society, while at the same time aligning globally with forces interested in the political oppression and economic exploitation of the German Volk.

For this reason, Adolf Hitler's struggle for the liberation of Germany also had to be a struggle for liberation from Jewish domination.

In doing so, not only was the influence of major Jewish financiers regarded as dangerous, but so too was the mixing of German and Jewish blood, as it was believed that this would transfer Jewish traits to the German spirit.

This also determined the policies of the Third Reich. Everything undertaken has been solely aimed at eliminating extraneous influences and preventing the mixing of German and Jewish blood.

At no point in Germany, despite what is often claimed abroad, has there been a cruel persecution or extermination of Jews. There were still nearly as many Jews living in Germany after 1933 as before, continuing their businesses in peace. Some left for political reasons or due to unfavorable economic conditions.

Of course, it is true that just as political Jews were expected to abandon their harmful traits, so too were Germans expected to do the same. However, the German Volk rejected the idea that its morally established self-reflection and clear moral consciousness should be made to share in any guilt for Jewish domination.

As a Christian Volk, we must strongly reject the accusation that we lack Christian love in addressing the Jewish problem. The removal of Jewish domination was one of the preconditions for undertaking one of the greatest acts of Christian charity, namely, that in a great nation, not only were 60 million people freed from moral decline, but a healthy and decent social order was restored. In particular, nearly a third of the Volk was brought back from unemployment into productive work.

In the treatment of Jews by Germans, no violation of Christian love is to be found, just as it was not contrary to Christ's love when our Lord and Master, in His struggle against Mammon, drove the Jews out of the temple, where they were selling doves, conducting money exchanges, and thereby turning the house of God into a den of murderers.

6. Church and Race

The race question can also become a church question. However, this does not make it a matter of faith but merely of church practice. Just as the Christian Church is not harmed and does not contradict its nature when it is organized by nations, it likewise cannot be rejected that, under certain circumstances, special racial groups may be formed within the Church.

Since the Christian religion has generally become the religion of the Aryan nations of the West, the race problem usually plays no role in the Church. It only becomes significant under particular historical circumstances—today in America as the Negro problem, in Germany as the Jewish question.

In America, wherever the race problem has become apparent, the racial issue has been resolved by the Negroes forming independent churches. This has shaped the relationship with people of color in such a way that these Negroes largely remain segregated groups.

After the German Volk freed itself from Jewish domination, which was closely linked to national decline, one must understand that even within the German Evangelical Church, the desire has arisen to consolidate Jewish Christians—whose numbers in Germany are actually very small—into separate congregations and to entrust the pastoral care of Jewish descent to those of their own, since their presence in German congregations has become almost nonexistent after stepping down from their offices.

This matter has been exaggerated into an issue of fundamental importance by Jews and Christians around the world. As a result, Christians in Germany have been labeled as haters and heathens. In contrast, it is precisely on this point that one must refer to the faith and practice of the apostolic age. The Apostle Paul held the belief that the Church is one in Christ, its head, and that all belong to this Church regardless of status, gender, or race. At the same time, however, church practice dictates that everyone should remain within the confession in which they were raised, that they should not be treated unjustly regarding salvation, and that the Jewish question should be resolved in a manner similar to Paul's approach—not through direct negotiations with the Apostles, but rather by choosing to engage in missionary work among the Gentiles with Barnabas, while James, Peter, and John were to go among the Jews.

7. The State

The state is closely connected with the Volk, so closely that the same community is often referred to alternately as "Volk" and as "State." However, the two must be consciously distinguished from one another.

Even externally, their boundaries are different. The Volk cannot be precisely delineated, whereas the state possesses fixed borders defined by treaties and boundary markers. There are also states that encompass only parts of a Volk and others that include multiple nations within them.

The Volk is an organism, while the state is an organization. The Volk is represented by the entirety of all people, insofar as they are connected by birth or by their living relationships, while the state is represented by its officials, who govern, and in the laws through which they govern it. The common life of the Volk is held together by the orders of morality, law, and custom; in state life, the legal orders prevail.

The national character (Volkstum) encompasses the entire natural existence and the whole of culture in its five domains: technical-economic, aesthetic, intellectual, social, and moral life. The state exercises its functions directly within the social cultural domain, specifically in maintaining the public order of the Volk through the judicial system, leadership in national defense, and, beyond that, it may also place the broader life of the Volk—its natural life as well as its culture—under its care, supervision, and promotion.

8. The Total State

A "total state," in the strictest sense of the word, is understood as a state that, on the one hand, completely controls the life of the Volk from above and, on the other hand, is not limited to its immediate governmental functions but directly manages certain spheres of life. Instead, it encompasses all areas of life, both the natural foundations and the culture of the Volk, and does so to such an extent that all leading figures in every major field, down to the lowest levels, are state officials, and all functions are regulated by state laws down to the smallest details.

The purpose of a total state can never be that it itself fulfills all individual areas of life internally. The state cannot itself be the content of technology and economy; in the end, these always concern the physical well-being of individual citizens, who, however, should not act merely selfishly but also in a way that benefits the community. Never can the state wish to be the sole object of artistic life; it may well be considered a significant factor, but in addition, the entire fullness of reality remains the object of artistic creation and contemplation. Likewise, it is inconceivable that the state alone should be the object of knowledge; of course, it is naturally an outstanding subject of science, but just as all other areas of existence must be studied, so too must it. Even in social life, the state can only be a particularly outstanding but not the sole content of thought and action; rather, this extends to all the relationships of human coexistence. And likewise, in religion, the state can never be regarded as the object of worship. No matter how reverently it is viewed as standing under divine guidance, divine life, which encompasses the entire world, as superhuman life, is still something entirely different from the state.

In today's world, strong tendencies exist toward the expansion of state power in the direction of a total state. This is understandable, as humanity has never before lived together in such large masses as it does today. Within these masses, there is a particularly high risk that centrifugal forces will dissolve the community. This danger is further heightened by the fact that subversive forces, through their agitation, introduce artificial oppositions among the masses and thereby destroy the sense of common belonging. In contrast, it is understandable that statesmen who feel a particularly strong responsibility for their nations desire to strengthen the authority of the state as much as possible. However, today, as at all times, the totality of the state meets its limits in the fullness and diversity of life, in which nations move and act.

Even in today's Germany, an unmistakable tendency toward the totality of the state is present. This is explained not only by the general global situation but especially by the unique situation of the German Volk. Our nation, in the years of humiliation after the World War, was caught in such a process of internal decline and was torn apart by so many opposing movements and parties, was primarily through the Marxist class struggle divided to such an extent that the renewal of German life was only possible through a very strong state government.

In today's Germany, one can only speak of a "total state" in a very limited sense. Under no circumstances does this term imply that the Volk is ruled from above by a tyrannical government. Rather, the current Reich government has emerged from a free popular movement. It has been placed at the head of the Reich through free, democratic elections and sees itself as nothing other than the representation of the German Volk. The Führer and his collaborators have therefore frequently stated that today in Germany, it is not the state that governs for the Volk, but rather the Volk that is decisive for the state and shapes it according to its nature. Thus, when we speak of a "total state," this only means that the Volk governs itself through the instrument of the state. Therefore, under no circumstances can there be any talk of a "deification" of the state in Germany.

9. Church and State

The relationship between state and church has developed differently among various nations depending on historical evolution.

Two main types stand in contrast to each other: on one side, the state church, as realized in England, where the church is governed by the state, and accordingly, church officials are also state officials, and church laws are state laws. On the other side stands the free-church system, as realized, for example, in the

United States, where approximately 200 churches founded by immigrants exist completely independently alongside the state administration.

In Germany, the state church system was previously predominant. However, in the course of the 19th century, the church began a process of independence. Yet, the state continues to provide direct support, for example, through military chaplaincy, but especially in its schools and universities, for the flourishing of church life.

Since 1933, no fundamental change has occurred in this regard. The constitution of the German Evangelical Church, dated July 11, 1933, which was drafted by churchmen and proclaimed by state law, provides for an independent Reich Church with its own legislation, whereby the Reich Bishop is not appointed by the head of state but elected by the National Synod. The new German Reich Church is therefore not a state church, but rather an independent German Volkskirche, legally recognized by the state and established through free elections of the church congregation.

This legal status has so far remained unchanged. Only as a result of internal church disputes and personal conflicts that have arisen in recent years, the highest positions in church governance are currently unoccupied, so that the church is temporarily being administered directly by the Reich Church Ministry.

How the situation of the German Evangelical Church will develop in relation to the state in the future cannot be determined at this moment. However, it is to be assumed that historical development will continue as it has begun, meaning that in the not-too-distant future, there will stand a great, strong church that is independent but cooperates in a trusting manner with the state government for the benefit of the Volk.

10. Political Freedom

In nations and states that emphasize their freedom, this freedom is primarily understood to mean freedom of speech, association, and assembly, as well as the freedom of production and trade, of science and art, and finally, freedom of religion. However, all these freedoms are restricted to the extent that public order is not disturbed, public morality is not violated, and fellow citizens are not insulted.

If these states are governed parliamentarily, they are simultaneously based on the right to free elections of representatives and the formation of political parties. However, this freedom is practically restricted by the fact that certain groups, especially those dominated by various economic interests, emerge as power factors upon which voters and parliamentary factions depend. Furthermore, in the politics of liberal states, the interests of international capital often act as dominant factors, influencing not only individuals but entire nations as well.

In Germany, since 1919, the parliamentary system prevailed, and through the Reich constitution, all conceivable freedoms were guaranteed. However, this resulted in a chaos of opinions and parties, which paralyzed the strength of the Volk and divided the entire nation into hate-filled opposing groups. The allegedly free Volk as a whole possessed no sovereignty but was under the rule of foreign nations and was an object of exploitation for world-dominating financial powers.

The German Volk, through free elections in 1932 and 1933, cast off the chains that bound it. Our nation has since not relinquished its political freedom, but the new government is repeatedly affirmed through popular referenda. Through these free elections, the German Volk created a government to which it submits in free obedience, while the government, in turn, considers itself closely connected to the Volk and responsible to it.

As a result, our Volk has regained new strength, reclaimed its sovereignty in international affairs, and shaken off the dominance of foreign states and international capital.

All civil liberties for individual Germans have been preserved, of course with the restrictions that exist in all countries, even the most liberal ones. However, greater vigilance is exercised here than elsewhere to ensure that these freedoms do not destroy public order and the national community (Volksgemeinschaft). If stricter control is exercised here today than may be found in some other countries, this can be explained by the terrible experiences we had during the time of misery and oppression with unrestrained freedom of expression.

All those who criticize our state from abroad today should realize that it was foreign powers that oppressed us, and that this strict discipline and consolidation of all forces has been, and still is, a prerequisite for regaining and maintaining our freedom.

11. The Freedom of Religious Confession

Among the personal freedoms granted by all Christian states of the present day is religious freedom. Even where certain people's churches (Volkskirchen) are predominant and where, therefore, most members of the Volk adhere to the tradition of the people's church (Volkskirche), they are permitted, in accordance with their freedom of conscience, to change their religion.

This is also the position of the state in present-day Germany. The program of the National Socialist Party, which is authoritative for the state in its religious policy, presupposes that Christianity is the religion of the German Volk. However, it also proclaims religious freedom, with the self-evident restriction that religious freedom does not apply insofar as a religion is immoral or endangers the existence of the state.

The state therefore grants both the Evangelical Church and the Roman Catholic Church full freedom of religious practice and, in particular, the proclamation of the Gospel. The restrictions that have been and must be imposed here are only the most self-evident ones. If a clergyman abuses the freedom of speech granted to him as a preacher of the Gospel to work against the state, or if religious conflicts take such forms that they endanger public order, then the state must, of course, intervene. If the present German state has a particularly watchful eye in this regard, this is explained by the catastrophic plight into which we had fallen due to the unchecked actions of the parties during the time of humiliation. Those friends of Germany abroad who now believe they must fight for the allegedly endangered freedom of Gospel proclamation in Germany should recall these circumstances.

12. Christian Freedom

Essentially different from the political freedom of religious practice is the freedom that belongs to the essence of the Christian religion. This is the free elevation of the human spirit into the freedom of the divine spirit, which at the same time means the humble integration of the human into the divine spirit.

This freedom can be experienced just as much within personal and political servitude, and in the greatest spiritual and physical hardship and distress, as it can in connection with worldly well-being. However, it can also result in the person who experiences it striving for external freedom.

However, this external freedom can vary greatly depending on the situation of a person and of a Volk, and it is not tied to a particular political system, such as that of Western democracies, from which one would have to conclude that they are the necessary expression of Christian freedom.

In Germany, since Luther's treatise on the freedom of a Christian, inner freedom has been the fundamental possession of Evangelical Christians. This possession has also found its foundation in more recent philosophical ideas of freedom, and this Christian freedom is reflected in the German Volk's uprising against oppression by foreign nations, as well as in the free establishment of the new state system, which has not come over us as a tyranny, but has been shaped out of the will of the entire Volk.

13. Church, State, and Economic Order

The church has the task in every Volk of combating the spirit of Mammonism and educating the Volk to an unconditional subordination of external life to inner life. At the same time, it is its duty to participate in the alleviation of external distress in noble competition with worldly organizations. In this, its special task is to give welfare care its deepest inner meaning and thereby provide a counterbalance to all schematism, which inevitably adheres to welfare enterprises when they expand on a large scale.

However, it is not only the church institutions that are responsible for alleviating external hardship. It is equally the concern of secular associations and state agencies to engage in care for the suffering Volk. These organizations thereby perform an act of charity, which, in a Christian Volk, is to be understood just as much as a fulfillment of the Christian commandment of love as the works carried out by the institutions of the church.

For a long time in Germany, great work has been done by ecclesiastical institutions and associations in both directions—both in fostering inwardness and willingness to sacrifice, as well as in direct charitable activity. Likewise, state welfare has long since developed in a truly Christian spirit.

However, both ecclesiastical and civic charitable activity were severely harmed in the postwar period by the exploitation of the Volk by foreign nations and by the division of the Volk into hostile political parties, to the point that they were largely rendered impossible. The misery brought upon over six million fellow countrymen and their families by unemployment became a catastrophe for the entire Volk, against which all attempts at remedy ultimately proved powerless.

Here, the National Socialist movement and the new state in Germany have brought about a complete transformation. National Socialism has fought materialism in a truly Christian spirit and has instilled in the Volk a willingness to sacrifice and personal modesty. At the same time, through job creation, unemployment has been almost entirely overcome. The artificially created divide and hatred between the "haves" and "have-nots" have been eliminated, and aid and charitable organizations have been established on a scale unparalleled anywhere in the world. It is precisely in these achievements that one rightly sees in Germany an expression of positive Christianity.

At the World Conference for Practical Christianity in Stockholm in 1925, the assembled representatives of the Christian churches lamented the economic hardships of the world as well as the divisions between races and urgently called for relief. In none of the participating countries have these wishes been fulfilled to such an extent as in Germany. This is the great contribution that Germany has made to the movement for practical Christianity.

14. Church, State, and Education

The Christian churches in all nations have the legitimate desire that their youth be raised in a Christian spirit and instructed in the Christian religion, and that no obstacles be placed in their way from any side.

On the other hand, every state has an undeniable interest in ensuring that its youth are raised in a national spirit. To the extent that the state extends its care to the entire cultural life of the Volk, it must ensure that its youth participate as fully as possible in the various areas of cultural life.

However, since in a Christian Volk the Christian religion forms the innermost core of cultural life, a cultural state in such a Volk must also desire the Christian education of its youth. In this regard, state interest aligns with that of the church. In nations, however, where the maintenance of culture is largely left to private life and where church life also takes on more of the character of private associations, it may happen that the state concerns itself with the Christian education of youth.

For a long time in Germany, there have been five spheres in which evangelical youth (and similarly, Roman Catholic youth) receive their education in the Christian religion. The first is the family, where the child experiences the earliest impressions of the Christian spirit. The second is the school, which is generally state-run. The few private schools that exist remain under state supervision and follow the state curriculum. Here, by state mandate, evangelical children receive evangelical religious instruction, while Roman Catholic children receive Roman Catholic instruction. This applies not only to denominational schools but also to community schools, where, otherwise, children of both confessions are taught together.

The three remaining spheres are more strictly ecclesiastical. These include the children's worship service or Sunday school, where children voluntarily gather and receive no secular instruction but are taught exclusively in religious matters. Additionally, there is the instruction given by clergy, which concludes with confirmation. Finally, the last sphere to be mentioned is the Christian youth group, which either affiliates with an individual church congregation or is formed from multiple congregations.

All five of these spheres still exist today, and now, as in the past, there is a rich abundance of opportunities for the youth of the German Volk to be educated in the spirit of the Gospel. Every child of Christian parents experiences, throughout life, numerous strong Christian impulses and gentle inspirations for both the soul and intellect. On the part of the National Socialist state, there is no intention today to abolish Christian religious instruction or otherwise restrict church education.

However, there has been a significant reorganization in the structure of German youth. Until 1933, there were hundreds of independent youth associations in Germany, both secular and Christian, each of which maintained its own separate existence and carefully distinguished itself from all others, leading to the fragmentation of youth into various groups that no longer understood one another. Most notably, there was a deep divide between the so-called "proletarian" youth associations, on one side, where the atheistic spirit of Marxism prevailed, and on the other side, the "bourgeois" associations, which also included Christian ones. Among these two camps, the same hatred was sown by the Marxists that was spread throughout the Volk through the so-called class struggle. Today, however, nearly the entire youth of the German Volk, without distinction of class, wealth, or religious denomination, has been united in the Hitler Youth, the largest youth organization in the world.

As a result, the other youth associations have either disappeared or been restricted. However, in the Evangelical Church, youth can still be gathered as before in connection with the church congregations, and members of these church groups can simultaneously be members of the Hitler Youth.

The Hitler Youth leaves religious education to the Church, the school, and the family. It itself is limited to political and physical education. However, this education is carried out in a manner that in no way contradicts the Christian values of the Volk but, on the contrary, fully aligns with them. For the Hitler Youth educates the children of our Volk in loyal brotherliness and firm camaraderie, in willing dedication to the community, and in strict obedience, physically to self-discipline and modesty, to renunciation and hardening—everything in direct contrast to the Marxist youth organizations, where young people were instilled with materialistic greed for physical comfort and hatred against the so-called "possessing class."

15. Church, Nations, and World Peace

If the churches are filled with the spirit of Christ, the Prince of Peace, then they must keep peace between nations as their highest goal.

To achieve this goal, they can best contribute by proclaiming the Gospel of peace and refraining from any political agitation that incites one Volk against another Volk.

Likewise, every government, if it is responsible, must desire the peaceful coexistence of its Volk with other nations. In this, its will aligns completely with the will of the Christian churches.

However, the means by which a peace-loving government can achieve this goal is, on the one hand, diplomacy that promotes peace, and on the other hand, an armed force appropriate to the size of the Volk.

Just as the presence of the police within a Volk is an indispensable prerequisite for maintaining domestic peace, so within the world of nations, the armed forces are the essential prerequisite for maintaining world peace. Moreover, it is desirable that there be no significant disparities in the armament of different nations, as defenseless nations can present an incentive for armed nations to commit acts of violence.

The German Volk is imbued with the same love of peace as the German Evangelical Church. The Führer, who has personally and extensively experienced the horrors of war as a front-line soldier, repeatedly expresses his sincere love of peace in his speeches and thereby proves himself to be a truly Christian ruler.

For the sake of world peace, however, the German Volk must be as adequately armed as all other nations. This is all the more necessary as it has been shown that, during the period of German defenselessness, other nations did not resist the temptation to commit acts of violence.

The defensibility of the German Volk does not merely serve to secure its own existence and maintain the balance between nations. Rather, it simultaneously serves the protection of the entire Christian culture. For to the east of Germany looms heavily armed Russia, whose current Bolshevist government, through its spirit of materialism and atheism and its radical will for world revolution, represents the gravest threat to the entire culture of the Christian nations; to the west lies France, which is in danger of succumbing to Bolshevist agitation. Thus, a militarily prepared Germany is simultaneously a bastion against the most dangerous enemies of world peace and all higher values of human culture. And every German soldier, who is ready to defend his fatherland and protect his Volk, is at the same time a warrior of Christ, defending the highest goods of humanity against barbarism and protecting the Christian churches of the world from destruction by anti-Christian forces.

Given the current situation of the German Volk, it cannot serve the peace of the world but must contribute to the preparation of a new war. It is contrary to all efforts of ecumenical conferences when Christians in other countries undertake, supposedly in the name of the Gospel and humanity, to disparage measures of the German government and thereby support the hostile sentiment against Germany, which is widespread in the world. Such attacks certainly do not arise from a Christian disposition but rather stem from the influence of dark international powers that, throughout the world—above all through the press they control—seek to incite the nations of the earth against the German nation. However, we must now expect all Christian brethren who are properly informed to show full understanding of our situation and to overcome prejudices everywhere in the world and help bring truth to victory.

III: Church, Word, and Grace

1. The Problem of Christian Unity

The unity of the Christian churches, its possibilities, supports, and obstacles have been sufficiently discussed in recent years. What has already been said on the subject shall not be repeated here. Instead, attention shall be drawn only to the following considerations: 1. One should not indulge in utopias and illusions but rather adhere to what is practically attainable. 2. One should not overlook the real progress made in the existing unity movement but rather appreciate it correctly. 3. One should not take steps within the ecumenical movement that work against its own goals. To this end, some facts shall now be presented, and concrete proposals shall be made.

2. The Christian Church Federation

A uniformly structured, doctrinally and liturgically uniform world church is unattainable. For the sake of the unity of the Church of Christ, it is also not necessary to achieve it.

However, it is useful for the various churches to continuously compare their constitutions, doctrines, and liturgical practices and to determine where they agree and where they differ.

Aside from attempts to reach agreement on matters of constitution, doctrine, and worship, a true unity is possible and already present in the innermost holiest possession of Christianity —the Gospel. This unity forms the essential foundation of the unity of the Church, and in comparison to it, the questions of organization, dogma, and ritual must be regarded as subordinate.

Achievable and already fundamentally present as an organization is a Christian church federation, in which each of the united churches retains complete independence. This federation does not mean a church above the churches but serves only for mutual understanding, consultation, and encouragement.

The establishment of such a federation is best promoted by first ensuring the most comprehensive possible unity of the churches within each nation.

3. The German Evangelical Church

The most significant contribution to the unity of Christianity in recent years has been the establishment of the German Evangelical Church. What had not been achieved in the land of the Reformation for four and a half centuries was realized in 1933 as a direct consequence of the national unification of the German Volk. This is an event that no one wishes to reverse and that will never be undone, but rather is now widely recognized in Germany.

The German Evangelical Church, encompassing nearly two-thirds of the entire German Volk, alongside which the small free-church groups form an insignificant minority of only about half a million adherents, is the people's church (Volkskirche) of the German nation and at the same time the largest evangelical church in the world.

According to the constitution of July 11, 1933, the German Evangelical Church is a unified church. At its head is to stand a

Reichsbishop, who is supported in the administration of the church by the spiritual ministry and the national synod.

The organic integration of the previous regional churches into the Reich Church is not yet complete and will only be definitively settled in connection with the reorganization of the Reich constitution.

However, it is certain that no one will be violated in their convictions. No uniformity will be required in doctrine or worship. Each sub-church, each local congregation, and each individual parish may retain its Lutheran, Reformed, or Evangelical-Unitarian stance and continue practicing its traditional forms of worship.

Beyond this, quite apart from the ecclesiastical legislation in the German Evangelical Church, the same freedom of personal conviction will prevail as has in fact existed in all major evangelical people's churches (Volkskirchen). Just as there have always been various groups, revival and sanctification movements, liberal and humanitarian circles, conservative and high-church associations coexisting within the German regional churches, so too will this remain the case in the unified Reich Church.

4. Obstacles to Church Unity in Germany and the World

As everyone knows, church unifications are always associated with the greatest difficulties. Wherever multiple churches form a union or even merge into a single church, there are groups of stubborn defenders of the old order. In most cases, church unification even leads to the separation of a defiant minority, which then founds a new small reactionary church.

Thus, it is not surprising that similar phenomena have occurred in the founding of the German Evangelical Church. In fact, since 1933, evangelical Germany has been afflicted by extraordinarily severe ecclesiastical struggles. However, no one opposes church unification, and as a result, no separation has taken place. In Germany, the sense of community in the evangelical church has always been so strong that all disputes and factional formations have taken place within the large regional churches, with only minor schisms occurring in exceptional cases. However, today, there are Christians within the constitutionally unified church who are not satisfied with simply existing as a faction within the church but instead seek to dominate the entire Reich Church with their position, tolerating no other standpoint.

The currents that exist in our church today, in terms of their goals and programs, are fundamentally different from those before 1933. In general, one can say: there are those who affirm the restructuring of the church in accordance with the new era, and those who reject it. These groups are usually distinguished as "German Christians" and "Confessing Christians."

The German Christians are not to be confused with the "German Faith Movement" or any other "neo-pagans." Rather, they stand firmly on the foundation of the Gospel. They are also not a continuation of any previous conservative, liberal, pietistic, or high church party. Instead, they unite Christians from all these groups and do not wish to be a party themselves. Their aim is to shape the German Evangelical Church as a living people's church (Volkskirche), in which various orientations have a place.

At the same time, they are loyal followers of the Führer and seek to bring National Socialism to prominence within the church. That is, they want a church that is not merely the church of a single social class but one that considers itself deeply connected with all members of the Volk, where the same sense of brotherhood prevails as in the entire Volk, and where the Gospel is proclaimed in the language of the Volk.

Among the German Christians, certain individuals have stood out from the outset, belonging to groups such as the "League for the German Church" (Bund für deutsche Kirche) and striving for a certain "Germanization of Christianity." They emphasized the mystical, rational, and humanitarian elements of Christianity in the spirit of older liberalism and are convinced that by doing so, they are simultaneously shaping Christianity in accordance with the German essence and cleansing it of remnants of Judaism. Today, they particularly emphasize something that the rest of the German Christians also recognize—namely, that God has visited the German Volk in a special way. Some among them even advocate for the establishment of a German "National Church," which is based solely on the proclamation of Jesus and is neither Evangelical nor Roman Catholic. This radical group, primarily found in Thuringia, should certainly not be confused with the German Christians as a whole, as it represents only a very small minority within the German Evangelical Church.

The German Christians have accomplished the great historical achievement of founding the German Evangelical Church (Deutsche Evangelische Kirche). The Reich Church (Reichskirche) was part of their program and was realized through them. In expanding the church, however, they proceeded too hastily. Above all, an overly rushed attempt was made to incorporate the existing regional churches (Landeskirchen) into the Reich Church.

However, this does not diminish their historical merit in having created the Reich Church, which has since not been challenged in its right to exist by any side.

However, in response to this new development, an opposition party has emerged since 1932, which, although forming a minority in the church, has nevertheless gained significant influence. The opposition group called itself the "Young Reformation Movement," the "Pastors' Emergency League," the "Confessional Front," and the "Confessing Church," but remains merely a faction and not an independent church. This group is composed not only of members from formerly conservative Christian circles but also, like the German Christians, draws adherents from various backgrounds. What unites them all is their opposition to certain contemporary religious developments.

Particularly strong since 1932 has been the opposition against the New Heathens (Neuheiden). These opponents continue to fuel the opposition. The claim made by the New Heathens that they are the true representatives of National Socialism is highly confusing, and as a result, there are confessional writings that have been led to believe that National Socialism is genuinely heathen. Consequently, in their polemics, they sometimes conflate Neo-Paganism (Neuheidentum) with National Socialism.

The belief that Christian faith is under threat in the new Germany has brought many followers to the Confessional Front in recent years. However, their opposition is not solely directed against the New Heathens outside the church but also against the German Christians, who are often labeled as "half-heathen" or even confused with the heathens, despite the fact that the German Christians themselves oppose Neo-Paganism.

Furthermore, the opposition is directed against the attempt to adapt the church constitution to the new social structure of the German Volk, meaning to shape it according to the new political forms. In contrast, the call resounds: "The Church must remain the Church"—though it is often forgotten that the existing constitutions of the regional churches before 1918 were modeled after the governments of the many former German states, and that even in the emergency constitutions that the regional churches adopted after 1918, these dynastic traditions were continued while simultaneously undergoing adaptation to the political forms of the Weimar Reich Constitution.

The spirit of the opposition group, however, acquired a peculiar coloration through the so-called "dialectical" theology originating from Switzerland, which had become widely spread among pastors in Germany. This theology is based on a pessimistic-agnostic philosophy. It emphasizes, in a manner neither found in Scripture nor in the confession of any church, the unknowability of God, the distance of man from God, the incompleteness of salvation, the separation between Church and world, the opposition between Church and State. From this perspective, all active engagement within the Church (except one's own) is rejected as human self-will, and all human action is generally criticized as presumptuous defiance of God. As a result, this theology also fosters a critical stance toward strong action, such as that which lifted the German Volk out of hardship, and toward the new state, which has been built through the strength of the German Volk.

However, the majority of those within the German Volk who belong to the Confessional Front know little about these theological views of their leaders and do not even understand the preachers who proclaim dialectical theology from the pulpits. The laypeople associated with this church group are, for the most part, of a very moderate conservative disposition and simply hold the conviction that one must belong to the Confessional Front if one wishes to contribute to defending the Gospel against the attacks of the heathens and the German Christians.

However, within a small group of the Confessional Front, and apparently particularly among its leading figures, an exceptionally strong radicalism prevails. Here, they are not content merely to be a faction within the church. They want the church itself to be their own. They call themselves the "Confessing Church," convene "synods," and have even established a "Provisional Leadership of the German Evangelical Church." Furthermore, they are convinced that their own viewpoint, shaped by the spirit of dialectical theology, aligns perfectly with the Word of God. They believe they act under the direct influence of the Holy Spirit and introduce new formulas of faith, which they demand that the preachers of the new church sign, just as was done with the old confessions of faith.

This radical group denies every other faction within the church its right to exist. Any cooperation with the German Christians is severed. Everything undertaken by the state to restore church order and promote the church—including the establishment of the Reich Church Ministry, the formation of church committees, and the Führer's call for free church elections—is viewed with suspicion and actively opposed. In short, this radical wing of the Confessional Front claims absolute power within the church and, by doing so, casts doubt on the very possibility of bringing peace to church life.

These radicals have significantly strengthened their power by establishing connections with foreign churches. As a result, the opinion has formed among foreign Christians that these circles are the true representatives of the German Evangelical Church, and that the image of the German situation they present corresponds to the actual conditions in which both the Reich and the Church currently find themselves. Due to the influence of the radicals, many foreign churches have come to believe that there is indeed a deep rift between the State and the Church, and that the church is being persecuted by the State. For this reason, foreign Christians feel obligated to take a stand for the leadership of the Confessing Church and against the State.

Thus, a situation has arisen that is entirely contrary to the intent of all ecumenical movements. A group is being supported in the name of united Christianity that constitutes the greatest obstacle to church unity in Germany, because it insists rigidly and exclusively on its own position against all other directions and seeks to enforce it with an absolute claim to power. In general, it is common for reactionary and exclusivist groups, such as the Lutherans from the Missouri Synod in America or the old Calvinist Free Churches in Scotland, to have no association with ecumenical movements. This fully aligns with Christianity's general tendency toward unity. However, if an exception is made in the present case, this does not serve unity, but rather the division of Christianity.

It is to be hoped that within the churches of the world, recognition of the true situation will prevail and that actions will be taken accordingly, leading in a direction that promotes church unity and serves the peace of nations.

5. The Church and the Word

The Church, in all its diversity and even in all its difficulties and disputes, has its unified foundation in the Spirit of God, which reveals itself in the Word.

Christianity hears the Word of God in Jesus Christ and in those who have hoped for him and foreseen him, as well as in those who follow him and bear witness to him.

The Christian Church sees the written expression of the Word of God in the Bible. In it, the New Testament is the direct testimony of Jesus Christ and his Gospel.

The Old Testament has never been equated with the New Testament in Christian churches—except in very small Jewish-Christian communities. As the New Testament itself testifies that Christ is the end of the Law, so all orthodox churches recognize that the Old Testament religion, in which the Israelite people worshiped God as their God and as a God of justice and law, has been surpassed as a religion of hope and anticipation by the message of God as the Father of all mankind and reconciliation with Him through Jesus Christ.

In contemporary Christian churches, the primacy of the New Testament over the Old Testament is therefore clearly expressed in both their worship services and their teachings. It can even be observed that in new liturgies, such as in the new prayer book of the Church of England, the spirit of the Old Testament has been overcome by the spirit of the New Testament, and the spirit of fear and servitude has been replaced by the spirit of sonship. There are also communities, such as the "Disciples of Christ", that more strongly oppose the Old Testament in favor of the New Testament than other churches.

The German Volk has once again been made aware of the problem of the Old Testament due to the ominous significance that Judaism has had in its most recent history.

We are, of course, aware that the Jews, who today are involved in world domination through their trade relations and whose spirit of Mammon we combat, are not to be confused with the ancient people of Israel, and even less with the prophets, whose spirit governs the Old Testament.

However, we are now more attentive than ever to what is peculiar to Judaism in the Old Testament and are vigilant that no theology gains the upper hand that proclaims to us more the God of wrath and judgment than the God of love and grace, and that transforms the Christian religion of fulfillment back into a religion of hope.

At the same time, we observe the fact that the Old Testament expresses not only the salvation hope of the Semitic peoples but also that of the Aryan peoples. And we further establish that the Jews crucified Christ and corrupted the Gospel, and that, in contrast, only very few Jews in later times converted to Christianity, whereas Christianity became the religion of the Aryan peoples of the West.

In all of this, we do not fundamentally deviate from the tradition of the Christian churches. On the contrary, we want to protect the churches from Judeo-Christian deviations and ensure the purity of the preaching of the Gospel.

6. The Church and Grace

Everything that is said about the life and work of the Church of Christ must always conclude with a confession of divine grace.

What the churches and the peoples accomplish in this world in the spirit of Jesus Christ is not their own work, but the work of divine grace. Even where human creative power is strained to its utmost—indeed, precisely there—a special working of divine grace can be observed.

In the German church and theology, since the time of the Reformation, divine grace has been spoken of with particular clarity, whereas in the churches of the West, as they themselves acknowledge, this thought has often receded behind human activism.

This has not changed even today. Especially now, when the German Volk has raised itself out of misery through an immense effort, we are aware that we stand under a special influence of God's grace. And the Führer of the German Volk, who places himself under the workings of divine providence far more clearly and far more frequently than many contemporary statesmen in other nations, expresses at the high points of his life as his personal experience that he humbly acknowledges the workings of divine grace.

THE 28 THESES

OF THE

GERMAN CHRISTIANS

translated with footnotes by

Corey J. Mahler

Originally published 1932

I: The Church and the State

1. The German Evangelical Church exists within the State. It cannot lead a secluded existence[4] *alongside* the State, as desired by Christianity-hostile[5] currents. It cannot remain neutral toward the State as desired by those who view the National Socialist State with mistrust. It *cannot* be a Church *above* the State, as the [Roman] Catholic position asserts. It also *cannot* be a Church *under* the State, as in the old State-Church system. *Only as a Church within the State can it be a People's Church.*[6] Thus, Luther's original[7] thoughts on State and Church become reality.

2. Because of its solidarity with the people, the Lutheran Church cannot adopt a concordat[8] stance towards the National Socialist State. As a People's Church, it trusts this State. A *Church leader* can be only one *who has the trust of the State leadership.* The State grants the Church support and free exercise;[9] for State and

---

4   "Winkel" has a number of different senses; one of which is "(interior) corner of a building," and it is from this sense that the figurative use as "a small group who regularly meet together" is derived, which is clearly what is in view here.

5   The same word ("Christentum") means both "Christianity" and "Christendom," so the implication is broader than either English term.

6   The term "Volkskirche" appears *frequently* in this document, and will be consistently translated as "People's Church," even though English certainly has no sufficient term for "Volk."

7   "Ursprünglich" has a broader sense than "original" in English, but the sense is clear enough (it shades much more toward the English "present or existing from the beginning" sense than the "not dependent on other people's ideas" sense).

8   This is a reference to the Reichskonkordat, which was an agreement between the National Socialist State and the Vatican. The intent is clearly to differentiate the stance of the Protestants from that of the Vatican, which is characterized as more of an arm's length relationship, whereas the Lutheran position is one of intimate and inseparable involvement.

9   This could also be translated as "freedom of action," but it should not be understood in the American sense of "freedom of religion" or similar; what

Church belong together as the two major order-enforcing[10] powers[11] of a people. Their relationship is one of trust and not of contract.

3. The People's Church *commits itself to blood and race* because the people are a community of blood and essence. Therefore, only those who are national comrades[12] according to the State's law can be members of the People's Church. Only those who can be State officials according to the State's law can be officeholders in the People's Church (the so-called "Aryan paragraph"[13]).

4. A People's Church does not mean excluding Christians of other races from Word and Sacrament,[14] or from the great Christian community of faith. *A Christian of another race* is not a

---

is meant here is that the State will not interfere in the Church *with regard to matters that belong to the Church.*

10 "Ordnung" is usually translated into English as "order," but it has a central place in German thought and carries far greater weight than the English term does for English speakers (cf. A most famous German saying: Ordnung muss sein—There must be order).

11 "Kraft" is a word with a broad lexical scope; in modern usage, "Ordnungskräfte" would refer to "law-enforcement agencies," but that is clearly not what is in view here; rather, here what is meant is that it is the State and the Church, which—together—form the necessary order, foundation, or bedrock of society.

12 "Volksgenosse" must be understood in the specific National Socialist sense, which is that a *Volksgenosse* is a member of the *Volksgemeinschaft*, which is to say 'the people's community.' "Volk" is 'nation' or 'people' or 'race' (it has specific connotations of blood in the German) and "Genosse" is 'comrade'; thus, membership in the Volksgemeinschaft is (largely) a matter of blood.

13 The "Aryan Paragraph" was a required clause in the organizing or governing statutes of entities (e.g., corporations) under the National Socialist State, which restricted membership (or certain other rights) to members of the Volksgemeinschaft—"Aryans", in the sense employed by the National Socialists. It was this paragraph that the so-called "Confessing Church" used as an excuse for their schism from the Church in Germany.

14 To the Lutheran, "Word and Sacrament" is both a set phrase and a term of art: It means the blessings of God, participation in the Gottesdienst (Divine Service), and, more generally, the Christian life. To bar someone from Word and Sacrament is to declare him no Christian; to include someone in Word and Sacrament is to declare him a brother-in-Christ.

lesser Christian, but rather *a Christian of a different kind.*[15] Thus, the People's Church takes seriously that the Christian Church does not yet live in the perfection of divine eternity, but is bound by the orders God has given to this life.

5. Because the German People's Church respects race as a creation of God, it recognizes the demand to keep the race pure and healthy as a commandment of God. Therefore, she considers marriage between members of different races a violation of God's will.

II: The Proclamation of the Church

6. God demands the whole person.[16] The proclamation of the Church aims to place people under the will of God.

7. As the Church of Jesus Christ, her foremost duty is to preach the Gospel of Jesus Christ to the German people, whom God has created as Germans.

8. The Gospel of Jesus Christ is that God is our Lord and Father, that this God has revealed Himself in Jesus Christ, and that we humans find the way to the Father solely[17] through Jesus Christ. The Church is bound to this proclamation.

---

15 "Kind", here, should be taken in the traditional (even in English) sense of 'kind'—'a group of people or thing having similar characteristics'; obviously, here, what is meant is *race* (see Point 3).

16 This term "the whole person" must clearly be read in light of the previous point; what is meant is that the entirety of a person—including his nature, which includes his race—is to be placed under the will of God, which is to say be made subject to it.

17 One need not, but one most certainly could, take this as a reference to the Protestant (Lutheran) declaration of Sola Fide (or Solo Christo, perhaps, in this case).

9. God ordains[18] (all) people to the fundamental orders of life,[19] of family, people (race),[20] and State.[21] Thus, the People's Church sees the *comprehensive demand of the National Socialist State as God's call to uphold the values of family, Folk, and State.*

---

18 Although the German verb „stellen" has the core sense of 'to put', 'to place', or 'to position', in this context, it can faithfully be translated as 'to ordain', for what Gods *places* into the lives of men He *ordains*, for *to ordain* means simply *to prescribe*, which is to say, when speaking of God and His Creation, '*to place* into being in a certain way'.

19 "Lebensordnung" is another German word that simply does not have a simple translation in English. "Leben"—'life'—and "Ordnung"—'order'— English has (although see fn. 2–3 for an importance difference between "Ordnung" and "order"), the compound is greater than the sum of its parts. An 'order of life' is a fundamental part of the organization of human life *created by God*—to oppose such an order of life is to oppose God Himself.

20 Certainly, English has the words "folk" and "race", but neither truly encompasses the German "Volk", which is a term laden with philosophical and other meaning, and can be understood only if one grasps that what it encompasses is the very core concept of a people as a nation, which is to say as blood and soil. From this point forward, I will translate "Volk" (n.b., this translation decision is for the lone word, not for compound words) as Folk, with the same scope of meaning fully intended by the translation.

21 Any Lutheran reading this Point will immediately recognize the (echoes of the) three-estates theology of Lutheranism. Although the three estates in Lutheran theology are the Church, the Household, and the State, we see in this point a political mirror of the theological tripartite division; in essence, this is an application of Lutheran three-estates theology (a matter of the Kingdom of the right hand of Christ) to the political realm (the kingdom of the left hand of Christ), but still with an eye to the theological, as, again, *both kingdoms belong to Christ.*

III: The Foundations of the Church

10. The foundations of the Church remain *the Bible and the Confessions*.[22] The Bible contains the message of Christ, the Confessions testify to the message of Christ.

11. The definitive revelation from God is Jesus Christ. The New Testament serves as the record of this revelation, which is why it holds normative power for all of the Church's teachings.

12. The Old Testament does not have the same value.[23] The specifically Jewish national morality[24] and national religion have been superseded. The Old Testament remains important because

---

22 I have chosen to pluralize this word in the (idiomatic) English translation because I believe this is warranted in the Lutheran context, which recognizes the Ecumenical Creeds and the Book of Concord as the norma normata of the Christian faith. For the English reader, this makes clear a matter that the German reader would intuitively grasp from the German diction.

23 This may sound shocking to (some) modern ears, but it is the historic position of the Christian Church, and it has been variously stated by various writers (e.g., 'What the Old Testament conceals, the New Testament reveals.' or, in the words of Augustine, "The Old Testament is the New Testament concealed; the New Testament is the Old Testament revealed."). Whereas the Old Testament contains *many* prophecies about Christ, it is the New Testament that reveals the fullness of God's plan of salvation for mankind. The Christians of the Old Testament were saved by faith in the Messiah *Who was to come*, but, we, New Testament believers are saved by faith in the Messiah *Who has come*, or, in the words of Christ, recorded in Matthew 13: "But blessed are your eyes, for they see, and your ears, for they hear. For truly, I say to you, many prophets and righteous people longed to see what you see, and did not see it, and to hear what you hear, and did not hear it."

24 The use of "jüdische Volkssittlichkeit" and "[jüdische] Volksreligion" is a clear reference to the traditional tripartite division of the law/Law in the Old Testament: ceremonial, civil, and Moral. In this case, 'Jewish national morality' is a reference to the civil law, which compelled Old Testament Israel to enact certain penalties for certain crimes, and 'Jewish national religion' is a reference to the ceremonial law, which compelled Old Testament Israel to engage in certain rituals, primarily with regard to Temple worship. Christians are not bound by the ceremonial or the civil law, and this is made abundantly clear throughout the New Testament (e.g., Acts 10), but Christians are bound by the Moral Law, which flows from the nature of God and is, thus, unchanging.

it records the history and decline of a people that repeatedly separated itself from God despite His revelation. The prophets of God[25] show us all: The position of a nation relative to God is decisive for its fate in history.

13. Therefore, we see in the Old Testament the defection (apostasy) of the Jews from God and, therein, their sin. This sin is made evident to the entire world through the crucifixion of Jesus. As a result, God's curse has been upon this Folk (i.e., the Jews) up to the present day. However, we also see in the Old Testament the initial glimmers of God's love,[26] which is fully revealed in Jesus Christ. Because of this understanding, the People's Church cannot abandon the Old Testament.

14. The Augsburg Confession and the other Confessional documents of the German Reformation testify to the content of the Christian proclamation. We are connected, through these Confessions, to our fathers in the faith. A Church without a Confession would be like a State without a constitution and laws.

15. Confessions are always bound to a specific time with its questions. Certain questions, which the fathers' Confessions answered, are no longer relevant to us today. Certain questions, however, to which the fathers' Confessions could not yet respond, are posed to us today. We are therefore striving to find a Confessional[27] answer of the People's Church to the questions of

---

25 The German—"Die gottgebundenen Propheten"—is admittedly stronger than the idiomatic English, which the literal English translation should make sufficiently clear, but to call a man a "prophet of God" clearly has the same import, at least *for any Christian reader.*

26 This is a reference to the many prophecies in the Old Testament concerning the redemption in Christ, not least of all Genesis 3:15—the Protoevangelium. See also fn. 12-1.

27 To give a *Confessional* answer to the questions of the day means to give an answer that is consonant with the Confessions of one's fathers in the faith, not necessarily to give an answer that is simply a restatement of things already contained in those previous confessions (see fn. 2).

our time from the Confession of the fathers: *Not back to the faith of the fathers, but forward in the faith of the fathers!*[28]

IV: The Way of the Church

16. The Peoples Church opposes Liberalism.[29] Liberalism undermines faith in Jesus Christ because it sees Him as only a man. It knows Jesus only as a preacher of high morality or as merely an heroic personality. It places human reason above God. For us, Jesus Christ is the Son of God, His appearance the miracle of human history.

17. The People's Church also stands against a new form of orthodoxy.[30] This "orthodoxy," with its inflexible adherence to

---

28 Although it should be clear what it meant by this saying, it does, perhaps, warrant some explanation or clarification: When the German Christians declare that they (we) must move *forward in the faith of the fathers*, what they are saying is that although the faith of the fathers must be maintained, guarded, and protected as an inestimable treasure, it must also, from time to time, be supplemented with confessions, or even Confessions, of our own that address the questions of the day. This is undoubtedly at least as true today as it was when it was written nearly a century ago.

29 Although the capitalization in German is incidental (as all nouns are capitalized), what is meant is the ideology that was then called Liberalism, and which is still, today, called by that same name by those versed in such matters. Specifically, it is theological Liberalism that is targeted by this point, because theological Liberalism, largely an attempt to 'reconcile' Christianity with the Enlightenment, sought to undermine the foundations of the Christian faith by subjecting the Scriptures to 'Biblical criticism' and 'reason', by focusing on the supposed 'ethical teachings' of Jesus to the exclusion of the rest of Scripture, and by attempting to 'reconcile' the content of Scripture with modern culture and society.

30 In English, we would place this use of "orthodoxy" in 'scare quotes', as I have done in this footnote and in the following instance of the word in the paragraph text. What is meant is not sarcasm, but mockery—the German Christians are condemning the stale and stagnate 'religion' of certain establishment or institutional churches (read: corporate entities), which they see as hindering the proclamation of the Gospel and the furtherance of Christ's Kingdom. Additionally, this should be taken together with Point 16

(mere) dogma,[31] obstruct the path to Christ for those who are struggling and seeking, and hinders a living proclamation of the Gospel.

18. The People's Church also *opposes attempts to replace* faith in Christ *with a religion shaped from the racial experience.* All religion, as a search and questioning for God, is racially different. But Jesus Christ, in his miraculous person, is the fulfillment of everything that is alive in the human soul in terms of longing, questioning, and anticipation. The dispute over whether Jesus was Jewish or Aryan does not touch the essence of Jesus at all. Jesus is not a

---

to be a condemnation of so-called "Neo-Orthodoxy," which arose in Europe in the wake of the First World War.

31 This word—"dogma"—must be understood in the context of the rest of the document, and, particularly, in the context of Point 15. What is *not* in view here is the Word of God or even the text of the Confessions (i.e., the Book of Concord); rather, what is in view here is the inflexible *dogmatic* pronouncements of certain institutional churches, which are not simply restatements of the Word of God or the text of the Confessions. It would not be wrong to see in this point an implied, if also subtle, criticism of Rome. Hence, I have added (as a parenthetical) the word "mere".

"wearer" of human nature,[32] but reveals to us in His person God's nature.

19. Therefore, the religion of the German people can only be Christian in nature. Christianity[33] manifests differently across races and ethnicities.[34] Thus, we are striving to establish a form of Christianity that is uniquely German.

20. This [concept of] German Christianity is personified in Martin Luther. In Luther's Reformation, we see the emergence of

---

32 To translate the German "Art" as "nature" is, admittedly, a sort of unhappy compromise. There is no English word that captures the fullness of the German, but *nature* does, to my mind, come closest, *if* the English term is taken in the fullness of its meaning. In German, one can describe the *Art* of making a particular dish in a regional *manner*—Schnitzel Wiener *Art* (Schnitzel prepared according to the Viennese style/manner/tradition), the *Art* of a particular *species*—Der Löwe ist eine *Art* der Katzenfamilie. (The lion is a species of the cat family.)—, the *Art* of a *genre* or a *style* of music— Diese *Art* von Musik gefällt mir. (I like this kind/genre/style of music.)—, the *Art* of the *nature* or the *characteristic* of a thing—Es ist nicht unsere *Art*, untreu zu sein. (It is not in our nature/characteristic of us to be unfaithful.)—, the *Art* of a *method* or an *approach*—Wir brauchen eine neue *Art* diese Probleme anzugehen. (We need a new method/approach to address these problems.)—, or the *Art* of a *style* or a *fashion* (of a [particular] time)— Die Architektur dieser Gebäude ist von der gotischen *Art*. (The architecture of these buildings is of Gothic style.). To say that the term *Art* exceeds the lexical scope of available English translations is to understate the matter, but "nature"—again, taken to the *outer extent* of its meaning in English—is, to my mind, sufficient for our purposes here, so long as the reader considers it aright.

33 Again, "Christentum" has a broader scope in German, so this entails both Christendom *and* Christianity.

34 This word, much like the word "gender", has taken on various connotations among different groups (particularly in recent decades). However, the terms themselves are not unusable or 'poisoned' due to these misuses—*abusus usum non tollit*; nevertheless, it is important to be clear what is meant. When I use "ethnicities", I do not mean to distinguish, at least not in a stark fashion, between "race" and "ethnicity"; rather, I use them similar to how I would employ "sex" and "gender"—gender is the *rightful and natural expression* of sex; thus, ethnicity is the *rightful and natural expression* of race. German is a race; Germanic is an ethnicity. Race forms a necessary subcomponent of one's ethnicity, but it is not the sum total of it. The culture and civilization of the Germans, an ethnic construct, relies upon the German race, but is a Gestalt that exceeds the merely genetic.

a distinctively German form of the Christian faith. *German Christendom is synonymous with Lutheranism.* As German Lutherans, we are both fully German and fully Christian.

21. Currently, (there are) various deceptions with regard to humanity (that) are being advanced. It is false to assert that people have no responsibility towards God, and thus bear no guilt before Him. It is false to believe that individuals have the power to redeem themselves.

22. The bonds of sin, the force of fate, and the power of death are conquered only through faith in Jesus Christ. Through Him, we are granted forgiveness of sins, a [deep] connection with God, and eternal life.

23. This statement is not a denigration but rather a realistic appraisal of humanity. Our true dignity lies in our bond with God, which is renewed through Jesus Christ.

24. This is the Christian message of salvation[35] that people of all times and all Folks[36] need. Salvation is firmly grounded upon the crucifixion and resurrection of Jesus.

---

35 If one were so inclined, much could be made of the fact that the term used here for 'message' or 'dispatch'—"Botschaft"—also means *embassy*, but that must be left for another time and place.

36 I recognize the unfortunate nature of the plural of "Folk" in English being "Folks"—and I am sorely tempted simply to import the German noun—, but it remains correct.

25. This proclamation, which takes both the real God and the real man[37] seriously, prevents the return of Materialism[36] and Liberalism[38] by way of religion.

26. Belief in Christ, if it does not lead to action, is of no value to a People's Church. The true expression of faith in Christ is a resolute struggle[39] against all forms of evil and a courageous[40] commitment to service and sacrifice.

---

37 The German word "Mensch" has no direct equivalent in English (the lexical scope includes human, person, man, and human being), but the closest equivalent for the *core* meaning is the specific submeaning of "man" as a generic term for a human being. This is part of why I have chosen to translate it "man" here, when, elsewhere, I have translated it otherwise. The reason for this is that the authors of this document would never have thought of the modern problem of certain persons questioning whether or not Christ was (and is) *male*. Thus, it would be misleading to the modern reader to translate this instance as "human" or "person" instead of "man". This is, rather obviously, an affirmation of the unio personalis—the union of God and Man in Christ—but it is worth highlighting that fact.

38 This must be taken not just as a condemnation of Materialism qua Materialism, but also as an implicit (and not particularly subtle) condemnation of Marxism, which we must remember was the major enemy at the time of the writing of document (may the attentive reader understand).

39 The German "Kampf" could, naturally, be translated as "fight", "content", or even "battle" (or a handful of other English words), but here I have rendered it "struggle" as that was a word in common use in these circles at the time, and it may even be a reference to Hitler's description of his work as a "struggle"—his *Kampf*.

40 The German "mutig" includes, in addition to the "brave" used in the literal translation and the "courageous" used here in the idiomatic translation, such concepts as *gritty* and *bold*.

27. Thus, the People's Church defines[41] Positive Christianity (Point 24 of the Party Platform)[42] as faith in Christ, salvation through Christ, and actions inspired by Christ.

28. This German Christianity represents the sole basis upon which the German people can [also][43] unite in faith.

---

41 I have chosen to translate the German "verstehen", which literally means 'understand', 'see', or 'recognize' (among other things), as "define" in the idiomatic translation as I believe the authors were doing more than merely stating their *understanding* of Point 24; rather, they were asserting both what they took Point 24 to mean and what they held it to mean for themselves and for their churches.

42 Here is an English translation of Point 24: "We demand freedom of religion for all religious denominations within the State so long as they do not endanger its existence or oppose the moral senses of the Germanic race. The Party as such advocates the standpoint of a positive Christianity without binding itself confessionally to any one denomination. It combats the Jewish-Materialistic spirit within and around us and is convinced that a lasting recovery of our nation can only succeed from within on the framework: The Common Interest Over Individual Interest."

43 This also is clearly meant as a reference to the political unity of the German people under the National Socialist State—as the National Socialist State brought political unity, so the German Christians would bring religious unity.

THE JEWISH QUESTION IN THE GERMAN EVANGELICAL CHURCH

by

Cajus Fabricius

Originally published in Berlin, 1934

The "German Christians" are a vibrant movement for the unification and promotion of the National Socialist church Volk, whose course should not be constrained. Therefore, they do not, as a rule, publish any "official" literature. The contributions of their members also appear under the sole responsibility of the respective authors.

— The [Original German] Publisher

Introduction

Dear Brothers of the Rheinish Pastoral Brotherhood!

You addressed a letter to the Reich Church Government around the turn of the year 1933/34, in which you accuse the Protestant state churches of Saxony, Brunswick, and Schleswig-Holstein, along with the German Christians, of heathenism. You substantiate this claim extensively from *The 28 Theses* "On the internal structure of the German Evangelical Church," which were accepted by the three state churches and by the leadership of the German Christians. You believed that you needed to support the Reich Bishop in his role as guardian of the pure doctrine, and you have exercised this office with the result that you declared the three state churches to have placed themselves "outside the foundations of the German Evangelical Church" by accepting the theses.

However, it was not enough for you to merely submit your letter to the Reich Bishop. Instead, you considered your statements to be so true, so important, and so significant that you wanted to bless the entire German people and perhaps all peoples of the earth with them. You had your letter printed as a pamphlet and offered it—1000 copies for 13 RM—for mass distribution. You called on the theological faculties to participate in your heresy court by providing opinions. Finally, you enclosed your pamphlet with the Pastoral Bulletin to stir up all pastors and parsonages. It seems that this last action has particularly brought about disastrous effects. In any case, you have thereby become co-responsible for the fact that numerous pastors read a "pulpit announcement" of the so-called Pastor's Emergency League during the first Sundays of the new year in their services, in which they refused obedience to the Reich Church Government, citing "heathenism and heresy," using words that clearly echoed your declaration.

Because you appear with such great claims, my brothers, and because you seem to have stirred up quite a number of people, we German Christians must address your letter. We do this not for our own sake. We are accustomed to endure blows without caring for them. But we are concerned that you dare to accuse entire German state churches of heathenism and that your letter is capable of spreading confusion and discord throughout the German people, even across all of Christendom.

For what we as German Christians desire is not confusion and discord, but order and truth. A great progress has already been made on the way to order since the first weeks of this year. The Führer, Adolf Hitler, addressed the church leaders on January 25, speaking to their consciences, and through the power of his personality and the persuasive power of his words, he succeeded in having the heads of all state churches stand behind the Reich Bishop and promise to ensure order. But this does not absolve us from the obligation to speak to the matter. On the contrary, we are now doubly obligated to help complete the order in the church by bringing the truth to light without reservation. For under no circumstances must even the slightest hint of suspicion arise that in Germany the freedom of conscience is being compromised by state power or that anyone in the Reich Church is being hindered by a heretical church authority from confessing their Christian faith. This compels us to investigate every accusation made against us down to the last detail, so that no even the slightest residue of alleged heresy remains attached to us.

The spirit in which we wish to act must be the spirit of brotherly love. For we belong to the Christians who wish to restore the spirit of the early church in today's Christendom, of which it is said: They were "one heart and one soul." We are particularly of the opinion that, especially in National Socialist Germany, where by a work of God unity has been established like never before, the Evangelical Church must not give the impression that it is a home for hatred and confusion.

Because we are filled with such a spirit of brotherhood, which can be shaken by nothing, we will not allow you, dear brothers, to divide us, even though you accuse us of the worst thing that Christians can accuse each other of, namely, heathenism. We act according to the obligation we take upon ourselves in the Lord's Prayer: We forgive those who sin against us. We love you, even though you want to be our enemies; we bless you when you curse us; we do good to you when you hate us; we pray for you when you insult and persecute us. Our prayer is: Father, forgive them, for they know not what they do.

For it is so, my brothers: You do not know what you are doing. You are not masters of yourselves. With clear Christian consciousness or even with theologically trained thinking and with holy responsibility before God, one cannot produce a work like yours. There is a foreign, uncanny power in you that has led you astray. Perhaps it is the power of original sin, which, like us, you have a very serious understanding of, and which you no doubt believe exists not only in us but also in you. Or perhaps an evil spirit has come upon you, or perhaps a legion of unclean spirits. We do not know, and perhaps you do not either.

But whatever the spirit may be that governs you, it is in any case part of that force which always desires the evil and always results in the good. You spread error, but you serve the truth; you want discord, but you serve peace; you want to judge us, but you justify us. The one great thing that your letter proves is this: If only what you accuse the German Christians of, the "heresies" of the German Christians, is true, then the German Christians belong to the most orthodox Christians who have ever existed. For these "heresies" do not exist. And if what you indicate as your own opinion is really your opinion, then you belong to the most deceived Christians of all time.

But you will grow impatient, my brothers. Therefore, let us get to the common work. I believe that the common work will bring us together.

You generally accuse the German Christians and the three state churches that you attack of having abandoned the foundations of the Reich Church, the Holy Scriptures, and the Reformation Confession. For this reason, you base your own statements on Bible verses—which, however, occur only occasionally—and on numerous and detailed references to Lutheran confessional writings, namely, the Apology of the Augsburg Confession, Luther's Catechisms, the Smalcald Articles, and the Formula of Concord. This gives your statements the appearance of confessional faithfulness and simultaneously creates the impression that our supposed heresies have already been refuted in the confessional writings of the Reformation era. But I recommend to all who are able to open up the referenced passages and thoroughly check them. They will be shaken when they notice how things really stand with the confessional justification of the heresy court proceeding against us. Just this review is so enlightening that one could spare oneself all further discussion. But for the sake of brotherly love and truth, we still want to examine the matter both in general and in detail.

The 28 Theses of the German Christians bear the title: *"Theses on the internal structure of the German Evangelical Church."* They clearly express that these are practical instructions for shaping the church of a particular country in a particular historical situation, but not a systematically complete Christian confession of faith. In all deeply moving times of church history, it has been the case that people did not write systems of doctrine but provided answers to pressing questions of the moment, answers that arose from the depth of faith.

Thus, all confessional writings of Lutheranism must also be understood. They partly serve the purpose of dealing with the Papists, partly the practical task of church youth instruction, and partly the settling of disputes within the church. Even less is the Gospel transmitted to us as a closed, systematic teaching. Despite their eternal content and their unified basic stance, the words of Jesus were not sentences of a life wisdom that is balanced in every respect, but revelations of divine life to certain people at certain occasions.

The 28 Theses of the German Christians also carry this occasional character. Therefore, everyone is mistaken and missing the essential point if they seek a complete Christian confession of faith in them, which provides conclusive answers about ultimate truths. You, my brothers, are particularly strong in this mistaken notion and thus great in missing the point.

This is already evident from the structure of the whole. *The 28 Theses* fall into the following parts: "1. Church and State, 2. Preaching of the Church, 3. The Foundations of the Church, 4. The Way of the Church." You divide it into: "1. Concerning the Church, 2. Concerning the Holy Scriptures, 3. The Doctrine of Jesus Christ." Even from this, it is clear that you seek statements on the innermost questions of the Christian faith, while *The Theses* primarily address the practical concerns of the present church life. This failure to engage directly must be kept in mind throughout the whole investigation. But now let us get to the individual work.

I treat you with the greatest consideration. You are free to speak completely. I do not tear any of your sentences from their context, but I repeat everything you have to say literally and fully. In every case, you precede some of your expressions or sentences from *The 28 Theses* with quotation marks and then present your heresy court. I print every one of your words. I also put everything in bold that you emphasize by bolding. Then, I will follow piece by piece with my responses, which I set apart from your statements with greater emphasis. You have the floor first.

I: Concerning the Church

First Citation & Criticism

1. "The state and the Church born together as the two great organizing forces of a people" (from Thesis 2).

This statement contradicts the scriptural and Reformation understanding of the Church. The Church can only be understood in relation to Christ, from God's revelation in His Word. For this reason, the Church cannot be described as one of the "two organizing forces of a people," as this characterization completely misses the essence of the Church. The Church, according to the Reformation, is never anything other than a community of people within the nations, whom the Holy Spirit, through God's Word, calls, gathers, enlightens, sanctifies, and preserves in Jesus Christ in the true, unified faith.

We base this understanding on the following: the Apology of the Augsburg Confession, Articles IV, VII, and VIII concerning the Church (cf. Müller, *Symbolic Books*, pp. 152–153), and the Large Catechism, Part II, Article 3 (Müller, p. 457).

Response of Fabricius

My brothers! It speaks directly to our hearts when you place value on the Reformation's understanding of the Church. We believe with you in the holy Christian Church. We simply wish to describe the essence of the Christian Church with somewhat deeper-reaching words than you do when you formulate your expressions by combining phrases from Luther's Small Catechism. We turn to Luther's Large Catechism and read (Müller, p. 457 ff.):

"I believe that there is a holy little flock and community of pure saints on earth, under one head, Christ, called together by the Holy Spirit in one faith, mind, and understanding; with various gifts, yet united in love, without sects or schisms. Of this community I am also a part and member, sharing and participating in all its treasures and blessings, brought and incorporated into it by the Holy Spirit because I have heard and continue to hear God's Word, which is the entrance into this fellowship. For beforehand, before we came to this, we were entirely under the devil, as those who knew nothing of God or Christ. Thus, the Holy Spirit remains with the holy community or Christendom until the Last Day, through which He calls us and uses it to lead and spread the Word, by which He creates and increases sanctification, so that it grows daily and becomes strong in faith and its fruits, which He produces."

This essence of the Church is presupposed as a matter of course in *The 28 Theses* of the German Christians. It is not explicitly stated because *The Theses* do not aim to be a complete confession of faith.

However, what applies to the general essence of the Church does not contradict the statement about the two organizing forces within a people but harmonizes with it in the best possible way; indeed, it even follows from the general essence of the Church that it is one of the great organizing forces within a people. For wherever people are united in the Holy Spirit of Jesus Christ, who bind themselves in brotherly love and grow daily in sanctification, there arises a power of community and order that constitutes the most solid element of a people's unity.

And you too, my brothers, acknowledge—despite your somewhat narrower conceptual definition—that the Church is a "community of people" who are "gathered" by the Holy Spirit. Is not even your Church an "ordering power among the people"?

In that case, we would fundamentally agree. We would not be heretics, and your accusation would only stem from the fact that you misunderstand us, reproaching us with an essence of the Church that, for us, is self-evident and thus left unspoken.

But the matter seems to be different. For you assert: The concept of the two ordering powers "contradicts the scriptural, Reformation understanding of the Church." According to you, your Church has nothing to do with order, power, people, or the state. Your Church must be some sort of theological or philosophical school, in which the hearers are merely taught the doctrine of the lordship of Christ and of the Holy Spirit. Jesus Christ and His Spirit, for you, are evidently not a living power that sanctifies you through and through, penetrates soul and body, and unites many separate spirits into one heart and one soul. Your Church, as a "community of people within the nations," may well be some kind of Christian-Internationale, one that exhibits pronounced indifference toward all national life. And it seems you are also displeased that Church and State are mentioned in the same breath and are recognized for their similar and mutual influence on the soul of the people. You likely do not acknowledge the creational structuring of humanity into nations, nor the corresponding structuring of the Church into national churches. And you probably regard the State as an ungodly power, permeated by sin and perhaps even possessed by demonic forces, from which the hearers of God's Word must guard themselves.

These appear to be the assumptions underlying your rejection of the concept of the two ordering powers. I will refrain from further tracing the course of your reasoning. However, I categorically deny your right to judge our thoroughly Reformation-based stance.

And because we are not only Reformation-minded but also biblically minded, and because you too claim to be Bible-believing, I would like to remind you of the 12th and 13th chapters of the Epistle to the Romans. There you will find the living interplay of the two ordering powers: the Church of Christ with the law of love, and the worldly authority with legal discipline and punishment. And I especially remind you that Paul, although he knows this worldly authority only as pagan and not as Christian, nevertheless regards it as God's order.

However, we must speak more extensively about the position of the Church in relation to the national structure of humanity. Therefore, please take the floor again.

Second Citation & Criticism

2. "Only one who possesses the trust of the government can be a church leader" (in Thesis 2).

This statement contradicts the Reformation confession of Church and Church governance, because it makes a worldly-political viewpoint the standard for suitability for a church office. In the Church, only spiritual principles can serve as the standard for suitability for a church office. Whoever has this spiritual suitability will certainly have the right, Christian attitude of obedience toward the authority, by which they are worthy of its trust.

We refer to: Apology (IV) VII and VIII de ecclesia. (Müller, p. 156), Apology XIV de potestate ecclesiastica (Müller, p. 288). Schmalkaldic Articles, tract. de potest. et jurisd. episc. (Müller, pp. 340–342).

Response of Fabricius

Dear brothers! If it were truly the case—as you seem to assume—that the Church in a nation does not represent an ordering power, but rather has nothing to do with power, order, people, or state, then, yes, precisely then, the state must ensure that only men lead the Church who guarantee that public order and the power of the people are not endangered by the Church. However, if the Church were to be a Christian-Internationale, emphasizing its indifference toward all national life, then the government of a nation must, with particular seriousness, assure itself of the loyalty of the church leaders to the state. Otherwise, it could happen that church leaders use their international connections to work against their own people and homeland.

But if, as is actually the case, the Church, together with the State, represents a great ordering power in a given country, then it is simply self-evident that the closest relationship of trust must exist between the government and the Church leadership.

If you counter by saying that only spiritual principles can serve as the standard for suitability for a church office, this does not contradict our thesis. On the contrary, it is self-evident that spiritual suitability is decisive. This is so self-evident that we did not even state it explicitly. But in addition to this primary condition, there are numerous secondary conditions in all church communities. It is not only generally assumed that the clergyman is a citizen of the country in question, that the national language is his native tongue, but it is also assumed that he possesses a high level of education, and indeed secular education, even pagan education. In all concordats of the Roman Catholic Church, in all state agreements of Protestant churches, and in all church and state legislations, numerous provisions are made that have nothing to do with spiritual suitability, but which are inevitable if state and Church are to stand in an orderly relationship with one another.

You are therefore fighting against self-evident state and church orders. But now, the floor is yours again.

Third Citation & Criticism

3. "The people's Church professes blood and race, because the people are a community of blood and essence" (in Thesis 3).

The Christian Church has never confessed anything other than the revelation of the triune God. Blood and race, however, are not according to the confession of the Reformation the revelation of God; therefore, one cannot possibly speak of a "confession of the Church" to blood and race. Rather, the Church confesses faith in God, the Creator, not in creation, and it grounds the affirmation of creation through its faith in the Creator, but not from a worldview, i.e., not from an understanding of the world from within itself, as is plainly the case in the aforementioned sentence.

Compare: Large Catechism II, 1st Article. (Müller, p. 450.)

Response of Fabricius

Dear brothers! What should one say to this? Is it an oversight or malicious intent when you omit Thesis 5, where the race is clearly called the "creation of God"? Can one continue the conversation with people who follow such methods? I will do so, for the sake of brotherly love.

Now, my brothers, we certainly confess with you and all of Christendom to the triune God. This is so much the foundation of all our confession that we did not even express it in our theses. But the triune God, however, is for us, as for all other Christians — and hopefully for you as well — no lifeless concept, but Spirit, strength, and fullness of life.

We confess — and surely you also do — according to Luther's Small Catechism, especially to body and soul, eyes, ears, and all members, reason and all senses as creation of God. And not only this, but also clothing and shoes, food and drink, house and home, wife and children, fields, cattle, and all goods we confess as creation of God. And when we open Luther's Large Catechism, we find there many other examples of things that are the creation of God. There, Luther, among many other things, names "life," further "sun, moon, and stars, day and night, air, fire, water, earth and what it bears and can do, birds, fish, animals, grain, and all kinds of plants." Luther also includes — and this is what you, my brothers, must especially take note of — "good governance, peace, and security" as part of God's creation. Dare you deny that blood and race are also creation of God? And do you wish to dispute our right to value these facts, because today our people, as a community of blood and essence, is important to us?

If you do not allow us to speak of blood and race as the creation of God, then you do not know what creation is or what the Creator is; then the Creator is probably to you merely a philosophical or theological thought of a distant God, who has to do with this world only in that He reveals Himself in the Spirit of certain people as the concept of the infinite.

But now you have the floor again.

Fourth Citation & Criticism

4. "The Christian of another race is not a Christian of inferior rank, but a Christian of a different kind" (in Thesis 4).

The Reformation confession does not recognize Christians of different kinds, but only Christians of different confessions. In this, it bears witness to itself as the teaching of truth and can therefore ask all Christians the question of truth. The doctrine of "race-appropriate Christianity" established in this sentence not only obscures the truth claim of the Reformation confession, which is asserted with the utmost seriousness based on its understanding of Scripture, but also renders the evangelical church incapable of being a preacher of the pure, unadulterated Gospel as the truth of God.

Response of Fabricius

My brothers! You probably want to claim here that in the one Church of Christ, the difference between peoples and races means nothing.

You will be overwhelmingly refuted by the fullness of historical facts.

Of course, the Gospel is the one great truth for all Christians. But equally evident is the fact that Christianity divides into groups that naturally align with ethnic and racial boundaries.

Even the division into different confessions, which you expressly acknowledge, is determined by ethnic and racial peculiarities. I will only remind you of the most well-known examples.

Already in the earliest Christian times, there were not only the pagan Christian communities of the Aryan peoples but also Jewish-Christian communities whose members adhered to circumcision and some other Old Testament ceremonies, recognized the absolute validity of the Old Testament, and emphasized the humanity of Jesus and His Jewish origin. Even in Russia, Jewish-Christian communities have existed for centuries, advocating similar principles in varying degrees. In Greek-Orthodox Christianity, the Gospel was clothed in a Hellenistic garment. Christianity became a cultic immersion into the immortal life of the deity and a recognitive immersion into the God-manhood of Christ. In the Roman Catholic Church, the spirit of the Roman Empire, the spirit of law and world domination, was noticeable. The Reformation was not only a new revelation of the Gospel, but it also represented an awakening of German inner life, which opened up to the Gospel and had already been active in a very peculiar way in German mysticism before and then in many awakening and sanctification movements, which emerged in part very radically, into the light. And finally, in the multifacetedness of English Christianity, with its emphasis on

196

individual personality and the individual congregation, not only the spirit of the Gospel is expressed but also the distinctiveness of a seafaring and world-conquering people. These are the relationships between confession and ethnicity, which every theologian must be familiar with.

However, there are also some less well-known individual cases, where not only unconsciously or semi-consciously, but deliberately and intentionally, an appropriate expression for one's own Christianity is sought. I particularly draw your attention, my brothers, to the new edition of the national songs of the German Community Movement. There, numerous songs have been deliberately excluded just because of their English-American origin and replaced with German original songs. Here, a sacred possession of the Community Movement has been tampered with and transformed for national reasons, and to an extent that does not seem justified by purely factual reasons. I ask you, my brothers, to carefully consider this fact before you take it upon yourselves to condemn German Christians and Evangelical State Churches because in them the concept of a race-appropriate Christianity has been spoken of back and forth.

So much for the connection between confession and ethnicity and race. However, beyond the division by confessions, there exists a far-reaching division in Christianity by peoples and races, which is simply determined by the local cohabitation and the linguistic and ancestral connection of certain groups of Christianity. Particularly instructive in this regard are the United States of America, where on the one hand, a very strong mixing of peoples and races has occurred in both the state and some large churches, but on the other hand, it is precisely in the churches that the ethnic and racial character has asserted itself extraordinarily tenaciously, even regrouping itself under these aspects. The large number of independent American churches is essentially conditioned by the fact that descendants of various peoples, such as Germans, Scandinavians, Finns, Poles, Bohemians, Russians,

Greeks, and many other former immigrants, have formed and continue to form self-contained and separated church bodies. And something similar applies to race. Although many African-Americans have mixed with Europeans to varying degrees, such that one can observe a whole spectrum of colors from pure white through all shades of gray to pure black, and although in some large churches like the Episcopal Methodist Church, whites and blacks are united, a significant number of independent Christian black churches have formed, largely due to the fact that cohabitation between races in a congregation was felt by both sides as a disturbance to inner peace, even as intolerable. One could, aside from America, also mention the Evangelical mission fields, where precisely with respect to the full impact of the Christian message, the ethnic and racial particularity of the newly converted communities is carefully considered and nurtured.

But we need not look too far afield, for we can remind ourselves of the most immediate examples to show to what extent church boundaries are conditioned by national borders, and indeed how sometimes, in this regard, even too much of the good has been done. In our German fatherland, there are still a number of regional churches within the national church, whose existence is not conditioned by confession, race, ethnicity, or even tribal affiliation, but is rather solely based on long-past dynastic facts and the familial relationships of dethroned princely houses, i.e., on small and very small political circumstances of earlier times. These German conditions represent one of the strangest facts in the Church of Christ on this earth, and if you, my brothers, have the need to address unjustified external divisions in the Christian Church, then please pour the bowl of your wrath over this situation within the German Reich church and help with the work of unification between the state churches so that it progresses quickly. In doing so, you will promote the unity of the Church of Christ more than if you hold unnecessary heresy trials over German state churches.

Now, you have the word again.

Fifth Citation & Criticism

5. a) "A member of the Volkskirche (People's Church) can only be one who, according to the law of the state, is a member of the people." b) "An officeholder of the Volkskirche can only be one who, according to the law of the state, can be a civil servant" (the so-called Aryan Paragraph). In Thesis 8.

a) This statement replaces the sacrament of baptism and the faith in Jesus Christ, worked by the Holy Spirit, with the condition of belonging to a race for entry into the Christian community. In doing so, it denies the effectiveness of the Holy Spirit and thereby abolishes the Church of Christ. A church that confesses this statement is no longer the Church of Christ, but a sect based on the racial principle in the form of a state-bound "organization for the promotion of German folk religion" (see Thesis 19), which bears the name of Christianity but is in truth a relapse into paganism.

The actual connection of the Church to the reality of the creation-based differences of races and peoples should not lead the Church to establish a legal binding. This Judaistic heresy has already been explicitly rejected in the New Testament (Acts 15 and the Epistle to the Galatians). The racial difference of Christians can neither be made the norm for belonging to a Christian community nor the norm for suitability for an office in the Christian community. The norm for belonging to a Christian community is the confession. Therefore, a Volkskirche that is not a confessional church is no longer a Christian church.

b) The suitability and calling for an office in the Christian Church cannot be determined by the civil servant law of the state. By doing so, the necessary freedom of the Church, which is inherent in its essence, in establishing and filling church offices, is restricted and destroyed by an external law. According to

Scripture, however, the Church must not bow to the spirit of this world, to the "elements of this world" (Galatians 4:3; Colossians 2:8), so that it does not become incapable of fulfilling its mission to deliver God's message to this world.

The Aryan Paragraph in the Church, in any form, is a heresy that destroys the substance of the Church. A Church that accepts the Aryan Paragraph has become a Judaistic, nationalist sect and will share the fate of all Judaistic sects: dissolution and relapse into sub-Christian piety, i.e., paganism.

Response of Fabricius

Oh, you foolish Galatians, so must I cry out with the Apostle Paul, who has bewitched you, that you do not obey the truth? Yes, my brothers, you are the Galatians of our time. You have now clearly made this known. You are ruled by the same spirit that ruled the Galatians, and this spirit is called—Juda. But Juda is not just an abstract term to you; it is a force of life that has taken possession of you. You show this by the way you now proceed against us with heavy artillery. You bombard us with the worst accusations that can be hurled against Christians. You accuse us of denying baptism and the Holy Spirit, yes, you call us heathens.

Until recently, I considered the Jewish question in the German Evangelical Church to be quite a minor issue, because the number of Evangelical pastors of Jewish descent in Germany is so insignificantly small. It is still difficult for me to depart from this view. But you are on the best way to teach me otherwise. Your attack seems to prove that this small number of pastors of Jewish descent possesses a very uncanny power. Therefore, this matter must certainly be taken very seriously.

Of course, my brothers, the way you proceed does not unbalance us. Your cannonade passes by; it threatens us—but it does not kill us. Here, indeed, precisely in a decisive offensive, you again make the mistake of talking past us. When we speak of the

"Volkskirche," that is, of the German Evangelical Reich Church and its legislation, you speak of the universal Christian Church and its innermost essence. You quickly confuse the term "Volkskirche" with the expression "Christian community" and act as if we desire that people of Jewish descent be excluded from the Christian Church. With this, this whole point is effectively settled in our favor. It is settled even more definitively if the confusion of terms is not a mistake, but a deliberate intention on your part. If you apply such tricks, one should actually not continue negotiating with you. But nevertheless, for the sake of love, I do not want to break off the conversation but rather engage in the matter with all seriousness.

Dear brothers! Let us, in a truly fraternal way, remember the common ground on which we stand. The standard recognized by both you and us is, as it says in the Reich Church Constitution, the gospel of Jesus Christ, as it is testified in the Holy Scriptures and newly brought to light in the confessions of the Reformation. Now, how do we understand the gospel in relation to the Jewish question in the German Evangelical Church?

The New Testament, and especially the Letter to the Galatians, gives very clear direction to our attitude and actions here. There was, indeed, in the earliest Christianity a very serious Jewish and Aryan question. The Jews wanted to impose themselves in the Christian communities, even among the Gentile Christians, with the absolute acceptance of the Old Testament, with circumcision, and with various other observances of the law. The Apostle Paul had to fight the hardest battles with his Jewish countrymen because of this. He had the fiercest disagreements with them and suffered intensely both from their accusations and from their persecutions. And how does Paul resolve the Aryan and Jewish problem from the perspective of the Gospel? He says in the Letter to the Galatians that the church of Christ is one in its head: "There is neither Jew nor Greek, there is neither bond nor free, there is neither male nor female; for ye are all one in Christ Jesus"

(Galatians 3:28). This, however, does not mean to Paul the abolition of all differences in the pale concept of uniform humanity. On the contrary, he tells the servants: "Let every man abide in the same calling wherein he was called" (1 Corinthians 7:20). He emphasizes the difference between the sexes so strongly that he even gives men and women special instructions for worship (1 Corinthians 11:3–16). Thus, he does not think about denying the serious tension between Jewish Christianity and Gentile Christianity in the practice of this world and in the building of the churches, nor does he seek to force Jewish Christians and Gentile Christians into one congregation. On the contrary, Paul proceeds here with the utmost prudence, the most serious sense of responsibility, and the most loving attitude. He reports in the Letter to the Galatians (2:9): "And when James, Cephas, and John, who seemed to be pillars, perceived the grace that was given unto me, they gave to me and Barnabas the right hands of fellowship; that we should go unto the heathen, and they unto the circumcision." Here, then, they pledged by handshake that in the emerging Christian Church, the missions to the Aryans and to the Jews should be strictly separated, and that they did not want to disturb or influence each other in preaching and church planting. This was agreed upon for the sake of love, because confusion between Jewish Christians and Gentile Christians in the congregations, such as in Corinth and Galatia, repeatedly led to the greatest difficulties. The correctness of the agreement made was immediately confirmed when Peter showed a wavering stance in Antioch and thereby fell into a sharp conflict with Paul.

The direction given here to Christian action in the church is as follows: All Christians are one in Christ, the head of the church, but they organize themselves in this world according to the division of mankind into nations and races. However, this is not nonsense, not a reprehensible adaptation to the world, not a "Judaistic" enslavement under the "elements of this world." Rather, Christians, precisely in their communion with Christ, are lovingly oriented towards this world and the racially and ethnically divided humanity, and they want to have in the church a peaceful community of people with each other, and, if love demands it, also a peaceful community of reconciliation.

Now, of course, my brothers, you who are otherwise so Bible-believing, you will object in this case: The circumstances in the New Testament times were different from ours. Back then, the Jewish and Aryan question was a problem in the Christian community, but today it is brought into the Church of Christ by the state and thus by the world. Certainly, my brothers, the situation is different today. But that does not change the great principles that flow from the Gospel, nor our obligation to act in this world from a holy sense of responsibility that takes into account the circumstances of the time. Moreover, you should note that even in the New Testament times, the difficulties had a significant root in the very worldly fact that the Jews were spread throughout the Roman Empire and lived mixed with people of other nations and races. And on the other hand, you yourselves, my brothers, show through the confusion you cause in the church that the difficulties today also arise not only from the "godless" world but simultaneously from within the church itself. But I will now, in order that nothing essential remains unsaid, carefully go over our present situation.

Today, the German people, who were in deep decay and close to collapse, have been awakened to new life through the National Socialist movement and, under the leadership of Adolf Hitler, have grown into a strong, disciplined, and orderly unity. However, part of the blame for the decay lies in the fact that the German people were under the dominance of individuals who liked to call themselves "fatherlandless comrades" and were more concerned with international interests than with the welfare of the German people. These ruling circles were closely intertwined with international Judaism. The German resurgence was only possible if, during its course, those international powers—and with them, the dominance of Judaism—were shaken off. The liberation of the German people was simultaneously based on the fundamental conviction that the general prosperity of the nations of the earth is ruined by the dominance of rootless international powers, and that recovery is only possible if the peoples everywhere return to their natural foundations, to blood and soil, and rediscover their natural organization into nations and races—a conviction that, by the way, not only has followers in Germany but worldwide and has been advocated and practically realized for decades, especially by Zionist Judaism.

In this situation, it is self-evident that the German people are concerned that the dethroned powers may, in some way, try to regain influence. These are the national conditions in which the Jewish question in the German Evangelical Church must be considered today.

The situation of the Evangelical Church in Germany is today as fortunate and favorable as it has perhaps never been before. National Socialism, and foremost the Führer, has taken a stand on the basis of Positive Christianity. The state is no longer pagan; it has become Christian. The terrible danger of Bolshevism, with its church-destroying effects, has been averted. The godless associations have been banned. Many people who had left the church under communist pressure are returning. There is widespread openness to the Gospel among the people, which was not present before. The people are ready to come to the church, and the church is ready to go to the people. There is a great historical opportunity to fill the masses of the people, after a long period of spiritual desolation, with the spirit of the Gospel. The Führer himself, in his great speech of January 30, 1934, urged both the Evangelical and Catholic churches to make the religious and moral forces of the Gospel effective among the people.

But this great historical opportunity would pass, the entire happiness of the moment would be shattered, and incalculable harm would result if the German people did not have absolute trust in the Evangelical Church. Therefore, suspicion must not arise as though the powers that have brought Germany to the brink of the abyss, and among them the Jewish power, have found refuge and a home in the church.

This practical-church perspective, that is, the sense of responsibility of the Church of Christ toward our people, the will for peace between the church and the people, is decisive under the present circumstances for the way the Church of Christ must prove itself in the German Reich through the power of love. These are the changed circumstances under which we, like the apostles, must give each other the right hand to live peacefully together and, if necessary, peacefully reconcile. From here, all measures must be taken and assessed that relate to the solution of the Jewish question in the church.

The measures themselves can have various content and forms. They can be church laws, ecclesiastical administrative measures, or even voluntary decisions by the parties involved. The content and form of these measures can be determined, in detail, not from the Gospel but only by the requirements of the hour. Their historical meaning, however, can only be that every Jewish influence in the German Evangelical Church is eliminated, and any possibility of the dominance of this spirit is excluded.

The immediate effect of such measures on the individuals concerned would be of very limited scope, given the vanishingly small number of Evangelical Christians of Jewish descent in Germany, and personal hardships of any significant importance would not occur under normal circumstances, especially since church laws in this area, just like corresponding state laws, will always contain a number of limiting provisions.

As for those Evangelical Christians of Jewish descent who do not hold or claim church office, a legal reorganization of their relationship to the state or the German Evangelical Church would in no way interfere with their practice of the Christian religion. It has long been a self-evident custom in all Evangelical churches in

Germany that Christian foreigners, and even Christians of other confessions, are fundamentally not denied any ecclesiastical act. No one is turned away from baptism or confirmation, no one is refused a church wedding or church burial, and no one is even barred from participating in the sermon or the Lord's Table. A refusal of this kind is always perceived as unloving and tactless. The same moral norm will, of course, always apply to Evangelical Christians of Jewish descent living in Germany. However, it must be expected of these Christians that they demonstrate the greatest modesty and unpretentiousness and in no way display challenging behavior. This demand, however, does not represent an exception in Germany today. For it is also expected of every citizen of genuinely Aryan descent that they do not make personal claims but instead exercise the greatest restraint, that they remember their duties more than their rights, that they distance themselves from all lawlessness, and that they conduct themselves in a disciplined manner within the larger whole.

As for the question concerning pastors and church officials of Jewish descent, this is also a matter that is inherently so insignificant, so simple, and so self-evident that no fuss should be made about it, let alone turning it into a fundamental or even doctrinal question. There must be an order within the German Reich Church that removes any offense that German fellow citizens might take to leaders of Jewish descent in the congregations. Since this is a particularly hotly debated issue, I would like to let someone speak in my place who also holds great respect among the opponents of German Christians. This authority can be quoted as follows: "The question can only be approached in such a way that, based on 1 Cor. 8, we may today, for the sake of the prevailing 'weakness,' expect church officials of Jewish descent to impose upon themselves the necessary restraint, so that no offense is caused. It would not be advisable today for a pastor of non-Aryan descent to hold an office in church governance or a particularly prominent position in public mission work." (Pastor's Journal 1934, p. 46.) It is evident here that even among the opponents, the correct insight is beginning to dawn. For despite all the reservations with which this speaker surrounds his concession, his viewpoint largely approaches ours. He senses what is at stake for the German people and has at least a faint sense of the responsibility that we feel so strongly.

But for you, my brothers, this very leader of yours must be a heretic and a heathen. For you are radical. For you, it is a matter of the utmost faith, following from the international character of the Church, that no distinction may be made between German and Jewish descent in the German Reich Church. You care little whether the German Evangelical Church falls into confusion, consumes itself in hatred, or even perishes, as long as the Jewish question is answered in favor of the Jews and not the Germans.

But, my brothers, you can be sure of this: you do not convince. You may have succeeded in confusing a number of people who read your leaflet with the superficiality with which one reads newspapers. But you have not won over deeper thinkers, and many of those whom you had deceived have already realized their mistake and regret having been misled by you.

Yes, my brothers—I must say this in conclusion—you not only fail to convince, but by your arguments, you place yourselves in a light that deeply calls for pity. Through your actions, you have simultaneously incurred a terrible guilt. You have brought about a disaster in one of the happiest moments that Evangelical Christianity in Germany has ever experienced, a disaster that one must shudder at when considering the possible consequences.

But despite all this, we are confident that in the end, this disaster must serve to bring about good, and your wrongdoings must ultimately work to our benefit.

II. On Holy Scripture

First Citation & Criticism

1. "The decisive revelation of God is Jesus Christ; the document of this revelation is the New Testament. Therefore, it holds normative significance for all proclamation of the Church"(from Thesis 11).

This thesis compromises the unity of Holy Scripture and thereby abandons the foundation of the Reformation's confessions. According to the confession and doctrine of the Reformation, the document of the one, sole, and therefore "decisive" revelation of God in Jesus Christ is the whole, indivisible, and unified Scripture of the Old and New Testaments.

We appeal to: Apology of the Augsburg Confession, Article IV, 5 (Müller, p. 87); Article XII, 53 (Müller, p. 175). Formula of Concord, Preface (Müller, pp. 517 and 568 ff.).

Response of Fabricius

Dear brothers! You appeal to the Reformation confessions and cite several passages where the value relationship between the Old and New Testaments is not addressed. However, you should know that during the Reformation era, the Law—meaning the essential content of the Old Testament—was subordinated to the Gospel, which is the essential content of the New Testament, to such an extent that there was debate over whether the Law should even be preached to believing Christians. In the Formula of Concord—specifically in passages you regrettably do not cite (Müller, pp. 533 ff., 633 ff.)—we read, for example (p. 633):

"Since the distinction between Law and Gospel is a particularly glorious light that serves to rightly divide God's Word and properly interpret and understand the writings of the holy prophets and apostles, it is necessary to diligently maintain this distinction so that these two doctrines are not mixed or the Gospel turned into a Law, which would obscure the merit of Christ and rob troubled consciences of the comfort they otherwise have in the holy Gospel when it is preached purely and clearly, enabling them to withstand the terrors of the Law during their greatest trials."

I believe this alone is sufficient to dispel all doubts about the orthodoxy of the German Christians, as they distinguish the New Testament from the Old. However, in order to address any remaining concerns, I would like to point to a contemporary development in a foreign Protestant church. Observing related situations and developments in other countries often provides clarification and reassurance. The case in question concerns the Church of England and its Book of Common Prayer, which, as is well known, serves as the fundamental confession of the church in England.

Although the Old Testament has traditionally played a far greater role in English worship services than in the worship services of the German regional churches, you will be astonished —and perhaps even alarmed, my brothers—to learn that in the new edition of the Book of Common Prayer, in use since 1928, the spirit of the Old Testament has been significantly overshadowed by the New Testament. Not only have numerous Old Testament references, such as those to Adam and Eve, Noah's Ark, and Abraham, Isaac, and Jacob, been omitted from many of the new parallel formularies, but numerous prayers have been entirely removed from the prayer book. These prayers had predominantly interpreted human suffering in an Old Testament sense as the result of God's punitive wrath. In their place, prayers have been introduced that interpret suffering, in accordance with the New Testament, as a means of discipline by God's fatherly goodness (Corpus Confessionum 17, I, pp. 1–449).

My brothers, I urge you to carefully consider this English development, which must surely concern you as much as it concerns us Germans. Please write to the Archbishop of Canterbury and express your concerns about the declining prominence of the Old Testament in his church.

We German Christians, however, refuse to be condemned as heretics by you. For our position aligns with the confessional writings of the Reformation.

But how do your and our views of the Old Testament truly compare? We would like to hear more from you on this matter.

Second Citation & Criticism

2. "The Old Testament does not have the same value. The specifically Jewish moral customs and national religion have been superseded. The Old Testament remains important because it transmits the history and decline of a people who, despite God's revelation, repeatedly separated themselves from Him. The God-bound prophets show us all, through this people: a nation's relationship to God is decisive for its destiny in history" (Thesis 12). "Thus, we recognize in the Old Testament the apostasy of the Jews from God and thereby their sin. This sin is made manifest to the entire world in the crucifixion of Jesus. From this, the curse of God rests upon this people to this day. Yet, at the same time, we recognize in the Old Testament the first rays of God's love, which is fully revealed in Jesus Christ. For the sake of this understanding,

the national church cannot dispense with the Old Testament"
(Thesis 18).

The devaluation of the Old Testament presented here arises from human arrogance, which refuses to submit to the entirety of God's Word. According to Reformation teaching, the sole standard for evaluating and interpreting Scripture is Scripture itself—not a historical-religious criterion rooted in humanistic thought.

This teaching about the meaning and value of the Old Testament is, despite contrary claims, effectively an abolition of the Old Testament as the Word of God in the testimony of Moses and the prophets, of the Law and the promise. With the abandonment of the Old Testament's salvation history, the New Testament also collapses; with the abandonment of the Old, the New bond falls; with the abandonment of the promise, the fulfillment falls as well.

To acknowledge the Old Testament merely as an illustrative teaching example of God's actions is to reinterpret it rationalistically and thereby dismiss it. The Reformation confession insists on the unity of Scripture and the genuine revelatory nature of the Old Testament. Both are surrendered here. Therefore, this teaching about the Old Testament must be rejected.

Response of Fabricius

Oh foolish Galatians, I must exclaim for the second time: who has bewitched you? You remain under the bondage of the letter of the Old Testament, like the Jewish Christians in the time of Paul. You are under the dominion of the "elements of this cosmos" and have not yet attained the freedom of the children of God.

If you label the position of the German Christians regarding the Old Testament as heretical and speak of our alleged "abolition" of the Old Testament, then you must also acknowledge that the position of Jesus and the Apostle Paul, indeed of all the writers of the New Testament, was heretical and that they too "abolished" the Old Testament. For the German Christians are doing nothing other than what Jesus and His apostles did. They interpret the Old Testament in light of the New, view the Law from the perspective of the Gospel, and understand the history of the people of Israel from the standpoint of the community of Jesus Christ. They accept what in the Old Testament prepares for the New and reject or regard as subordinate what diverges from the Gospel.

Shall I remind you of well-known facts? In the preaching and conduct of Jesus and His disciples, the external ceremonies, the legal order of the Law, and the national restrictions of the Jewish worldview are disregarded and surpassed by the worship of the heart, moral brotherly love, and a vision for all peoples. Above all, Jesus' words and life demonstrate a free stance toward the Sabbath commandment—one of the holiest commandments of the Old Testament and a cornerstone of Judaism. Similarly, Paul opposes another sacred commandment of the Old Testament and another cornerstone of Judaism: circumcision.

With what conscience, my brothers, do you dare to attack the German Christians, who hold the same position regarding the Old Testament as Jesus and the apostles? The expressions you use to rebuke us are not quite as harsh as those in your treatise on the Church. Thus, our sin against the Old Testament seems to you perhaps not as grave as our sin against Christians of Jewish descent in today's Germany. You do not speak of "heathenism," but merely of "human arrogance," "rationalist reinterpretation," and "humanistic thought"—attitudes that border on paganism. Yet we will defend ourselves against these accusations as well.

You must recognize that in the same sense as us, Paul was also a "humanist" and "nationalist"—that is, a "believer in reason." Especially at the beginning of the Epistle to the Romans, one notes an emphasis on reason, where true knowledge of God is founded on rational conclusions, and the sinful apostasy from God is characterized as irrational. Paul also does what you most severely criticize us for: he dares to treat the chosen people of the Old Testament as an example among nations and thus equalizes them with other nations. In Romans 2, he goes so far as to say that Gentiles who do not have the Mosaic Law nevertheless fulfill the requirements of the Law through their conscience. His conclusion is (Romans 3:9): "Are we any better? Not at all. For we have already made the charge that Jews and Gentiles alike are all under sin."

Shall I continue with further proof texts, my brothers? I will refrain, lest I become overly lengthy. One could and should cite many passages of the New Testament to refute you. And this is precisely the outcome of the principle you invoke, which is also our principle: "The sole standard for evaluating and interpreting Scripture is Scripture itself." However, for every Christian who is not a Jewish Christian, this principle means that the Old Testament is to be explained in light of the New, not the New Testament in light of the Old. You, my brothers, proceed in reverse: you make the New Testament dependent on the Old when you say, "With the abandonment of the promise, the fulfillment also falls." If we were inclined to treat you as you treat us, we would have to say to you at this point: you abolish the New Testament by subordinating it to the Old. But we refrain, for we do not wish to repay evil with evil. Yet we must say this: your position is that of Jewish-Christian communities, both in antiquity and in modern times.

My brothers! I conclude your second treatise with horror, noting that your view of Holy Scripture goes even further astray than your doctrine of the Church. There, you expressed your solidarity with Protestant Christians of Jewish descent and demanded their legal equality with Germans. There, it was still possible to assume that the Christianity of these Christians of Jewish descent was genuine evangelical Christianity. But now you teach us otherwise. The Christianity you represent, and which you wish to impose upon us German Christians, is in a fundamental point—in its stance toward Holy Scripture—Jewish Christianity.

III. Doctrine of Jesus Christ

First Citation & Criticism

1. "But Jesus Christ, in His wondrous person, is the fulfillment of everything that lives in the human soul as longing, question, and intuition" (Thesis 18).

Such a claim is a denial of human sin according to the testimony of Holy Scripture (Matthew 15; John 8). It stands in contradiction to the doctrine of original sin as presented in the confessions of the Reformation: Apology of the Augsburg Confession, Article II, On Original Sin (Müller, pp. 78–79); Schmalkald Articles, Part 3, Article 1, On Sin (Müller, p. 310); Formula of Concord, Article I, On Original Sin (Müller, pp. 519ff., 579ff.).

Furthermore, it constitutes a misinterpretation of the redemptive work of Christ and a trivialization of the forgiveness of sins, as has been characteristic of heterodox liberal theology. In this way, the Reformation doctrine of justification is abandoned.

Response of Fabricius

What is this, my brothers? The further our conversation progresses, the more peculiar your theology becomes.

So, you truly deny the immense and immeasurable longing for salvation and the Savior that has always existed in humanity, and which still exists today, resonating toward us from thousands of documents and millions of living souls? Do you also deny— despite your professed adherence to Scripture—the well-known biblical passages that confirm these human realities? Surely, you are familiar with what Acts records about Paul's sermon in Athens, where it states (Acts 17:26–28): "He made them to seek the Lord, if perhaps they might feel after Him and find Him, though He is not far from any one of us. For in Him we live and move and have our being." And surely, you also know that Paul goes even further in Romans (2:14–15) when he observes that Gentiles not only have a longing for God but even fulfill God's law, though they do not possess the Old Testament.

You deny, my brothers, the existence of all this, claiming it contradicts your so-called biblical doctrine of sin and the doctrine of original sin in the Reformation confessions. But your appeal to Matthew 15 and John 8 is incomprehensible. Those passages do indeed speak of sin, but not exhaustively, and they say nothing at all about the relationship between humanity's longing for salvation and sin. As for the church's teaching on original sin, I would remind you of the master of this doctrine, St. Augustine. According to him, one can interpret all of humanity's original sin as a misguided search for God. Even the strictest doctrine of original sin would therefore fully permit us to speak of the nations' longing for salvation.

It is difficult to conceive, my brothers, how you arrive at such strange theological assertions and what you aim to achieve with them. You must be advocating a theology or philosophy completely detached from the Gospel and alien to life, one that acknowledges no foundation for salvation other than a Lord in heaven, distant from humanity and the earth, and therefore not only diminishes but outright denies all longing for God in humanity.

Perhaps, however, your peculiar doctrine concerning humanity has another purpose—namely, that you wish to recognize no preparation for salvation outside the Word of God and the chosen people of Israel. This interpretation of your theology is likely correct, as it aligns with your stance toward Judaism and the Old Testament. But I urge you to further reveal your thoughts.

Second Citation & Criticism

2. "The debate over whether Jesus was a Jew or an Aryan does not touch the essence of Jesus at all" (Thesis 18).

Anyone who thinks they can bypass this question does not stand on the foundation of Holy Scripture. Such a person attempts to evade the scandal of Christ and to sidestep the offense of the Gospel.

For the debate over whether Jesus was a Jew or an Aryan is unequivocally resolved by Scripture. Therefore, it must be declared by a church that stands on the foundation of Scripture that Jesus was born as a Jew and, according to the flesh, was a son of David (Matthew 1, Luke 3, Romans 1). For a theology grounded in Scripture, the birth of Christ as a member of the chosen people is a redemptive-historical necessity. It follows from God's faithfulness to His word of promise.

Response of Fabricius

Oh, you foolish Galatians, I must exclaim for the third time. For truly, my brothers, you are once again on the path of Judeo-Christianity. In the Jewish-Christian congregations of both ancient and modern times, it was emphasized as essential—or, to use your term, as a "redemptive-historical necessity"—that the Redeemer was of Jewish descent.

However, this does not correspond to the "clear" testimony of the New Testament, as you claim. In the New Testament, there is no uniform tradition on this point. The Apostle Paul adheres to the Jewish tradition of the Davidic lineage of the Messiah.[44] In contrast, in the infancy narratives of Matthew and Luke, which you cite, there are genealogies of Joseph from the line of David on the one hand, and on the other hand, accounts of Jesus' birth from the Holy Spirit and the Virgin Mary, emphasizing the essential nature of His divine rather than His human origin. And entirely in Jesus' own words, nothing is said about Jewish descent as a redemptive-historical necessity. On the contrary, in a debate (Mark 12:37), even the Davidic lineage of the Christ is questioned. Overall, the divine connection and the heavenly origin of Jesus and His Gospel are emphasized far more than His earthly and human origin.[45]

This stance of the New Testament aligns with the position of the German Christians. But you, my brothers, label us heretics and accuse us of attempting to evade the scandal of Christ. In doing so, you do not prove us to be heretics; rather, you demonstrate that you yourselves stand more on the foundation of the Old Testament than on that of the New Testament.

As for the scandal of Christ, the New Testament does not speak of it in the sense that the Jewish descent of the Redeemer was a stumbling block for the Gentiles.

---

44 [Paul does more than this; i.e. he notes of the Israelites, his kinsman according to the flesh, that Christ, according to the flesh, comes from them (Rom. 9:3-5). Thus Christ was and is clearly "Jewish" in the sense of descending genealogically from Abraham and David. See Patrick Fairbairn's discussion of the Joseph-Mary lineage in *Typology of Scripture* for more information. Christ was likewise "Jewish" in the sense of being born "under the law" (Gal. 4:4), i.e. the Mosaic Covenant and the Levitical cultus, observing the related ceremonies, such as circumcision and Passover, and worshiping the God thereof—although he also abrogated these same things at the cross and fully put them away, never to return, in the events leading up to and concluding in the ruin of Jerusalem in AD 70. Christ was not and never was "Jewish" in the sense of being an adherent of Pharisee religion or of later Talmudic religion.—Editor]

45 [Fabricius does not appear to be denying *the fact* that Christ was Jewish; rather, he seems to contest *the emphasis* placed upon this fact by the critics. —Editor]

Incidentally, it is good, my brothers, that you speak of the scandal. I will not address it now, but at the conclusion of our discussion, I will have a very serious word to say about the scandal. For now, however, I would like to hear more from you about our supposed heresy concerning Jesus Christ.

Third Citation & Criticism

3. "Jesus is not the bearer of human nature, but reveals in His person the nature of God" (in Thesis 18).

Such a doctrine of the humanity of Christ is heretical and a false teaching. It is the docetic Christology, which was rejected by the ancient Church through the ecumenical confessions, because it denies the reality of the incarnation of the Son of God. Whoever claims: "Jesus is not the bearer of human nature," is asserting: "Jesus is not 'truly man, born of the Virgin Mary."

Scripture clearly bears witness to the true incarnation of Christ in Israel. He belongs to the Jewish people, as certainly as He assumed our human flesh and blood, which, according to God's will, always has a "racial" nature.

It is precisely the Lutheran confessions that, for the sake of the doctrine of the Eucharist, have once again firmly confessed the true incarnation of Christ as a necessity for salvation: Formula of Concord, Article VIII, Of the Person of Christ (Müller, p. 545 ff., 674 ff.).

Whoever denies the true incarnation of the only-begotten Son stands outside the evangelical Church of the Reformation.

Response of Fabricius

But, my brothers, what kind of theologians are you? You are speaking now in a particularly theological manner, but your theological attempts are completely misguided.

You remember that there was once a heresy known as "Docetism." This was a view similar to the current beliefs of Theosophists and Anthroposophists, according to which the divine Christ only seemingly united with the human Jesus. Now you claim that the German Christians are Docetists and place themselves outside the Church of the Reformation because they, in a carelessly formulated phrase, said that Jesus Christ is not the bearer of human nature but reveals in His person the nature of God.

Here I must again remind you fundamentally that *The 28 Theses of the German Christians* are not a systematically complete Christian confession of faith, but that they take many essential elements of faith as self-evident. Thus, the fact of the full humanity of Jesus is presupposed as self-evident. Moreover, the theses are entirely for the practical use of the Church, and it is perfectly understandable that one might express themselves carelessly about the contents of the living Christian consciousness, meaning one is not anxiously worried that what is said might be interpreted heretically by nitpickers and fault-finders. There are many similar careless formulations in the history of the Christian religion, and even very important passages where famous figures have carelessly formulated their faith in Christ and thereby exposed themselves to the possibility of being accused of heresy. One of the strangest passages of this kind is precisely the phrase in Luther's Small Catechism, which you, my brothers, in your ignorance, have quoted yourselves. Luther's expression "truly man, born of the Virgin Mary," which you use against us, does not correspond to the orthodox tradition of Christianity. For according to this tradition, not only the man, but the God-man is born of Mary.

And furthermore, you should note: Christian faith, as countless great examples teach, always essentially depends on the fact that, in the assumption of full humanity by Jesus, the fullness of the deity is revealed in Him. Therefore, in theological formulations of the creed, the divine nature of Jesus Christ is generally emphasized more than His human nature. In fact, there are expressions in Christian liturgies that only refer to the divinity and not the humanity of Jesus Christ. When we sing, "Glory be to the Father, and to the Son, and to the Holy Spirit, as it was in the beginning, is now, and ever shall be, world without end," there is no mention of His humanity, but only of the eternal divinity of the Son. In the Eastern liturgy, the congregation is repeatedly called to devote itself "to Christ, the God," with all their soul. And when, finally, I may remind you of the most well-known, it is that evangelical Christianity sings: "If you ask who He is, He is called Jesus Christ, the Lord of Hosts, and there is no other God." And if you, my brothers, refer to Article 8 of the Formula of Concord because it expresses the full humanity of Jesus, you should note— and you must actually know—that in this very article, to explain the mysterious presence of the Savior in the Eucharist, it is stated that the human nature of the Son of God participates in the divine property of omnipresence.

No, my brothers, with such theology as you proclaim, you cannot harm us. Your weapons shatter upon our resistance. Now, however, we go on the offensive again. We note that in the present context you once again refer to Jesus' Jewish origins. By doing so, you clearly show what it is that you are concerned with when you assert the full humanity of the Savior as fundamental. Your entire theological attempt here is merely an emphasis on your claim regarding the essential nature of Jesus' Jewish descent. In doing so, however, you are once again demonstrating that you are influenced by a sectarian tendency which presents the Jewish origin of Christ alongside his humanity as a historical necessity, and thus, as a foundational dogma. But this is—Jewish-Christianity.

So here, at the end of your third doctrinal piece, I must again state with horror that you are on the path of Jewish-Christianity in a second essential point of the Christian faith—in the doctrine of the person of Christ—and that you not only impose this Jewish-Christianity on Christians of Jewish origin, but that you want to impose it on the Protestant German people, indeed on the whole of Christendom, as true Christianity.

Conclusion

Dear brothers! We are now at the end of our conversation, and I wish to say a brief word of farewell, not a word of anger and hatred, but a word of reconciliation and brotherhood.

Whoever speaks publicly in Germany today bears a tremendously heavy responsibility. For the nations are watching us, Christendom is watching us, humanity is watching us. Through God's guidance, our people have risen up powerfully in an unprecedentedly great struggle for liberation. In doing so, it has become a strong bulwark against all the international powers of decay and dissolution. Our people have also become a strong defense for all of Christendom against the onslaught of anti-Christianity. Thus, everything that happens in Germany is significant for the whole world. Therefore, we must do everything that strengthens and sanctifies our people internally, while diligently avoiding anything that could provoke offense. For what disrupts us here at home will quickly become an offense to all nations.

The matter of offense is a terribly serious issue. You know, my brothers, what Jesus says about it: "It is impossible that offenses should not come; but woe to him through whom they come! It would be better for him that a millstone were hanged around his neck and he were thrown into the sea, than that he should offend one of these little ones." With these words of Jesus in mind, please consider what it means if, under the current circumstances in Germany, pastors of Jewish descent are to be imposed upon evangelical congregations. Even one of your leaders, as already mentioned, has spoken of offense in this context. But consider further what it means when a pronounced Jewish-Christianity is to be imposed on the German evangelical Christianity today as the true Christianity.

I do not accuse you, my brothers; but I do accuse the spirit that has deceived and seduced you, and I ask the Lord of spirits to deliver you from this spirit and show you the way of truth. You have already had to serve the truth through your error by causing the truth to be told to you. Now, however, we ask you to do only that which directly serves the building, the strength, and the peace of the Church of Christ in our people and among all peoples.

THE REICH IN STRUGGLE

REPORTS AND PROPOSALS ON THE
LIFE QUESTIONS OF THE NATION

Confidentially shared by

Professor D. Fabricius

Eighth Issue

Originally published in Berlin,

January 1, 1938

Contents:

These pages are not intended for public dissemination but serve to provide personal information to their recipients, who are expected to use the material presented here in their actions for the benefit of the Reich.

The Church as a Military Force

A church is the military force in the inner life of a people. The Führer referred to it as the strongest support of national identity on the Day of Potsdam.

Whoever seeks to harm the church weakens the will to defend his people.

A representative of the church who commits a crime is as culpable as a soldier before the enemy.

A government that relies on the church adheres to the ABCs of statesmanlike wisdom.

In a conflict between church and state, the church prevails.

A Confessional Song of the SA

1. The autumn storm sweeps across the stubble field,
It blows over fields and fallows.
A new millennium begins in the world,
You slumbering Germany, awaken!

2. The Pope sits in Rome upon his throne,
His priests sit among us still.
What has the son of a German mother
To do with Pope and priests?

3. Our ancestors were burned as heretics
In honor of the militant church.
In Asia's deserts, in the Jewish land,
German warriors bled out!

4. The Aller ran red with Saxon blood,
The Stedingers were slaughtered.
The peasants' blood was sold as indulgence
And carried by monks to foreign lands.

5. Time passed, yet the priests remained,
Robbing the people of their souls.
Whether Roman or Lutheran they claimed to be,
They taught the Jewish faith.

6. We need no mediators to reach heaven,
The sun and stars already light our way.
Blood, sword, and the sunwheel
Are fighters in every distant land.

7. (Refrain): As before.

Such songs are heard today in German streets. Dark forces seek to impose them on the SA. Yet many stormtroopers resist them. The German people will not march with an SA that sings such songs. Instead, it cries out for a saving deed to root out those dark forces.

A Party Within the Party

Although the formation of new political parties in Germany is strictly prohibited under severe penalties, party life is once again flourishing. The old German hereditary sin of mutual slander among German brothers is bearing strong fruit once more. Especially under slogans such as "alien worldview" and "native worldview," people are fighting each other with the same malice as before, creating divisions within the nation that run at least as deep as the former class conflicts. These divisions are further emphasized politically, as ideological issues are now disastrously intertwined with nationalistic concerns.

Above all, a party emerges that can be described as radical-socialist or national-Bolshevist. This party rejects Point 24 of the NSDAP program. It does not support the position of Positive Christianity but rather advocates a freethinking heroism. It abandons the fight against "Jewish materialism" and the notion of "inner renewal," as it promotes naturalistic and materialistic ideas itself. It also does not recognize the freedom of religious confession, treating Christian compatriots as second-class citizens and insulting and opposing Christian churches.

What is new and simultaneously far more dangerous than in the past is that this new party does not form a separate organization that is clearly distinguishable from other groups. Instead, it exists vaguely, partly outside and partly within the NSDAP, even misusing the organization of the NSDAP for its agitation. Moreover, it does not seem to be a workers' party but rather more of a civil servants' party, as it primarily seeks to spread among political officials of the movement and state administrators.

It is difficult to determine the exact leadership of this party. Some attribute it to Rosenberg, but this is likely incorrect. One of the leading figures, and increasingly the sole leader, appears to be Frau Ludendorff. This woman had previously offered herself to Adolf Hitler as a leader, as Rosenberg reported in the National Socialist Monthly in 1931. At that time, she was rebuffed, which was a blessing for the German people. An anti-Christian party could never have gained the trust of the German people and could therefore never have assumed leadership in the national uprising. It was a great achievement of the Führer that at that time, nationalist sects of this kind were eliminated. Today, they are resurfacing and attempting to distort the Führer's work. Now, Frau Ludendorff seems to be truly becoming the "leader." In her following are numerous party comrades who have fallen for this woman's sophisticated propaganda and have credulously accepted her sensational "revelations," especially the claim that "Christianity is a Jewish scheme." Even the "German Faith Movement," although outwardly opposing Frau Ludendorff, largely moves in her wake, as it is even poorer in original ideas than the wife of the field marshal.

The growing radicalism that developed within this extreme party during 1937 is undoubtedly linked to Frau Ludendorff's renewed propaganda. Conversely, the radicalism of this extreme party explains all the intolerable events for the German people that occurred in 1937.

It would not be an exaggeration to say: the fate of this radical party within the party determines the fate of Germany. If it continues to rise, the unity of the Reich is threatened. If it is eliminated, the Reich moves toward a great future.

The Naturalistic "State Religion" of the "God-believers"

The Black Corps (Schwarze Korps) from December 9, 1937, published an article under the headline "To the Churches," in which it takes the stance of the "God-believers" (Gottgläubigen) and, following the precedent of the Erfurt Program of the Social Democrats in 1891, declares the Christian churches to be private associations. The religion of the "God-believers," however, is defined as follows:

"The National Socialist state seeks to affirm divine order in all areas of life. It promotes what is natural and combats what is against nature. That is our state religion."

Anti-Christian Agitation in the Hitler Youth

In Breslau, a Bannführer (regional leader) named Hirsch, formerly an adjutant to the Reich Sports Leader, is currently active. This Bannführer has repeatedly stated that he considers "religious influence" to be one of his primary tasks. However, by "religious influence," he does not mean a Christian or church-affiliated influence but rather one of a free-religious nature, openly opposing the Christian churches. This has resulted in Hitler Youth members leaving the church.

It can be assumed that a Bannführer does not act independently in such an important matter and that he is informed about the guidelines set forth by the Reich Youth Leadership. However, the religious activities of Bannführer Hirsch contradict the public declarations of the Reich Youth Leadership, which has stated that religious neutrality is to be maintained. It also goes against the reasoning provided by the Reich Youth Leadership for excluding theologians.

For this measure, the leadership justified itself by appealing to neutrality, explaining that there was a possibility that theologians might violate this neutrality. At the same time, it was assured that propaganda for neo-paganism would not be tolerated. In the current case, not only is there a possibility of neutrality being violated, but neutrality is actually being breached as neo-paganism is being preached, and the churches are being attacked.

If such agitation continues to spread, it will inevitably lead to the Hitler Youth gradually becoming a free-religious sect rather than representing the youth of the German people. Furthermore, there will likely be a rapid decline in membership because neither the youth will tolerate for long the internal dissonance this causes, nor will parents in a Christian nation be willing to expose their children, at an immature age, to anti-Christian agitation.

Dance on Day of Repentance and Day of the Dead

The Day of Repentance (Bußtag) and the Day of the Dead (Totenfest) are among the most traditional holidays of the German Evangelical Church. From the solemnity of these days has always flowed an abundance of moral strength into the life of the people. It was a long-standing custom that all festivities ceased on these days.

This year, public dancing was permitted starting at 7 PM. Reports indicate, however, that the people did not make extensive use of this opportunity to dance, so the anticipated profit for the hospitality industry failed to materialize. Good customs are so deeply rooted in the German people that they are not easily abandoned.

The intent behind this measure is interpreted in the same way by everyone in Germany—whether Evangelical, Roman Catholic, or anti-Christian—namely as a gesture by influential authorities against church customs.

It is not known who ultimately initiated this new regulation. However, there are indications that responsibility lies with the radical party within the party—that is, the same faction responsible for other similar incidents in the year 1937. This is confirmed by the tone in which the National Socialist Party Correspondence discussed the Day of Repentance, criticizing the servility of previous state governments toward church demands. Further conclusions can be drawn from the way SA comrades distributed free entrance tickets to dances on the Day of the Dead to perplexed fellow citizens.

In the interest of the reputation of the state government and the party, it is advisable not to repeat such an experiment in the coming year.

Success of the Church Exit Movement in 1937

Despite intense agitation from both above and below, the number of church exits in 1937 remained very low. It is, of course, only a small number of German compatriots—and not the best among them—who would abandon the great Christian faith community of their people on command or due to opportunism. Even the appeal by the Chief of Staff of the SA on August 15th in the Berlin Stadium, urging his entire leadership corps to leave the church, was reportedly followed by only a small fraction.

Precise figures are naturally not yet available. However, from partial data, it can already be concluded that the number of exits remains well below one percent of the church-affiliated population. Since 95 percent of the German population belongs to Christian churches, this means that significantly less than one percent of the total population has left.

On the other hand, it is evident that the trust of Christian Germans in the agitators advocating for church exits has not only dropped far below one percent but has sunk significantly below zero—that is, it has transformed into complete distrust and even the bitterest aversion. In cases where the agitators are party members or, worse, party officials, this sentiment inevitably turns against the movement as a whole.

Every old fighter within the party is filled with the deepest dismay when he sees leading party members today in the role of committees like Konfessionslos (Non-Confessional) and other groups that, even before the war, brought together Jews and Marxists to destroy the churches. These groups rightly recognized the churches as the strongest bulwark of the people against their revolutionary plans.

The SA Chief of Staff Activities in America

The guidelines of the SA Chief of Staff for "cultural service planning" were recently disseminated to the American public through the press.

Now it has been irrefutably established abroad that "neo-paganism rules" in Germany. All attempts to prove the contrary by distributing literature abroad are, therefore, fruitless for the time being.

This will undoubtedly have consequences for foreign policy as well. How will England and America respond to Germany's demand for colonies when they hold concrete evidence that the Germans not only fail to bring Christian culture to non-Christians but instead "bless" their own people with pagan barbarity?

"A Mighty Fortress is Our Gold"

On December 5, the SS held a celebratory event at the Centennial Hall in Breslau on the theme of "German Piety." During this event, beautiful words about respecting foreign religious convictions were spoken in remembrance of the comradeship of the trenches. Among the recited words was a quote from Luther, in which the idea of tolerance was hinted at. Following this, the melody of the hymn "A Mighty Fortress is Our God" played.

In the same days, on Street No. 48, the "Black Corps" sold a publication. It contained the phrase, "One billion Reichsmarks for church taxes—A mighty fortress is our gold." The latter expression is evidently a reference to a Jewish parody written by the emigrant Alfred Polgar in 1919 for the magazine Kleine Zeitung, directed at the Rothschild family.

Thus, this mockery of Luther's hymn and the Christian churches served as the SS's commentary on the beautiful words of tolerance. This was the message on the street, set to the melody of the Centennial Hall.

The Minister of Churches Has Spoken

The Minister of Churches has fortunately made several statements on the church issue recently. In addition to some press comments, the results of a few expert discussions are as follows:

1. It is very commendable that the Minister has reminded us of Positive Christianity as the foundation of National Socialism. Unfortunately, this is no longer believed by anyone today, as long as the anti-Christian radicalism dominates within the party. In 1935, anyone who made this point was labeled as either dishonest or crazy. Since then, the situation has significantly worsened.

2. It is important, as the Minister also did, to emphasize religious freedom alongside the Christian foundation. But no one believes us in this regard, as long as Christians are treated worse than other citizens in Germany, especially as long as holders of spiritual office are publicly insulted by organs of the movement in ways that would lead to severe punishment for anyone else (think of officers, judges, teachers, merchants, workers).

3. It has been noted that in press reports about the Minister's statements, the equality of all religious communities has been emphasized in a way that apparently does not reflect the Minister's own opinion. It is of course correct that no citizen should be disadvantaged or advantaged because of their religion. But as far as

the standing of religious communities is concerned, it is clear that for a government of a Christian people, which itself represents the position of Christianity, the two large Christian churches, to which almost the entire nation belongs, play a different role than any arbitrary association of a few thousand freethinkers.

4. The Minister's announcement that the state will withdraw subsidies from the churches has acted as an anti-church threat in the tense domestic political situation and has overshadowed the Minister's positive statements, which have been eagerly seized upon and exploited in the most awkward way by the anti-Christian "Black Corps."

5. The Minister's suggestion that a declaration of adult church members before the political community might be required as a condition for their legal membership in the church has caused a great deal of commotion. It is assumed that this plan did not originate with the Minister himself but comes from the anti-Christian party, which apparently hopes to use this method to reduce the churches. Such an act would be meaningless in a national church, where, as the Minister himself states, children grow up in the faith of their parents and consciously enter the community of adult church members through confirmation. By the way, the procedure is essentially the same in free churches. The church itself is not afraid of such a measure, nor of any other anti-church measures. However, from the state side, it must be understood that at this moment, when the party and the state are considered anti-church due to the actions of the radicals, the demand for such a public declaration before the civil community would also be perceived as anti-church, so any such declaration would take on the character of a religious confession in front of an anti-church state. The collection of such declarations would thus be akin to a vote against the anti-church state. Therefore, from the state's point of view, experiments of this kind should be avoided.

6. All in all, it can be stated: The very commendable efforts of the Minister for church peace will be in vain as long as the anti-

Christian party dominates the party. The church issue will not be resolved within the church but outside of it, and only by eradicating that anti-Christian party and eliminating its influence.

"We Are Not Destroyed in Germany" (Bolshevik Accounts)

In April 1934, the following news circulated in the German public: "According to newspaper reports, the Bund Proletarischer Freidenker (League of Proletarian Free Thinkers) recently held a meeting in Hirschenstand in Czechoslovakia. On this occasion, a certain comrade Lobenhart from Aussig gave the main lecture. During his speech, he also touched upon the relationship between the free-thinker movement and the German faith movement, and elaborated on the following: 'We were politically destroyed in Germany, but not ideologically. Everyone knows that the German faith movement sees our free-thinker movement as hopelessly similar, for we work, this is our work.'"

One only needs to think through the ideas suggested in these words and compare them with the facts that have become known since 1934. Then, one understands what interests the Bolsheviks are pursuing in Germany and how they are actively involved among us.

1. **"We work."** This phrase, when uttered by a Bolshevik, means that there are individuals within the German faith movement who consciously and internally align themselves with the proletarian international. This fact is confirmed by reports in the publications of the German faith associations, which indicate that entire groups of former free-thinker associations, which were banned in 1933—extreme Marxists who had left the churches— have now joined the German faith associations. These Marxists still view Bolshevism as their ultimate goal, while considering the present German faith movement as the preparation for this goal. It is assumed that the number of these secret Marxists in Germany is

241

considerable. The twelve million people who cast Marxist votes on March 5, 1933, have not yet disappeared.

In calling themselves "German believers" today, these Marxists are executing the cleverest and therefore most dangerous disguise possible in today's Germany. They pretend to be so devotedly German and National Socialist that they make a religion out of Germanism and National Socialism. This legitimizes them everywhere not only as completely reliable but even as one hundred fifty percent National Socialists, and they hope to thereby secure positions of power within the Party, its organizations, and affiliated associations.

At the same time, they gain significant influence over masses of unsuspecting German compatriots who, in complete innocence and good faith, join German faith associations because they believe they can only become true National Socialists by making National Socialism into a new confession. These ignorant compatriots can be used by the Bolsheviks as the most useful tools. They work, without knowing it, not only willingly but almost instinctively for the distant goals of Bolshevism.

In rare cases, Bolsheviks also infiltrate opposing fronts, such as the Protestant Confessional Front and Catholic associations. They exploit the tensions that have arisen due to the growing influence of the German faith movement within the National Socialist movement and incite hostility not only from one side but from both sides. This serves to make the religious struggle in Germany as malicious as possible, directing the attention of the state and the police hostilely towards the churches, and away from the German faith movement and its masterminds. However, overall, Bolsheviks do not need to personally engage in the church fronts. Their work under the guise of "German faith" is sufficient to create a growing hostility between the state and the church, which may lead to a deadly conflict that benefits Bolsheviks on both sides.

2. "This is our work." The inner attitude of the national free-thinkers aligns in many essential ways with the fundamental views of international free-thinking. The sources (Feuerbach, Marx, Haeckel, Nietzsche) are essentially the same everywhere, whether one subscribes to the International of the Godless or to the "German Knowledge of God" of Mrs. Ludendorff or to any other national-free-thought program. The worldview is generally materialistic or naturalistic. Within this framework, one finds the same absolute emphasis and glorification of the human being on one side, and of natural things and natural laws on the other. The difference between "godlessness and belief in God" is fluid. In Russia, one usually adheres fanatically to full atheism. In Germany, there are traces of Christian faith, but there is also a tendency to ascribe the label "divine" to human beings or natural phenomena. Within this shared stance, the differences between "international" and "national" are of secondary importance. In Russia, salvation is expected from the world proletariat, primarily from the Russian proletariat. In Germany, one finds the fulfillment of humanity in the German people but extends the reverence for nature far beyond the borders of the German people, raising oneself to the sky during solstice celebrations and occasionally emphasizing the infinite universe revealed to us by Copernicus, where the Earth and its people are nothing.

On the whole, we are moving in the same intellectual realm, namely the ideas of the Enlightenment, as they are found in various forms in the dogmatic tradition of free-thinking world movements, Freemasons, Reform Jews, and Communists.

However, more than the positive cultivation of one's own modest intellectual heritage, all these movements vigorously agitate against Christianity. Everywhere, one notices the fight against the Roman Church, against the papacy, dogma, and cult, against monasticism, the Inquisition, witch trials, relic worship, and the like. But most critically—and this strikes at the core of the Christian religion—they fight against belief in a transcendent deity, against humility in humans, and against human guilt. This is seen as a degradation of the self-aware revolutionary proletariat.

Many German believers confuse the class-conscious proletariat with the heroic human and ascribe to the latter the same characteristics, only to then fight against the Christian experiences of sin and grace (which, according to Chamberlain, are genuinely Aryan experiences). In doing so, the German believers are now prone to labeling what they oppose in Christianity as "Jewish," but substantively, they differ in nothing from their Jewish-Marxist comrades.

After all this, it is beyond doubt that the propaganda of the German believers against the "Jewish God" of Christians, against the churches of the anti-Christian International, must be considered as part of that campaign. Therefore, the statement: "This is our work" is fully justified, regardless of any personal or organizational connections that may exist between national and international free-thinkers.

3. "We are not destroyed." What the Bolsheviks declared in the spring of 1934, after the political collapse of Communism in Germany, to their consolation, not only still holds true today, but since then, events have unfolded that the Bolsheviks not only have the greatest interest in but can now gladly record as successes: an increasing penetration of anti-Christian agitation within and outside of the National Socialist organizations, even from higher and the highest levels; propaganda of the German faith associations in the broadest public, sometimes even with the appearance of official party support; a rising agitation for leaving the church both inside and outside the movement; widespread vilification of the churches, their institutions, and their officeholders in public, even by representatives and organs of the movement; on the other side, growing opposition within the churches, leading to numerous arrests and other measures against clergy and Christian laity.

In general, the Bolsheviks can watch this development calmly, as it seems to develop on its own. However, they are not merely passive observers; they use the international Jewish press to stir up

Christians worldwide against "pagan" Germany, and it is likely that they are not idle within Germany itself, but through their helpers, they are doing all they can to exacerbate the internal crisis and block all paths to salvation.

For the near future, the Bolsheviks have a strong interest in ensuring that the entire movement, from top to bottom, is transformed through anti-Christian agitation into a pagan organization, which enters into a life-and-death struggle with the Christian German people, causing the national community to fracture or, better yet, Bolshevizing the people spiritually. This way, they hope that Germany will soon fall into their hands as a ripe fruit.

Since all these tendencies in Germany have clearly intensified since 1934, particularly in 1937, the proletarian free-thinkers can now not only declare with satisfaction: "We are not destroyed in Germany," but they can also confidently assert: "We are making gratifying progress in Germany."

Is Remedy Possible?

The terrible crisis in which the National Socialist movement finds itself can perhaps still be turned to the better at this moment.

It is conceivable that through some energetic prohibitions from the Deputy of the Führer, who works in the closest cooperation with the Deputy of the Führer, the anti-Christian agitation could be contained, and thus the movement could be steered back onto normal paths.

To achieve this, a series of positive measures would need to follow, especially a proper professional training on the true foundations of National Socialist worldview.

It is conceivable that through work of this kind, in a few months, or even in a few "weeks," a complete change in the situation could be created, and the movement could be brought back from a state of internal division to its former strength.

The Result of the Year 1937

At the end of the year 1937, the mood of the German people regarding religion can be described as desperate, even catastrophic.

Indeed, the Christian churches, to which the German people belong except for about one-twentieth, proclaim their message with undiminished strength and work quietly and tirelessly in the preservation and strengthening of spiritual and moral life.

But the religious policy of the Party gives the public the impression of a fundamentally anti-Christian and anti-church stance. One believes that it should be inferred from this that not the movement as a whole, but a radical party within the movement, which is pushing upward, seeks to work in this manner from above.

As a result, the trust of the people in the Party has been so undermined that the previous enthusiasm has suffered greatly. Unshaken, however, is the trust in the Führer and in certain of his collaborators. New and great is also the trust in the Wehrmacht, in which, according to all reports, the Christian stance is decisive. Unshaken is also the hope among many of the people that perhaps soon the Führer will be informed of the gravity of the situation and then, through decisive measures, will bring about a complete change in religious policy.

But aside from this, there is an ever-growing realization among the German people, paralyzing all trust and hope, that through a fanatical inner religious war initiated by our movement, the soul of the people is being weakened, and as a result, moral life is threatened and the national strength is being destroyed.

This is the lesson of the year 1937. When will the decisive step be taken that will ward off the impending disaster? Perhaps it is already too late. Perhaps there is still time. In any case, it is high time.

INNER ARMOR

CONFIDENTIAL MEMORANDUM

ON THE OUTBREAK OF WAR

by

Professor D. Cajus Fabricius

Originally published c. September, 1939

Introduction

This memorandum is written in obedience to the will of the Führer, who, on September 3, 1939, declared that the German people must form an indestructibly solid community within a few weeks.

For the completion of military and technical-economic armament, the Reich government is taking admirable steps. The present document aims to address the third area, which is of fundamental importance in the existential struggle of a great nation: the inner and innermost life, the realm of worldview and religion.

The Führer knows and has decisively stated that this area is precisely the vulnerable spot of the German people, and that religious conflicts are therefore always life-threatening for us. This holds, of course, even more in a war than in peaceful times. The terrible outcome of the World War has shown how our people were internally corroded and ultimately collapsed under the influence of the Jewish-materialistic worldview of Marxism.

At present, however, as is well known, the German people are not only threatened by disintegration, but are in the midst of a severe internal conflict that holds the greatest dangers and must therefore be resolved without delay.

One might ask whether it is already too late to attempt to eliminate the internal tensions. There is no question that the proper moment was not during the war but during the peaceful rise of the Third Reich. I have indeed, over the past five years, left no stone unturned, tirelessly pointing out the existing crisis in public pamphlets and confidential memoranda, and showing the way to overcome it. But I have only had partial success. In any case, the question of timeliness is now irrelevant. This question cannot be postponed until after the war. It is one of the life-and-death questions of the German people, whose resolution depends on the internal cohesion of the nation.

Thus, the hour of decision has come. The situation will be addressed in the following pages with the openness and fearlessness that Adolf Hitler expects from his comrades. If I must at times be critical, it is not out of spite against any individuals, but from an unreserved dedication to my people and its National Socialist government. Moreover, it is not my intention to tear anything down but, on the contrary, to rebuild what has been torn down. I employ absolute objectivity and truthfulness and am prepared to substantiate the facts I present with extensive evidence. My depiction may only deviate from reality insofar as I perhaps do not portray the existing crisis as darkly as it is, and insofar as the terms I use are not as strong as they should be for the sake of the matter. I exercise this restraint to avoid unnecessary sharpness and exaggeration under any circumstances.

I am personally entitled and obligated to make the following statements both as a specialist in cultural sciences and theology, and as one of the oldest National Socialists among all German professors.

My position is further elaborated in the party-approved publication: "Positive Christianity in the New State,"[46] which has been published in German, English, and Japanese editions. Based on this publication, I achieved a remarkable foreign policy success in 1937 and 1938. At that time, the Anglican Bishop of Gloucester declared in several publications that National Socialism, as I represented it, could very well be acknowledged, and on this basis, England could live in peace with Germany. Such a statement even appeared in the Times, allowing me to advocate for National Socialism in the broadest public sphere of the British Empire and thereby help promote a peace mood towards Germany.

---

46 [This is the same as "Positive Christianity in the Third Reich."—Editor]

I now wish to express the justified expectation that in this present fateful hour, my statements and proposals will not go unheard by the Reich government, and I declare my readiness to personally use all the strength at my disposal to complete the inner unity of Germany.

First Part: The General Task

I: The Foundations of Inner Unity

It is one of the fundamental principles of every government of a Christian people that the Christian religion must be cultivated in the soul of the people, and that this religion grants the people inner strength, peace, and security. However, the most powerful form of the national community exists when the government itself is Christian and, thus, intrinsically connected with the people.

This connection is particularly recognized by the movements and governments that today fight against the corrosive influences of liberalism and Jewish materialism. Therefore, in Italy and Spain, the national government works closely with the Church, and the fascists in France and England are likewise Christian and church-oriented.

The same spirit imbues National Socialism. The spiritual faith in the God of Christianity, the serious judgment of evil, the high ideal of life, and the struggle against Mammon, as well as all other Christian principles, form the foundation of National Socialism, as it has been presented for all times in the Führer's book and in Program Point 24. This fundamental attitude is also considered to be in harmony with the moral and ethical sense of the Germanic race.

The division of Christian denominations should, according to the Führer's will, not disrupt the national community. Just as during the movement's time of struggle, convinced Protestants and devout Catholics worked together in peace, so it should continue to be. It is not expected or demanded that one of the denominations, or both, be erased to make room for a new unified religion. This is no more expected than the eradication of dialects in favor of a unified German language or the destruction of folk costumes for the sake of a uniform fashion. On the contrary, National Socialism respects the peculiarities of the tribes and emphasizes even more strongly that the various tribes are united in one empire. In the same way, it respects the peculiarities of the two denominations and highlights all the more that they, as "German Christians," peacefully coexist in one empire.

This is the foundation on which the inner unity of the Third Reich rests and will continue to rest in the future. On this basis, the Christian German people have chosen Adolf Hitler as their Führer. In this sense, our soldiers, as Christian Germans of Protestant and Catholic denominations, will stand together in unbreakable comradeship. In this spirit—and only in it—will the people at home endure as a united whole and constantly renew the confidence of the front-line fighters that they are fighting for a nation that possesses a high inner culture and, therefore, deserves to live in honor and freedom.

II: The Decomposition of Inner Life

In contrast to the foundation of German unity described above, in recent years an agitation has emerged that threatens the structure of the Third Reich with decomposition. This is not a popular movement but rather an artificial creation by a few individuals, who, with the help of a clever method, seem to be succeeding in rising to prominence and sowing discord from above into the people.

This refers to a group of Volksgenossen (people comrades) who can be called "Radicals," "National Bolsheviks," or, most appropriately, "folkish free-thinkers."

Even during the movement's struggle years, these circles caused trouble for the Führer, and the Führer successfully worked to keep the movement free from the dominance of their influence. This led to bitter hostility from a particularly extreme group led by Frau Ludendorff, whose association was soon banned after the takeover of power. After the takeover, there was hope that the power of the Reich and the Party could no longer be broken by freethinking activities. Thus, especially since 1934, these circles were allowed to renew their agitation, and their radicalism grew until the end of 1937, when it reached grotesque forms, especially after Frau Ludendorff opened a new association. During 1938, these efforts waned but surged again with increased intensity following the resolution of the Sudeten German question, reaching significant proportions again by 1939.

The teachings of these radical circles largely coincide with the dogmas of international free-thought. In both, a deification of nature and the natural human being forms the basis of their worldview and lifestyle. Essential to this standpoint is the philosophy of the Jew Spinoza, particularly in the materialistically simplified form presented by Ernst Haeckel. Also key is the judgment of humanity in modern world Jewry, which calls evil good and declares the feeling of sin to be a pathological "inferiority complex."

A shared trait of freethinkers worldwide is a bitter fight against Christianity, which also aligns with the interests of world Jewry. They oppose not only the priesthood, the teachings, and the cults of the Christian churches, especially the Roman Catholic Church, but also the Christian mindset, particularly the humility inherent in all true religion, because they believe this mindset makes individuals submissive to human orders and restrains the revolutionary instincts of the proletarian masses.

The radicals among us differ from foreign freethinkers only in that they call their ideas "German, Aryan, folkish, Nordic," emphasize "blood" in human nature, and call the unrepentant attitude "heroic," while rejecting everything they don't like as "Jewish," even though their own worldview is influenced by Jewish materialism and is far removed from the instincts of the Aryan race.

The connection between the so-called German believers and foreign free-thought is not only in ideas but also in people. As is well-known, large numbers of Volksgenossen from Marxist-associated free-thinker groups joined the folkish free-thinker associations in 1933 and now represent the same views as before, but with national, rather than international, emphases. This leads to the suspicion that there are still numerous Deutschgläubige (German believers) in Germany who are disguised Marxists. Furthermore, it is to be assumed that these Volksgenossen have underground ties to the International Free-thinker movement. This was openly stated at a Bohemian meeting of proletarian free-thinkers in the spring of 1934, where these comrades declared the work of the so-called German faith movement to be their own. It is possible that some of the disturbances troubling the German people in this context are due to the activity of these secret puppet masters.

Of course, this does not mean that the folkish free-thinkers, whether individually or in associations, are secretly international in orientation. On the contrary, the majority of them are likely loyal Germans, some even convinced National Socialists. However, in an honest portrayal of the situation, these connections must be exposed without reservation.

In recent years, these folkish free-thinkers have carried out activities that have become a danger to the nation, increasingly questioning the Volksgemeinschaft (people's community) won in 1933. While their numbers are still minuscule compared to the majority of the German people, they have managed to gain enough influence that their pernicious actions are felt in even the remotest corners of the Reich.

Their influence rests on the following circumstances:

1. They claim that their free-thinking worldview is the true National Socialist worldview, which opposes Christianity.

2. Although this is contrary to the truth, it is believed by poorly informed Volksgenossen—including Party members.

3. Based on this, they seek to infiltrate higher Party offices and use those positions to influence the state government and the people, with the clear intent to first create an anti-Christian, free-thinking leadership class and, with their help, gradually win the whole people over to their ideas.

4. They have had some success in their efforts to influence official positions.

5. Their methods are particularly aided by their peculiar tactics. They prefer to operate in the shadows, acting personally at times, officially at others, working privately at one moment and publicly at another, influencing others both through personal pressure and by appealing to voluntarism.

6. Those who resist them and their supposedly true National Socialism are branded as peace-disturbers, opponents of National Socialism, or even "enemies of the state"—though they themselves could more easily be accused of this—and they attempt to use this strategy to strengthen their own position and weaken their opponents.

The effects that have been caused by the actions of the völkisch free thinkers in the inner life of the German people, particularly the domestic political consequences, are catastrophic. The Party has been torn in two, an anti-Christian minority and a Christian majority, with the minority claiming and actually achieving significant control. Thus, an estrangement arises between the Party and its leadership. However, as the radicals outwardly give the impression that they speak in the name of the Party, they create a rift between the Party and the German people. As anti-

Christianity penetrates the people, a party formation and a tension emerge in the population that is at least as severe as the former tension between the National Socialist and Communist parties. And what is worst of all: due to the close connection between the Party and the state leadership, the Reich government is also compromised in the eyes of the public by the actions of the radicals, thus initiating an estrangement between the people and the government, which in the eyes of those who do not fully understand the internal connection, already exists and is considered a settled fact, particularly abroad. But the division is also carried into the consciences of countless individual Volksgenossen, who are faced with the decision between their Christian faith and the supposedly anti-Christian National Socialism. This situation, however, does not produce unified personalities, as a strong National Socialist Germany requires, but uncertain and helpless minds who do not know what they want and what they are obligated to do. Large numbers of the most valuable German men and women, with the noblest Christian upbringing in all classes of the people, have already chosen against the supposedly anti-Christian National Socialism in this conflict, although they belong to those who form the best core of the people.

The tension that has been noticeable in recent years between National Socialism on the one hand and the Roman Catholic Church as well as the Confessional Front within the German Evangelical Church on the other hand has—alongside other circumstances which are not to be discussed here—its main cause in the confusion created (already before 1933) by the völkisch free-thinkers, who presented their anti-Christian stance as the true National Socialism. It is well known that Catholic Christians and also Catholic priests in the Old Reich as well as in the East Mark were among the oldest and most loyal champions of National Socialism, and in the Evangelical Confessional Front, numerous holders of the golden party badge stood and continue to stand. It would therefore be completely misguided to suspect either of these organizations of being anti-party or even anti-state. However, since the radicals repeatedly linked the völkisch free-thinker position with the official party line in their proclamations, it is not surprising when opponents of völkisch free-thinking simultaneously appeared as opponents of the Party. The church conflict between the Confessional Front and the German Christians within the Evangelical Church is also fundamentally caused by this situation, as a line of connection was drawn between the German Christians and the völkisch free thinkers.

The radicals therefore bear the main responsibility for the church opposition, and when the anti-Christian free thinkers within the Party occasionally cited the church conflict as the reason for their anti-church measures, they were moving in a vicious circle, as they themselves had largely caused the church conflict and, through their actions, only increased the tensions within the Party and the people, rather than overcoming them.

In any case, it seems that within the churches and church groups, a significant progress toward improvement and a growth in the correct understanding of the situation has begun to take place. In all church camps, it appears that people have learned to distinguish between the real political National Socialism, which is based on Christian principles, and the false, pretended National Socialism with its Jewish-materialist-influenced worldview, and everywhere the former is acknowledged while the latter is fought. In this regard, one can say that a great united front of sentiment (without a unified external organization) has formed throughout the Christian and, that is, nearly the entire German people, a united front that includes all conscious Roman Catholic Christians as well as Evangelical Christians of all stripes, a united front against the common enemy, the radical free-thinking with a völkisch character.

It should also be reported in this context from the Evangelical Church that, with the onset of the war, the various groups—from the Confessional Front to the so-called Thuringian German Christians—immediately united for common work, after efforts in this direction had already been present throughout the entire year of 1939.

All in all, the internal situation of the German people, as it exists at the beginning of the war, can be summarized as follows:

A small group of radicals, who are under the influence of international free-thinking and thus Jewish materialism, is on the way to undermine and empty the high intellectual culture of the Christian-National Socialist German people by all means and ultimately by state power.

These radicals have succeeded in filling broad sections of the population with a gloomy and depressed mood. Although trust in the Führer and some of his associates is unwavering, trust in the movement has been largely destroyed.

In view of the struggle of the German people for their existence, it becomes clear that we must ask for which German future our best men must bleed and die—whether for a Germany that preserves the deep inner content of its culture and its high moral discipline, or for a Germany that, under the dictatorship of a naturalistic worldview, falls into miserable decadence and possibly—like post-revolutionary France—sinks into an extinct people due to such an inferior worldview.

Finally, it must be pointed out how extraordinarily serious this situation must be taken with regard to the foreign standing of the Reich. It is well known—and the Führer pointed this out in his great speech of January 30, 1939—that abroad, there is talk of the "persecution of the churches by the state." Even though the Führer has vigorously opposed this claim and although much has been done from certain quarters to reassure foreign countries about the situation, the "neo-pagans"—as they are called abroad—through their seemingly official appearance, continue to provide such notions abroad with new nourishment, and it is to be expected that our enemies will not fail to incite Christians all over the world against the "pagan Nazis" during the war.

III: The Restoration of Internal Unity

The threatening internal situation requires immediate and final remedial action. The ruthlessly advancing radicalism demands radical and comprehensive countermeasures.

The resolution of the disturbing tension and the removal of the deep discontent cannot be postponed until after the end of the war; rather, everything must be done to eliminate it in a few weeks, or even better, in a few days. Therefore, all measures to be taken must, under no circumstances, bear the character of temporary pacification or even tactical appeasement, but must make it clear that the tyrannical rule of the radicals is permanently over. For it would obviously be disastrous if the heavy burdens, which naturally fall upon the entire people at the beginning of such a great war, especially upon the German women, were to be further compounded or even enlarged by concerns about the internal future of a victorious Germany.

Moreover, there is a danger that the radical course will be maintained during the war. Some even fear that it will intensify. In any case, there is concern that it will intensify in the event of a victory. This latter fear arises in light of the fact that immediately after the successful resolution of the Sudeten German question, a heightened attack by radicalism on the internal culture of the German people has begun.

Therefore, the end of this internal crisis requires an urgency comparable to the swift defeat of Poland by the German Wehrmacht. What measures must now be taken to quickly overcome the internal division of the people?

Undoubtedly, reassuring statements from the Führer and his immediate collaborators would be desirable, through which the Reich government would clearly distance itself from all undertakings against the Christian religion of the German people. But such statements alone would not be sufficient. For the party members loyal to the anti-Christian radicalism in 1939 simply ignored the reassuring statements of the Führer from January 30 and, at the same time and later, in their secret decrees and public proclamations, even reached new heights in their struggle and their violations, as irrefutably shown by several facts that will be reported in the second part of this memorandum.

One might also hope for orders from the Ministry of Churches and other ministries. But the ideological rulers, as will also be demonstrated through examples, disregard the wishes of ministers, even Reich law and criminal statutes, just as much as they disregard the solemn statements of the Führer and the principles of National Socialism.

Therefore, nothing remains but for the highest authority of the Reich, that is, the Ministerial Council for the Defense of the Reich, to take up this fundamental issue and bring about a change of course with the greatest energy.

It is desired that some individuals, who possess both the trust of the state government and the church leadership, dedicate themselves with full force to the best interests of the Reich. It is recommended to appoint a Reich Commissariat, endowed with extraordinary powers, which would be directly subordinated to and responsible to the Ministerial Council.

The name for this office should be proposed as "Reich Commissariat for Internal Peace" or "Reich Commissariat for Internal Armament" or a similar designation that hints at the program.

The task of this office would, on the one hand, be to clear up all phenomena that stand in the way of the internal unity of the people, and on the other hand, through continuous public proclamations, particularly through literature, the press, and radio, to positively express the viewpoint corresponding to the true sense of National Socialism, as will be developed in the second part of this memorandum in various directions.

Of course, all public proclamations from this office, even if they include a change of course in any respect, must be designed in such a way that they do not undermine the authority of the state or the party, but rather uphold and promote it.

Second Part: Specific Facts & Measures

What has been outlined so far will be explained in the following by a series of specific facts. These facts form only a very limited selection from an enormous amount of material. It is not the time and opportunity to compile everything that has happened in this area over the past five years. Only what is significant for the present and the future is presented here, and above all, only the most fundamental and important points from the main areas of public life are highlighted.

Furthermore, specific measures are proposed, some of a positive nature, others of a negative nature, which are necessary to restore the normal state that guarantees the internal unity of the German people in both war and peace. These measures partly entail the repeal of previous orders. This corresponds to the situation found in all administrations, namely that old measures are replaced by new ones, and my proposals naturally do not constitute an attack on the party or the state, but instead aim to serve the Reich and the movement by prompting the modification or repeal of measures whose existence is likely to compromise the state and the party, because they do not align with Reich law and the principles of National Socialism.

I: Church

1. The Church is the armed forces in the inner life of a people. Just as the army is responsible for protection against external enemies, the Church protects the individual and the people through inner forces against moral decay, brutality, and barbarism. National Socialism fully recognizes this significance of the Church. Accordingly, the Führer declared in 1933 in Potsdam that the two great Churches were the firmest pillars of the people, expressed in 1934 that he highly values the impact of their moral forces in public life, and pointed out on January 30, 1939 that the Churches in Germany enjoy the protection and promotion of the state, particularly through their financial security.

In contrast to this position of the Führer and National Socialism, the Radicals under the influence of volkisch free-thinking have pursued openly anti-church goals for several years, especially in their main organ, the "Black Corps." They demand not only the separation of Church and State in a liberal sense that is unfavorable to the Churches, but also (because the Churches still seem too powerful to them) the "Declaration of Religion as a Private Matter" following the pattern of the former German Social Democrats, meaning they wish to push the Churches out of public life and treat them as private associations, although the Churches are the largest public-law corporations next to the Reich. These efforts must now be decisively opposed, and the true position of National Socialism must be firmly established through Reich laws, as was already initiated in the Concordat with the Roman Catholic Church, in the Constitution, and in the law to safeguard the Evangelical Church.

2. In accordance with the fundamental position of National Socialism toward Christianity and the Church, the view was widespread in 1933 that every member of the people in Germany, and especially every National Socialist, must belong to one of the two great Churches. Therefore, in the early years of the Third

Reich, there was a strong return to the Churches, after more than two million members of the people had left the Churches under the pressure of Jewish-communist agitation during the system era. However, with the growth of anti-Christian radicalism, a new agitation for leaving the Church began, which—exactly corresponding to the advance of volkisch free-thinking—became particularly noticeable in 1937, subsided in 1938, and made a new attempt at the beginning of 1939.

The reasons used by the agitators were varied. Some of it was the supposed contradiction between Christian and National Socialist worldviews, some of it was the (partly caused by radicalism itself) internal church disputes, and some of it was the illusion of a German unified faith outside of confession.

The method of agitation, however, was exactly the tactic that is preferred by the volkisch free-thinkers, as described earlier. Particularly favored was the semi-personal, semi-official pressure from above to below within the Party, and to some extent in state authorities. According to reports, agitation even took place through the Block Wardens among Party comrades in some areas, and entire groups within the associations were allegedly taken to the district court to collectively declare their departure from the Church. Even though this last point is only reported as a rumor, the overall nature of the procedure is fully confirmed by the results. It was not, as before, the proletarian masses of workers who left, but primarily individual political leaders and officers of the movement, as well as some state officials.

As far as the internal condition of the people leaving the Church at the moment of their departure is concerned, it is of course not to be assumed that in all cases a pronounced anti-Christian, volkisch-free-thinking worldview was present. Rather, it is to be assumed that in the overwhelming majority of cases, the semi-official pressure and the associated current circumstances were the real deciding internal motivation.

The numerical success of this agitation, however, is negligible compared to the forces applied and the personal standing of some of the agitators. In the year of the strongest agitation, 1937, the number of those leaving was well under 1% of the population, and within the primarily targeted Roman Catholic Church, the number was even lower than in the Protestant Church. In 1938, it was even smaller. For 1939, it has not yet been determined. If one says that the Churches have lost just over 1% of their membership through the new departure movement, one would be quite close to the truth. However, if one excludes those who left not out of inner conviction but simply under pressure from above or due to circumstantial factors, one can get an approximate idea of how small the number of "German believers" in the sense of volkisch free-thinking may be and how immense the absurdity of the fact is that this small group can, to the extent that it actually does, violate our inner life.

However, the agitation for leaving the Church has been very successful in two respects. On the one hand, the propagandists of leaving the Church, by abusing the Party's organization for their purpose, have compromised the movement in such a way that the damage will be difficult to repair. On the other hand, the German people have clearly demonstrated that they remain unwaveringly loyal to the Christian Churches. In numerical terms, the result of this is that, after deducting the Jews as well as the departed Communists and German-believers, the number of Christians in Germany must, according to all reports, be placed between 95 and 100%.

For the moment, and for all the future, the practical demand arises that while it must of course be allowed for each individual to change their confession out of conviction, any agitation for leaving the Church must be prohibited because it destroys the national community. Such agitation must be strictly prohibited for Party members and state officials because it serves to undermine the reputation of the state and the Party among the people.

II: Sects

1. The fact that, alongside the two major churches in Germany, there are some Protestant sects does not diminish the unity of the German people. These sects together have only about half a million members, or far less than 1% of the total population. Furthermore, their members are generally harmless and decent people, and their leaders have repeatedly affirmed their loyalty to the state.

Some problematic groups, such as the so-called Bible Students, were justifiably banned shortly after the takeover. Further measures in this direction do not seem necessary today.

2. In contrast, the associations in which volkisch free-thinking has organized itself are dangerous, such as the association of Frau Ludendorff, which calls itself the "League for German Knowledge of God," the "Combat Ring of German Faith," and similar groups. These associations are also small in number. However, they represent the organization of the mindset that, as shown earlier, threatens the inner unity of the German people more than anything else. In response to the question of whether these associations might have great value due to their promotion of Germanness, it must be stated that they are defined by the dogmas of international free-thought and that, therefore, they are fundamentally incapable of understanding the peculiarities of the Aryan race. They are, as experience shows, particularly inclined to incorporate ideas from modern Enlightenment philosophy into the old Germanic traditions and their religion. Even if one or another previously internationally-minded compatriot has been won over by these associations to the German cause, this is insignificant compared to the destruction of the national community through the degradation of the Christian religion among fellow countrymen and Party comrades.

Furthermore, the Führer, together with the Wehrmacht and the Party, takes such great care to cultivate truly German sentiment, that no support from such questionable associations is necessary.

The seriousness of the hour demands that the work of these associations be terminated. Not for the sake of the churches, whose existence is by no means threatened by this activity, but for the strength and unity of the people, it is necessary that these centers of agitation cease their activities. Significant progress has already been made in this direction by official authorities. The Association of Frau Ludendorff was banned during the first four years of the Third Reich. The main organ of the so-called German believers, the "Breakthrough," was banned at the beginning of 1938. The propaganda of these circles, which in 1937 sought to expand with large mass meetings, was significantly restricted by official measures. The seriousness of the present situation requires that these measures now be completed in every respect, so that the agitation of those disturbing the internal peace is permanently silenced. Such an announcement will bring deep satisfaction to the German people and make an essential contribution to internal unity.

3. Even more dangerous than the associations of volkisch free-thinkers are individual Party comrades, especially those in influential positions, who use their position to spread the teachings of volkisch free-thought in the Party as a supposedly "National Socialist worldview" and encourage the organization of Party celebrations in a free-religious style as a replacement for Christian worship. These Party comrades are working—without calling it as such, and perhaps without knowing or wanting it—to turn the Party itself into an exclusive anti-Christian sect, where, in the end, only those who have separated themselves from the Christian churches can claim a home.

Party comrades who engage in this direction fall under the judgment of the Führer (Mein Kampf, p. 631 ff.), according to which those who push the volkisch movement into a religious crisis are more dangerous than international Communists because they bring disintegration to the movement and thus advance the interests of world Jewry. The Führer also specifies the measures to be applied to such Party comrades. They must be immediately removed from the ranks of the movement. This measure must now, as far as it has not already been implemented, be carried out with all energy, and it will significantly serve to raise the reputation of the Party among the people, which, due to the actions of such Party comrades, may have lost more of its popularity than through anything else.

III: Spiritual Office

1. In every respectable nation, those holding spiritual office are held in high regard. In National Socialist Germany, this is one of the most self-evident things. Accordingly, the Führer stated in his great speech of January 30, 1939, that every clergyman can be assured of his personal protection.

This now establishes the standard for the treatment of theologians in the Third Reich, both in the present and in the future.

2. Regarding the position of the clergy toward the state, the Führer declared in the same context that he considered the German clergy, with a few disappearing exceptions, to be loyal to the state. In line with this, and in view of the war, it should also be added that during the World War, the Protestant theologians, along with infantry officers, made the greatest blood sacrifices of any profession. One in three men fell. The Catholic theologians did not lag far behind. In the present war, it is expected that the Protestant clergy in office—the former volunteers from the World War—will largely be stationed in the field, perhaps more than half.

From this, it follows that it is the responsibility of the relevant authorities to ensure that pastoral care at home is not harmed by this. Pastors at home must be provided with adequate transportation and materials for printed publications so that they can handle the increased workload. Support for radio devotions should also be arranged for their assistance.

3. In contrast to the Führer's position, the radicals have, for several years, waged a campaign against the holders of spiritual office in both churches, which, in form and content, must be placed alongside the works of Jewish writers from the Weimar period. Particularly, the "Black Corps" habitually ridiculed and insulted them. On March 2, 1939, an article appeared—incidentally, thoroughly Marxist in its inspiration—deriding the theologians as "unemployed," followed by a supplementary statement on March 16, which insulted them as "drones."

This campaign must now, during the war and for all future, be brought to an end. It is desirable that the existing criminal law and the press laws be applied in the case of insults against theologians.

4. The agitation against the holders of spiritual office within the Party and its organizations has led to decrees that, due to their untenability, were not always fully implemented, but which consistently provoked deep bitterness among those affected and, on the other hand, severely damaged the reputation of the movement. These decrees were never directed merely against individuals who had made themselves objectionable in some way, but always against the entire clergy. Since 1934, theologians have been excluded from the SS, since 1937 from the Hitler Youth, and partly from the SA. Since the fall of 1937, clergy have been denied entry into the Party. Since the end of 1938, theological students have faced difficulties in joining the National Socialist Student Union, in which they had played a prominent role during the struggle. On Pentecost 1939, it was demanded at the National Student Day that all scholarships due to theologians, according to the foundations, should be revoked. Shortly thereafter, student bodies at numerous universities announced that theologians would be excluded from harvest assistance. Although this measure

was soon revoked, it naturally left a deep resentment among all involved. During the past two years, there was also a secret agitation for the removal of theological faculties from the universities. Related to these measures is a Party decree issued in late January 1939. According to it, no one may hold an office both in the Church and in the Party. This provision contained such harshness that it was only partially implemented. Specifically, it is reported that in the Sudetenland, the Reich Governor spared some clergy, who had greatly deserved the Party, from the application of this decree. Where it was applied, the most unpleasant situations sometimes arose, such as when a rural teacher resigned his position as organist, and from then on, the congregation was reminded of the anti-Christian nature of a Party measure by the clumsy organ playing of his replacement.

All these decrees contradict Reich law. For they degrade citizens to second-class Volksgenossen by denying them honors as though they were Jews, mentally ill, or criminals. Furthermore, such measures contradict the well-known decree of the Führer's deputy from the fall of 1933, which states that no Party member may suffer any disadvantage because of his religious beliefs. Finally, they serve to compromise the Party in the eyes of the people. Therefore, all of these measures must be definitively abolished.

IV: Cultus

During the period of struggle and the early days of the Third Reich, National Socialist groups often participated in Christian worship services in uniform, and even special church ceremonies were held for them.

With the increase in anti-Christian agitation, this practice not only nearly ceased entirely, but various prohibitions against such participation in Christian worship services were even issued. Furthermore, cultic celebrations in the style of free-religious communities (with a volkisch orientation) began to be organized and propagated as substitutes for Christian services. Important in this regard were the "Guidelines for Cultural Service Design" issued by the SA Chief of Staff on July 1, and the Christmas celebrations propagated within the Party at the end of the same year (which included a ban on Christian Christmas carols), as well as a youth consecration recommended for Easter 1939.

These attempts, which met with widespread resistance within the Party and its organizations, severely damaged the popularity of the Party and strengthened the impression that the Party, under the dominance of the radicals, was developing into a sect distinct from the Christian German people, which would, with minimal changes, continue the traditions of the free-religious communities known from the Marxist era.

In the course of the general return to normal National Socialist conditions, it is expected that both in the present and in the future, all orders opposing the participation of National Socialist organizations in church celebrations will be revoked, and that any propaganda for free-religious substitute cults, which even remotely carries the appearance of Party-authoritative legitimacy, will be abandoned.

V: School

The education and instruction of children in the confession of their parents, which is guaranteed by the Reich Constitution against the attacks of the November revolutionaries, is in accordance with the essence of National Socialism. Accordingly, after the seizure of power, the few secular schools that existed at the time were dissolved, and in the later propaganda for the community school, it was promised that Protestant children would continue to receive Protestant religious instruction, and Catholic children would continue to receive Catholic religious instruction.

In contrast, radical elements have launched a campaign aimed explicitly at removing Christian religious education from public schools. Undoubtedly, effective in this campaign are former Marxist elements in the teaching staff, who, given the circumstances, found it easy to adjust their free-thinker worldview from an international to a national perspective.

The agitation against Christian religious education became more noticeable after the foreign-policy victory in the fall of 1938, along with all the radical efforts. In November of that year, attempts were made in the National Socialist Teachers' League throughout the Reich, supposedly on orders from above, but in reality not in line with the wishes of the Reich leader, to pressure teachers to abandon Christian religious education by appealing to their National Socialist beliefs. This led to very severe confrontations within the Teachers' League. The number of those who succumbed to the pressure exerted on their conscience was small, and it dwindled further when the Reich Minister of Education confirmed the freedom of conscience for each teacher. The result was that, generally, only about 3% of the teachers withdrew from religious education. Only in a few places was the percentage higher, particularly in Bavaria, where certain difficulties arose as a consequence. However, the impression made on the population throughout the Reich was oppressive, as it now had a clear understanding of what was intended for the German youth, and naturally, it had to conclude that this was not merely a private matter, but an official Party initiative.

Since the beginning of 1939, attempts have been made in some parts of Germany to introduce substitute religious education, disregarding existing Reich law and the applicable curricula. In Württemberg, where, before 1939, due to questionable actions by the school authorities, a large number of pastors had to discontinue religious education in schools, a "Worldview Instruction" has now been introduced in some schools as a substitute for Christian religious education, partly according to a radically volkisch-free-thinking curriculum that recalls the teachings of the free-religious communities and also shows similarities with the drafts of Frau Ludendorff. In some areas of the Free State of Saxony, "interdenominational" instruction has been introduced, in which Protestant, Catholic, and German-believing children are supposed to participate, and to which parents and children are forced through punitive measures, although the general principle is that participation in religious education is voluntary.

Apart from this, reports have been circulating for some time that even within denominational religious education, many teachers are not adhering to the established curricula but are deviating into paths that lead to the thought world of volkisch free-thought.

It is evident that this is an issue that moves the entire nation, affecting the mood in every German family.

The insecurity and concern caused by this situation was already unbearable during peacetime. In wartime, it could become disastrous. German fathers and mothers must now be freed from this inner unrest, and above all, they must no longer live in the sad expectation that, after the victorious conclusion of the war, a final, fatal assault on the Christian education of the rising generation will be launched.

Therefore, it is to be wished and hoped that, despite all previous resistance, the Reich Ministry of Education will establish a state of complete order in religious education by first reminding of the validity of the previous curricula and then, as soon as possible, introducing new, up-to-date curricula for Christian religious education, in full agreement with the wishes of the churches and without carrying new sources of conflict for the future.

This matter is so urgent that the wish must be expressed that it be brought to a satisfying conclusion before the end of this year.

VI: *Training*

In present-day Germany, the greatest emphasis is placed on professional skill and maximum performance in all areas.

A curious exception is made in the most intimate and therefore particularly responsibility-laden field—religion—when it comes to the training within the Party. In this area, almost universally, not only are there no experts, but in most cases, even opponents of the Christian religion are the ones speaking. The ideas of volkisch free-thinking prevail widely, even among the few former theologians who have made themselves available in this field.

Where ideological training is undertaken within the Party, its branches, and affiliated associations, it is repeatedly observed— both from personal experience and reports from others—that misguided religious theories and distorted images of Christianity and its history are being devised.

As in other areas, it has been reported that since the incorporation of the Sudetenland, the agitation has intensified, especially after Alfred Rosenberg, in the fall of 1938, immediately following the foreign-policy victory, declared at a conference in Crössinsee to about 8,000 training leaders that the open battle against the churches must now be launched on all fronts.

It must be demanded that, as in all other areas, the National Socialist principle of expertise now be established in this sphere as well, and accordingly, all remnants of pre-National Socialist thinking still present in the movement's training be eliminated. This, too, will make an essential contribution to the restoration of the inner unity of the people in this hour of danger.

VII: *Literature*

1. In the spring of 1939, the anti-Christian radicals succeeded in delivering a decisive blow against German literature, insofar as it has a positive relationship with the Christian religion. This was expressed in the official announcement by the Literature Chamber No. 133 (especially §. 6) and even more so in the implementing regulation that modified and thus intensified this announcement.

What is required here is, in short, the following: Any bookstore that displays even a single book with any Christian content (even if it is literary fiction) in its window or on its counter, or advertises it, must express, through a special designation (such as "Christian" or similar), that it represents a worldview different from National Socialism.

This demand caused a tremendous disturbance in the German book trade. A large number of submissions were made to the relevant official bodies. The most important of these submissions argued that the intended announcement and its implementing regulation were ideologically untenable, as they claimed a contradiction between Christianity and National Socialism; commercially unfeasible, as Christian literature cannot be distinctly separated from non-Christian literature; and culturally unacceptable, as it clearly aimed at suppressing and ultimately destroying all literature affirming Christianity, thereby attacking the innermost life of the German people.

Since the regulations of the Reich Literature Chamber are published in the Völkischer Beobachter, wide circles of the population have learned about this case, and voices from the people have raised the concern: "This is about German culture!"

When a measure has already faced such criticism in peacetime, it is clear that it cannot be sustained even for a moment during the current great war. Therefore, one of the first actions that must be taken in the necessary cleanup of the inner life is the final abolition of Announcement 133 (which, apart from §. 6, contains many severe measures).

2. There is literature whose removal from the public domain in National Socialist Germany already seems long overdue, and particularly now, desirable.

This includes, for example, the books by the half-Jew Korvin: Der Pfaffenspiegel and Die Geissler, which, aside from their contempt for Catholicism, are also notable for their sexually provocative depictions due to their sadistic descriptions. These books, which have been part of the core collection of international free-thinker libraries for almost a hundred years, have surprisingly not disappeared from the book trade in National Socialist Germany. Instead, they have even been sold publicly and undergone new editions—a fact that is undoubtedly due to the activity of anti-Christian free-thought.

Also belonging here are the pamphlets by Frau Ludendorff, which lack any expertise, directed against the Christian religion, in which a worldview influenced by the materialist Ernst Haeckel and the Jew Spinoza is presented as "German knowledge of God."

One should also recall Gustav Frenssen, whose glorification of the Jew Walter Rathenau has not been forgotten. In the last two works of this writer, a worldview influenced by Haeckel (partly copied word for word) is proclaimed as the "faith of the North Mark."

VIII: Press

1. The daily press has been so intimidated under the pressure of anti-Christian radicalism and seems to be so thoroughly infiltrated by followers of this ideology that only a very few newspapers still publish articles and news that show we are a Christian people. In general, the daily press remains completely silent on Christian and church matters. At most, occasional notes with hostile content appear. For example, the starvation plan against the theologians in

Würzburg mentioned above (under III) was made known to the German people by the newspapers on May 26, 1939. In the spring of 1939, the church bulletin, that is, the announcement of Sunday services, also disappeared from the daily press. A measure which, whatever the justification might have been, was naturally understood by the people under the prevailing circumstances as an anti-church action.

The objection that confessional matters do not interest the public and therefore do not belong in the daily press is invalid, since the newspapers, on the other hand, publish an abundance of sports news, marriage announcements, fashion updates, and other topics whose circle of interested parties is far smaller than the two Christian denominations, each of which comprises about half of the entire population.

Even the so-called church conflict has never, even at its most intense times, manifested itself in such a way within the daily press that a near-total exclusion of everything Christian and ecclesiastical would have been necessary. In accordance with the fundamental position of National Socialism toward Christianity and the churches, all related matters in the press deserve a place commensurate with their public significance. Accordingly, any remaining restrictive measures must be eliminated.

2. A significant positive task will fall to the daily press once the position is established that is responsible for ensuring the internal unity of the people. One of the most effective means in the hands of this office will be to regularly, ideally weekly, publish articles in the entire press in which knowledgeable authors calmly discuss the foundations of the National Socialist worldview. Topics could include: "The Unity of the Reich and the Duality of the Denominations," "Fascist Style and Christian Belief," "What is Positive Christianity?" "God and Mammon," "Humility and Heroism," "Jewish Materialism," and similar subjects. Through such articles, more than through all negative measures (which are also necessary), all hearts burdened with concerns for Germany's

inner future will be soothed, and the wounds inflicted upon the national community will be healed.

The extent to which we are still far from such press work, even now at the start of the war, and how strong the force must be that directs a new course, is evident from the fact that the call issued by the leadership of the German Evangelical Church immediately after the outbreak of the war could only appear in church weekly publications, while its appearance in the daily press—despite the efforts of the church ministry—was forbidden.

3. Among the political weekly publications, the already frequently mentioned "Black Corps" deserves special attention in our context. The incitement of this publication has, despite being reportedly warned several times, repeatedly taken forms diametrically opposed to the knightly spirit of National Socialism, and the content of the worldview it consistently represents is pure anti-Christian free-thinking. Even in a series of articles under the headline "Confusion in Blood" from June 8 to 29, 1939, the Jewish-influenced naturalistic worldview of Ernst Haeckel was typically represented, as well as the opposite side, the fight against the intellectual concept of God shared by both Christianity and Aryanism, as well as against the serious understanding of evil that also unites them, and finally against the common high spiritual-moral life ideal. In the latter case, thoughts and expressions of Haeckel were reproduced down to the smallest detail, and, most remarkably, the social task was not expressed in the Christian-National Socialist principle "the common good before self-interest," but, faithfully to the model of international free-thought, in the golden rule of the Chinese philosopher Confucius. In this context, the paper's well-known stance on sexual matters was also mentioned, which has been widely recognized, particularly since the "Black Corps," in autumn 1937, discussed the divorce problem by elevating sexual instincts, especially the male sex drive, to the norm to such an extent that, as the paper itself hinted at the time, it caused outrage among all decent German women.

The danger posed by the existence of this paper to the people, the state, and the movement is particularly great because its anonymous contributors write under the name of a party organization, thereby giving their remarks, which are naturally of a private nature, an official party veneer. In recent years of German life, there is hardly a factor that has contributed as much as this paper to discrediting the movement, poisoning the atmosphere of public life, and destroying the national community achieved through National Socialism.

At this moment, it is a fundamental task for the responsible authorities to silence the voices of these anonymous writers forever and protect the National Socialist people from any resurgence of their spirit.

There is also much to restructure in the magazine literature. The "SA-Mann," which for a time struck similar tones as the "Black Corps," has already been banned. The organs of the German-believing associations would become superfluous with their own dissolution. Many other magazines would need to adapt according to the circumstances.

4. Church periodicals have lived under extraordinarily restrictive conditions in the last year, and their dutiful struggle against the national free-thought movement and the confusion caused by its actions has, in part, been hampered in an entirely unacceptable way. For example, in the spring of 1939, one of the best journalists in the Evangelical press, the head of the Evangelical Press Association for Saxony, an officer of the World War and holder of the gold wound badge, was dismissed for reasons that, as the records of the case show, were completely inadequate, essentially because he had occasionally, in (admittedly too many) articles, correctly characterized and rightly criticized the ideas of the national free-thinkers.

For the present and the future, it is to be expected that, in the course of pacifying internal German life, the barriers that have previously made life unbearably difficult for church press will also be removed.

IX: *Radio Broadcasting*

Since 1933, Christian devotions have been increasingly pushed back in radio broadcasts. By 1939, the last remnants had nearly disappeared. Occasionally, Christian hymns without words are still played. Otherwise, the fact that we are a Christian nation is rarely presented positively in radio broadcasts, just as in the press. The radio thus does not provide a complete picture of German culture in this regard.

For a time, one could hear Sunday morning services, which, in a cultic framework, usually offered secular lectures and presented the ideas of folk free-thought, making them hardly distinguishable from the worship hours of free-religious communities.

This development has made the same disheartening impression on the National Socialist German people as all similar phenomena. The foreign effects of this situation can be gauged by the fact that shortly before the war, a plan was proposed in England to broadcast German church services to Germany — a plan which might now be executed, and which is even more diabolical, as listeners of these services would soon make themselves liable to prosecution in Germany.

The war has thus far brought no change. However, a new hour has now come for radio broadcasting. The German people expect that, in such a difficult and significant time, sounds will emerge from the radio that help to bring forth the last sources of inner strength.

Therefore, it is expected that from now on, Christian devotions of either Protestant or Catholic nature will regularly be heard on the radio.

It would undoubtedly be particularly effective if church services from chaplains, both from the front and from the home front, were broadcast. This would create a wonderful harmony between the fighting army and the families at home. But even apart from the broadcasting of such services, it is desirable in a National Socialist Germany that, in the future, the Christian culture of the people finds its unadulterated expression in radio broadcasts.

X: Theater and Film

Until recently, one could still see on stage and on the screen works (such as the play *Queen Isabella* or the film *To New Shores*) in which the figure of the ridiculous or repulsive clergyman played a role, much like in the degenerate art of Jewish writers from the system period. The vices and foolishness of this clergyman were now only supplemented by his anti-national sentiment.

Such phenomena must always have been regarded in the Third Reich as remnants of a bygone era. Now, the time has come to finally put an end to such phenomena.

XI: Public Welfare

For several years, radical circles have turned their attention to the Inner Mission of the Evangelical Church. The Inner Mission—and the same applies to the Catholic Caritas—famously carries out an act of love in silence, which represents one of the most magnificent forms of social assistance and, in the best sense, practically realizes Positive Christianity and the principle "Common good before self-interest." In this context, religious devotion is an essential prerequisite for social self-sacrifice.

As early as 1937, the radicals demanded a law by which all institutions of the Inner Mission and Caritas should be placed under the control of the National Socialist People's Welfare (NSV), with the aim of completely secularizing their charitable activities. At that time, their attempt failed due to the united resistance of all concerned parties.

In the spring of 1939, the attempt was made again. Once again, not only the affected associations resisted, but also the responsible authorities of the Reich thwarted the plan.

Then, in July of that year, the Reich Governor of Mecklenburg attempted to seize all institutions, including their assets, and secularize their work. With the help of the Reich authorities, this initiative was also reversed.

For the moment, the danger of destroying Christian charitable work has been averted. However, the repeated attacks naturally leave a heavy concern in all who are aware of them, including the twenty thousand sisters now serving in hospitals, that after a victory, the radicals might still succeed in carrying out their destructive work.

All these efforts and all these concerns must now be conclusively addressed by strong measures from the highest authorities, so that the German people stand united in life and death with undiminished strength as an indestructible entity.

CAJUS FABRICIUS:
RECORDS OF HIS IMPRISONMENT, ETC.

Draft of a Telegram to Göring

Professor Fabricius has been in custody since November 9th due to the memorandum on internal armament. No offenses have been established during interrogations, nor have any been alleged. The dispatch of the memorandum was strictly confidential and only sent to a few high-ranking offices.

As Fabricius is known domestically and abroad as a Christian defender of National Socialism through several publications translated into English at state expense, prolonged detention could lead to renewed unrest within the country and intensified propaganda abroad concerning Christian persecution.

Thus, the situation poses an imminent danger. Therefore, immediate release is an urgent political necessity.

Notes by Professor Fabricius on the Circumstances of His Imprisonment and Possible Measures to Limit Its Duration Breslau, 29 November 1939

1. Circumstances of Arrest. During my arrest on the afternoon of 9 November, I was informed at the Breslau Police Headquarters that I was being "provisionally detained on the orders of the Reichsführer SS due to the memorandum 'Innere Rüstung'."[47] It was not clarified whether the content or the manner of its dissemination was decisive. During the interrogation on 10 November, which merely supplemented the earlier questioning in Berlin, only the question of which offices had received the memorandum was reiterated. At no point was the strictly confidential transmission to a few high-ranking offices deemed improper.

---

47 [This is the previous document, translated "Inner Armor."—Editor]

As indicated by the wording of the arrest notification, my detention was directly ordered by the head of the police. My records and the memorandum itself are held there. The Breslau police were unfamiliar with its content and acted solely on orders from Berlin. Therefore, anyone seeking precise information about the matter must inquire in Berlin.

My detention has only been officially communicated to me as "provisional." Upon my transfer to Nord Hospital, the detention was designated "protective custody," as I learned from the head physician. I was held in the police prison until Friday, 24 November, and then transferred to Nord Hospital for a mental health evaluation. However, I remain in custody indefinitely.

2. Public Perception of Detention. Had my detention lasted only 14 days, it might have been appropriate to keep it entirely private. However, as there is now the possibility of prolonged imprisonment in a jail, concentration camp, or mental institution, it is no longer suitable to conceal the situation. I do not feel ashamed of my imprisonment. Rather, I bear it as befits a follower of the Führer and simultaneously a Christian and theologian. My colleagues and students should likewise feel no shame about my detention.

I therefore request that the matter now be disclosed among my colleagues and students with transparency. In short: "On 9 November, arrested on the orders of the Reichsführer SS due to the memorandum 'Innere Rüstung'; held for 14 days in the police prison and then transferred to Nord Hospital (psychiatric clinic) for an evaluation of mental health; future uncertain, with indefinite prospects of return to police custody, transfer to a concentration camp, or prolonged institutionalization."

The police do not intend for my detention to remain secret, as evidenced by their requirement to list the police prison as the sender on correspondence. Even if we maintain discretion, the matter will become known through other channels.

This arrest, involving a theologian known domestically and internationally through publications translated into English at state expense, risks causing significant unease domestically and an international scandal. It could intensify accusations of "Christian persecution" and provoke calls for a "crusade" against "pagan Hitlerism." We cannot prevent such repercussions by silence but must act decisively to seek legal remedies to secure my immediate release.

3. Measures to Limit Detention. It appears possible to bring about a temporal limitation of my detention. In this regard, the following general circumstances must first be considered: The imposition of protective custody is not based on any judicial decision but is merely an administrative measure that can be lifted at any time if substantive considerations are raised by any party that make this appear necessary. However, if it is a matter of pretrial detention prior to an ordinary court proceeding, release from custody could be requested by any party, especially by the university, as there is no suspicion of flight risk, nor can any public danger be assumed for an old National Socialist whose absolute reliability can be certified by his dean. Furthermore, it is generally noteworthy that with regard to the foreign political scandal concerning "Christian persecution," there is imminent danger. But if there is imminent danger, the usual time-consuming procedural channels cannot be pursued; instead, expedited routes must be taken. Specifically, the following is possible:

a. The university requests release from detention in the interest of duty, because it is necessary that the teaching activities of the detainee not be further interrupted, particularly at a time when, with regard to the upcoming military training of students, the curriculum is already significantly condensed.

b. In light of the feared national and international scandal over "Christian persecution," any interested and responsible authority may file a request for immediate release. Such a request, due to the high political significance of the matter, is best directed to General

Field Marshal Göring as Chairman of the Ministerial Council for the Defense of the Reich. Additionally, the Reich Minister of Justice must simultaneously be informed and prompted to act, as he is, by virtue of his office, entitled to make decisive decisions in any arrest of theologians.

c. Annually before Christmas, the Führer grants an amnesty for political prisoners. My political offenses have never been clearly presented to me. Thus, I can only speculate on them. It is possible that the imprudent dissemination of my memorandum was assumed—though this was refuted during my interrogations. Furthermore, it may have been criticized that I have questioned administrative measures of some authorities, for instance, if I mentioned the unrest among the people and the damage to the Party's reputation caused by certain Party measures, which resulted in theologians being excluded from the Party and its subdivisions, or if I pointed out the disquieting effects triggered by certain measures of authorities within the Propaganda Ministry's sphere. If these are my political offenses, then I have amply atoned for them with six weeks of detention up to Christmas, and it is not evident why the detention should be extended indefinitely beyond Christmas.

Notes by Professor Fabricius on the Prehistory of His Imprisonment. End of November 1939.

Under the impact of the outbreak of war, I composed my memorandum, "Inner Armor," in the first half of September. It was the result of ardent patriotism and a profound sense of duty toward the Führer and the people. Its sole purpose was to serve the ultimate internal unification of the people, as demanded by the Führer. Above all, it was my repeatedly expressed concern that all causes of discontent within the population should be eliminated, particularly those that could undermine the reputation of the

Party and the National Socialist government. To this end, I had to point out a number of troubling developments in the religious and ideological spheres, arising from certain radical tendencies, including some official measures that—whatever their intent—had caused unease within the predominantly Christian (95%) German population.

In his book, the Führer spoke with disdain of a system of government in which it is not permitted to address harmful developments within state affairs. Thus, in National Socialist Germany, it is permissible to criticize official measures, particularly through confidential submissions to appropriate authorities. However, my memorandum was not centered on criticism of official measures; rather, it prioritized the interests of the state. To the extent that anything might have been perceived as critical, its intent was solely to complete the construction of the national community. Moreover, it was emphasized with all due clarity that the questionable measures in question were not ultimately rooted in Reich law or National Socialism but rather stemmed from other private influences.

The memorandum had both theoretical and practical purposes. On the one hand, it sought to systematically present the entire issue and examine its internal connections. On the other hand, and more importantly, it proposed practical solutions for resolving existing internal tensions. This practical aim was so central that I mentioned only those problematic developments within Germany's internal affairs that were relevant to the present and future. For instance, I did not address the numerous arrests of theologians that occurred with particular frequency in 1937, causing significant concern both domestically and abroad. I assumed such actions were a thing of the past and would not recur.

Since the memorandum addressed matters within the purview of multiple agencies, it was inappropriate to send it to just one office. Instead, several agencies, including the highest offices of the Reich, needed to be informed simultaneously. These offices were

291

expected to advocate for the implementation of the measures proposed in the memorandum. Thus, I sent the memorandum under strict confidentiality to a limited number of recipients, including relevant offices of the Reich government, the Supreme Command of the Armed Forces, the Reich Church Administration, and some deans of Protestant theological faculties. The strict confidentiality ensured that misuse, especially any transmission abroad, was impossible. I could not be held responsible for such a crime if committed by some traitor.

The distribution primarily took place in the second half of September, with some additional copies requested later by the aforementioned authorities. No one accused me of procedural impropriety in the manner of the distribution. I am unaware of any regulations governing the dissemination of such memoranda, and if such regulations exist, any violation would warrant, at most, a reprimand—urging future adherence to proper channels—not indefinite detention. The form of distribution cannot, therefore, be the reason for my imprisonment.

The memorandum was received without objection by the agencies to which it was addressed. In some cases, it was met with unequivocal approval. Dr. Meissner, Chief of the Presidential Chancellery, personally acknowledged receipt in writing and confirmed its forwarding to the Council of Ministers. It is plausible that General Field Marshal Göring also received the memorandum via this or another channel. At any rate, Göring reportedly acted in the spirit of close collaboration between the Reich government, the armed forces, and the church—a spirit embodied in "Inner Armor." The Minister of Education also personally received a copy. He neither confiscated the memorandum nor called for my arrest, nor criticized any procedural breach. Instead, his personal adjutant sent a note of thanks acknowledging its receipt.

The Berlin Reich Church Administration expressed unreserved approval, as did the theological deans who received the memorandum. Without exception, they gave it strong endorsement (margin note: "Not by me—author unknown?").

The Supreme Command of the Armed Forces showed particular recognition. An adjutant from the relevant department visited my Berlin residence, declaring that their department shared my position. He emphasized the importance of the memorandum, noting concerns over the potential rise of Bolshevist threats as a consequence of political and economic rapprochement with Russia, alongside increased public anxiety fueled by radical internal tendencies and foreign propaganda portraying the National Socialist regime as anti-Christian. The adjutant assured me of the armed forces' protection, particularly should any difficulties arise. He also took several copies of the memorandum to present to senior officers, thereby reinforcing his department's approval.

In mid-October, I sent a copy to the Ministry of Propaganda. The memorandum was confiscated on October 25 at the ministry's request. Subsequently, while staying in Berlin for a few days, I was interrogated on October 27 at the police headquarters.

During the interrogation, no political offense was alleged against me. On the contrary, the legitimacy of my actions was confirmed and even emphasized in the protocol, leading me to believe that the Gestapo had no objections after reviewing the memorandum's content and distribution.

The protocol confirmed: "I am convinced the memorandum was written from the Führer's perspective." This was supported not only by references to the Führer's statements cited in the memorandum but also by other facts, such as his recent declaration to Blood Order members: "We remain committed to Positive Christianity." Regarding the distribution, the protocol listed only the confidential recipients and confirmed that the memorandum could not have fallen into the wrong hands. No negligence or misconduct was attributed to me. The receipt acknowledgment from the Presidential Chancellery was noted and photocopied for the files, and the armed forces' assurance of protection was thoroughly documented.

Finally, the content of the memorandum was addressed. No guilt or fault was imputed to me in this regard. I was not accused of using overly sharp expressions, presenting matters unprofessionally, or adopting an anti-state stance. Only the possibility was raised that someone might think I had reported difficulties that would resolve themselves due to the war's onset. I was asked whether any similar issues had occurred since the war began. I noted the following, which was included in the protocol: Since the war began, for example, the theological faculty in Leipzig has been closed. Furthermore, when the Church Minister summoned leading members of the Berlin Church Administration to Dresden to resolve remaining internal church tensions in Saxony, they were forced to leave under threat of arrest by the Reich Governor. Similarly, radio broadcasts, such as in Breslau, continued to feature anti-church content during the war. This concluded the interrogation regarding the memorandum's content.

On October 28, I was called for a supplementary interrogation at the Berlin police headquarters, where it was recorded that I had received no rejections but rather endorsements from various parties.

I thus assumed the matter was resolved and even hoped for the memorandum's confiscation to be lifted.

However, on November 9, I was provisionally arrested in Breslau "by order of the Reichsführer SS due to the memorandum." During the interrogation the following day, no incriminating evidence was presented against me. Berlin merely ordered verification of the memorandum's confidentiality and the names of its recipients. Three weeks have since passed, and I still have not been informed of the reasons for my detention, now termed "protective custody."

LETTER TO LAMMERS

JUNE 23 1940

by
Cajus Fabricus

Professor D. Fabricius
Berlin NW 87 Händelallee 30
Berlin, 23.6.40
258

Herr Reich Minister Dr. Lammers
Personal
Berlin

Herr Minister!

The German victory over France gives me the occasion to submit the following to you.

The struggle that I have been conducting for several years in public print and in confidential reports, with the knowledge and support of the Reich government, for the National Socialist state, and at the same time for the preservation of German culture, has, in a "cultural-historical" sense, placed me in opposition to an intellectual orientation that originates from the revolutionary France of the 18th century. With its naturalistic and materialistic worldview and its struggle for the separation of state and church, this school of thought has, over the past 150 years, contributed to the French nation becoming a decadent and dying people. The National Socialist movement has opposed this spirit and has developed in the sharpest opposition to an ideal of the national community (Volksgemeinschaftideal) that arose from that French atmosphere.

In complete ignorance of these connections and in total misunderstanding of National Socialism, certain fellow countrymen (Volksgemeinschaft) have adopted these radical tendencies of French origin, rebranded them them with German characteristics, and distorted them into a false National Socialism. Against this tendency—thus, as one must say, against this "Inner France"—I have fought under the protection of the government, and not only I, but the greatest part of the German Volk has, as well as it could, defended itself against these tendencies.

After the war, however, the situation arose that political France capitulated before the victorious arms of the Third Reich, but the "inner France" was by no means defeated. On the contrary, it has reemerged in highly alarming forms. I have hope, because since the beginning of the war I have unwaveringly dedicated myself to worldview questions (Weltanschauungsfragen) in support of National Socialism and have personally endured painful experiences as a result. Even today, what has been done to me due to my personal commitment has not yet been completely eradicated.

I consider it my duty, Herr Minister, to draw your attention to this paradoxical situation in the present great hour of the German Volk and to once again request your vigorous intervention in this matter.

This concerns, as I may briefly recall, the following points:

1. I was in custody on the personal order of Reichsführer Himmler from November 9, 1939, to January 13, 1940. My release was by no means complete. Rather, I was given the exceedingly difficult condition to refrain from any political activity. In the event of non-compliance, I was threatened with lifelong imprisonment in a concentration camp. After a period of three months, on April 17, my freedom was further restricted, as I was forbidden to leave Berlin without the permission of the state police. Consequently, since then, I have been unable to carry out my profession as a university lecturer in Breslau.

2. In an order dated March 20, I was expelled from the party by Reichsleiter Bouhler and Hess (without prior proceedings). However, I see no justification for this step, which includes an

accusation of treason against the state. According to your directive, Mr. Reichsminister Hess, I have not received any written response or any formal notification from there to this day.

Mr. Minister! I humbly ask you to work toward restoring my freedom, which was taken from me by Mr. Himmler, and my honor, which was violated by Mr. Bouhler. In both cases, I place my trust in you as the executive of the highest authority over me, under whose protection I stand. In the second case as well, if my statements are correct, this is not merely a party matter but a general legal issue in which the justice of the accusations made against me remains in question.

Mr. Minister! I ask you to secure my rights and, at the same time, to clarify a case that, within the paradoxes mentioned, represents one of the greatest inconsistencies.

If I have made an error on any point, I ask to be informed of it. If further clarification is needed on any matter, I am always ready to provide the necessary information.

If I am not mistaken, then I believe I am not wrong in assuming that my case can now be brought to a conclusion in the very near future. My urgent expectation, as I have been informed, is that it will be presented for a final decision by the relevant authorities within a few hours. Thus, I may hope that the resolution of my case will no longer be subject to delay.

Heil Hitler!

C. Fabricius

AFFIDAVIT

JULY 16/17 1946

von

Dr. Cajus Fabricius

Nuernberg, Germany

Affidavit July 16/17 1946

AFFIDAVIT POLITICAL LEADERS-62(a)
AFFIDAVIT, 17 JULY 1946, BY DR. CAJUS FABRICIUS, PROFESSOR OF THEOLOGY: CHURCH STRUGGLE DURING PERIOD OF NATIONAL SOCIALISM NOT LED OR SUPPORTED BY EITHER STATE OR PARTY; STATE AND PARTY AFFIRMED THE CHURCH; ESTABLISHMENT OF THE GERMAN PROTESTANT REICH CHURCH AND THE CONCLUSION OF THE CONCORDAT WITH ROME AS EXAMPLES OF THE ATTITUDE OF THE STATE

I, Dr. Cajus Fabricius, born on August 16, 1884, in Graudenz, by profession a Professor of Theology, residing in Hirschhorn am Neckar, currently in the Nuremberg Court Prison, being duly sworn, depose and say:

a) About myself:
I am a Professor of Theology, ordained as an Evangelical clergyman in 1909, and a university lecturer in Berlin since 1911, later in Breslau starting in 1935. Through my theological publications and connections with numerous foreign church leaders (such as Macfarland-USA), I have consistently worked for the peace of the Church and the nations.

In 1932, I joined the NSDAP for Christian-social reasons but was imprisoned by Himmler in 1939 for two months due to my opposition to him. In 1940, I was expelled from the party by Bouhler without party court proceedings. Subsequently, I was placed under city arrest for five years and, in 1943, lost my position as a professor as a declared enemy of the state. Since June 17, 1945, I have been interned in Ludwigsburg.

b) Regarding the matter:

The Religious Attitude of the Political Leaders

1. During the National Socialist era, there were religious and ecclesiastical disputes in Germany.

2. This conflict was neither directed by the state nor the party. On the contrary, the state and the party stood on the foundation of Christianity and affirmed the churches.

a. The party's stance was programmatically established through...

i. Program Point 24: "We demand the freedom of all religious confessions... The party as such adopts the standpoint of a Positive Christianity... It is convinced that a lasting recovery of our people can only occur from within, based on the principle: Common good before individual good." (Cf. the Christian-Social Program of 1919.)

ii. In Hitler's book *Mein Kampf*: "Christianity is the religion of love; we fight against Mammonism. Religious disputes are 'lethal for the German people.' The 'völkisch friends' who drive National Socialism into a religious crisis are more dangerous than international communists."

iii. This was consistent with the official approval of my publication *Positive Christianity* in 1935. Fundamental ideas: The German people are and remain Christian! National Socialism is based on Christian principles. Antichristian freethinking is opposed to National Socialism.

b. From the side of the state, the following declarations and Reich laws were issued:

i. Government declarations from February 1 and March 21, 1933: "The two great Christian confessions are the most important factors for the preservation of our national identity. The government's concern is for the sincere coexistence between state and church. It sees in Christianity the unshakable foundation of the moral and ethical life of our people."

ii. The Reich Law regarding the establishment of the German Evangelical Church, dated July 11, 1933.

iii. The Reich Concordat with the Roman Catholic Church, dated July 20, 1933.

iv. The emphasis on positive Christianity in Hitler's speeches—especially in 1934—and his repeated appeals to the churches to make their moral influence effective among the people.

v. Hitler's speech on January 30, 1939: "The churches are not persecuted in Germany." They receive the financial support due to them. Every loyal servant of God "is under my personal protection."

vi. The Führer's order to all responsible state and party authorities around 1941: Everything should be avoided that might worsen the relationship between state and church.

vii. The note from the Foreign Office on December 1, 1941, countering the accusation of official paganism.

c. This fundamental stance of the party and the state was confirmed by the behavior of the German people.

i. Masses of fellow countrymen (Volksgenossen), who had left the churches under the pressure of the Marxist parties, rejoined in 1933. Couples who had not been married in the church had their marriages solemnized, and children who had not been baptized were baptized. Numerous political leaders became members of the Evangelical Church councils and synods. Many Evangelical clergy had already been members of the NSDAP before 1933 and had become political leaders. In the NS-student body, theologians took on a leading role.

ii. According to the 1935 census, 95 percent of the German people belonged to the Evangelical or Catholic Church. From 1933 to 1939, only 1.4% had left the churches. According to the 1941 elementary school statistics, 98% of all elementary school children belonged to the Evangelical or Catholic Church. The vast majority of political leaders, as statistically verifiable, remained loyal to the church.

d. The struggle was led:

i. by private individuals outside the NSDAP, primarily by Frau Mathilde Ludendorff—salvation through Jesus Christ, the Bible is not the word of God, among other publications—as well as by Gustav Frenssen: Faith of the North Mark—

ii. through private associations outside the party, e.g., Kampf und Deutscher Glaube, Bund für Deutsche Gotterkenntnis — Ludendorff — Nordische Glaubensgemeinschaft, etc.

iii. In these associations, after 1933, numerous secret Marxists from the then-banned Freethinker groups gathered, such as the Freethinker Association for Cremation. These efforts were consciously promoted by communist freethinkers abroad to undermine National Socialism. — Conference in Hirschenstand/Czechoslovakia, Spring 1934. There, it was declared: "We have been politically destroyed in Germany, but not ideologically. The German faith movement, that is us, that is our work."

iv. Through private journals, outside the party, such as "Durchbruch," "Blitz," "Am heiligen Quell deutscher Kraft," among others...

v. This struggle was also carried out by individual party members against the principles of the party and state. Among them were personalities in high party positions, such as Himmler, Ley, and later Bormann. They abused their positions to influence their personal circle and subordinates, generally in an anti-church manner. Such actions were also abusively carried out by some subordinate party functionaries without the approval of their superior office.

3. The struggle was neither supported by the state nor by the party. On the contrary, it was fundamentally rejected. See Hitler's *Mein Kampf* and the decree of Lammers (see above II, A 2 — decree of 1941, S.O. II, B 6). Unauthorized actions, such as Bormann's comment about National Socialism and Christianity from June 9, 1941, and the actions against monasteries and

crucifixes in individual regions in 1941, were swiftly stopped by the Führer. Positive support was provided by the communist foreign and secret domestic free-thinking movement (see above II, C, 3), as well as by individual private persons and groups outside the party (see above II, C 1).

a. The reasons for this struggle by private individuals, associations, and certain National Socialists against the church and Christianity were initially ideological ideas that, following Spinoza, the French materialists, Darwin, Feuerbach, Marx, Haeckel, and others, were rooted in international free-thinking and were now being propagated as German. This struggle was never conceived as a means to prepare for wars of aggression or to facilitate crimes against humanity, but had, more or less clearly, the ultimate goal of realizing some form of religiosity of an humanistic or naturalistic kind, in the sense of the above-mentioned philosophers. The state and the party had nothing to do with this worldview but were based on Christian foundations. Accordingly, the Führer wanted peace and humanity. In contrast, international communism aimed at the extermination of Christianity and the churches (Karl Marx: "Religion is the opium of the people") and civil war in all countries (The Communist Manifesto: "The proletarians have nothing to lose but their chains. They have a world to win. Proletarians of all countries, unite!").

b. Then, the disputes in question sometimes revolved around organizational power claims.

i. The illegal blending of German-faith anti-Christianity and National Socialism by some leading National Socialists provoked opposition within the churches, which in turn mixed anti-Christianity and National Socialism, fighting both simultaneously — for example, a position paper by the so-called Evangelical Confessional Front of 1936 and the papal encyclical "Mit Brennender Sorge" of 1937.

ii. The church opposition was intensified by the fact that political opponents of National Socialism — from the German

Nationalists to the Communists — used the church to fight against the National Socialist regime. This created the impression of politicized churches. It triggered a series of state-political measures and led some party members to the belief that, as right-wing National Socialists, they must leave the church for political reasons.

iii. This did not change the fundamentally positive attitude of the state toward the churches, and only a small minority of political leaders left the church for the political reasons mentioned above.

iv. The fundamentally positive attitude of both the party and the state is fundamentally expressed in the securing of both confessions, through the establishment of the German Evangelical Reich Church and the Reich Concordat with the Roman Catholic Church. This is the strongest counter-evidence against the assumption that National Socialism sought to eradicate Christianity and destroy the churches.

The above-mentioned facts are true. This statement has been made by me voluntarily and without any coercion. I have read it and signed it.

Fabricius

Subscribed and sworn to before me this 17 day of July 1946 at Nuernberg, Germany.

Paul S. Burger, Capt 0-451219
Name, Grade, ASN

I, BRITT BAILEY, being thoroughly conversant with both in English and German, certify that I have acted as interpreter for the swearing of this affidavit.

Britt Bailey

AFFIDAVIT

JULY 18/22 1946

by

Professor D. Cajus Fabricius

Affidavit July 18/22 1946

I, D. CAJUS FABRICIUS, born on 16 August 1884 in Graudenz, by profession a full professor of theology, residing in Hirchhorn on Neckar, at present Court prison Nuernberg, being duly sworn, depose and say:

A) Personal Data

I am professor of theology, ordained as a protestant clergyman in 1909, university teacher in Berlin since 1911, in Breslau since 1935. Maintaining relations with numerous foreign Church Leaders through my theological publications, I always strove for peace in the church and among nations. In 1932 I became a member of the NSDAP for Christian-Social reasons. I never belonged to the SA. In 1939, because of my opposition to the anti-Christian efforts of HIMMLER, I was imprisoned by him for two months, and in 1940 I was expelled from the Party by BOUHLER without legal party proceedings. After that I had five years city arrest (Stadtarrest) and in 1943 I lost my office as professor as an enemy of the state. Since 17 June 1945 I have been interned in Ludwigsburg.

B) Concerning the Case

The religious attitude of the SA. As an objective observer I have ascertained the following.

(1) During the period after 1930, especially after 1933, large numbers of Protestant theological students in the institutions where I was teaching, that is, the universities of Berlin and Breslau, were at the same time members of the SA. I myself— apart from my Christian-Social service for the unemployed—was

also induced to join the Party because of the outstanding character of these students. The fact that these future spiritual advisers of the people, young men of undoubtedly the most noble conviction, became members of the SA in such large numbers, proves irrefutably that the SA cannot have been a criminal organization.

(2) As a student of theology from Lauban in Silesia reported to me in 1936, since 1933 all the members of the Young Men's Christian Association from there—that is, an association of strongly Christian laymen—joined the SA together. It is not conceivable that members of this world-wide Christian organization, which has its headquarters in the USA, should have joined a criminal organization.

(3) At the end of 1933, I had a conference in Berlin with the two highest officers of the Salvation Army; the latter informed me that the asylums of the Salvation Army for the homeless and neglected in Berlin had been emptied in the course of 1933, because, as a result of the National Socialist rising, unemployment had considerably decreased. The Salvation Army voluntarily put these asylums at the disposal of the SA for its purposes. As is well known, the Salvation Army is a Christian organization, which has as its principal goal the conversion of those who have gone astray. And so, if the Salvation Army transferred its asylums to the administration of the SA, this proves that it did not consider the SA as a criminal organization, but on the contrary that it considered the brown batallions precisely as a Salvation Army.

Notes

(1) If in the period before 1933 individual Germans in great distress sought and found refuge in the SA, this does not mean that there they allied themselves with a gang of robbers. On the contrary, they wanted to extricate themselves from the desperate

situation in which the German people found itself under the pressure of the Treaty of Versailles, and—with the help of one party in one democratic state—to return to a decent and orderly life.

(2) If in later years isolated attacks occurred against Christianity and the churches, even within the SA, this, just as in the NSDAP altogether, is traceable to the acts of individuals, who fell away from the Christian principles of National Socialism, and must therefore be considered as illegitimate.

The above mentioned facts correspond to the truth. This statement has been made of my own free will and without any compulsion. I have read it through and signed it.

Subscribed and sworn to before me this 22 day of July 1946 at Nuernberg, Germany.

I, KVETA LIKOVSKA, being thoroughly conversant both with English and German, certify that I have acted as interpreter for the swearing of this affidavit.

THE 28 THESES OF THE GERMAN CHRISTIANS EXPLAINED

by
K. F. E. Walter Grundmann
Dr. Theo.

Originally entitled
The 28 Theses of the
Saxon People's Church Explained
Die 28 Thesen der sächsischen Volkskirche erläutert

Originally published in German in 1934

Disclaimer on Copyright and Historical Use

The following appendix, *The 28 Theses of the Saxon People's Church Explained* by Walter Grundmann, is included as a historical document for educational and scholarly purposes. This work was originally published in Germany in 1934 by Deutsch-Christlicher Verlag in Dresden.[48]

As the translator and publisher of this book, we have undertaken reasonable efforts to determine the copyright status of this work. If copyright protection still applies, the inclusion of this translation is made in good faith for research, documentation, and the preservation of historical texts. No claim to original authorship of the underlying work is made, and no intent exists to infringe upon any valid copyright holder's rights.

If any party believes they hold a legitimate copyright interest in this work, they are encouraged to contact the publisher at www.sacrapress.com/contact, and appropriate steps will be taken to address their concerns.

This translation has been prepared to ensure accessibility to researchers, historians, and the general public. The larger work in which it appears is a broader study of related historical, political, and theological topics from the same period. This publication is part of an initiative to document and analyze primary sources relevant to historical and theological studies.

By including this document, no endorsement is made of its contents, nor does its presence imply agreement with the perspectives contained therein.

---

48   See this archive: https://portal.dnb.de/opac/showFullRecord?
      currentResultId=auRef%3D116895004%26any&currentPosition=87.

Introduction

In our Volk, it is becoming ever clearer that with the beginning of the National Socialist Revolution, we have entered a turning point of immense magnitude. National Socialist Volk life is expanding ever further and is shaping a new man, who finds the meaning and content of his life in devotion to the Volk and in experiencing Volkstum and Race. All areas of public life—politics, economy, law, culture, and art—are being placed on new foundations, undergoing a transformation and a reformation. It is self-evident that the rise of a new era cannot pass by without leaving its mark on the experience of the religious question and the life of the churches. It would be a terrible state of affairs for the churches if the great national (völkisch) event were to pass them by without leaving a trace. That would be proof that they do not truly live within the Volk.

Precisely our Evangelical Church, which since Luther's days has been connected in a special way to the fate of the Volk and the State for better or worse, had to be drawn into the upheavals of our current völkisch life. There is no reason to be alarmed when there are conflicts and struggles within the Church. Rather, the task is to find the form in which the Church is truly built into the Third Reich.

In such a time, Church leadership must, of course, tell the Volk what it wants and which path it is taking. Amid the struggles within our newly established German Evangelical Church, the so-called Saxon course within the Saxon branch of the German Christians took shape during the autumn months of the past year. This well-known Saxon course was based on the recognition that the task of the hour is to integrate the heritage of the Reformation—entrusted to us Saxons in the motherland of the Reformation—in an unadulterated and contemporary manner into the Third Reich.

The representatives of this Saxon course aim to be entirely Evangelical-Lutheran Christians and entirely National Socialist Germans. When the great assembly of the faith movement of the German Christians took place on November 13, 1933, in the Berlin Sportpalast, the well-known statements of the study councilor Dr. Krause demonstrated how necessary this clear Saxon course was. Dr. Krause may have had an honest National Socialist will, but in his Christian stance, he revealed himself as one of those zealots who always appear in times of upheaval and reorganization.

The fact that he attempted to achieve a goal within the contemporary faith movement of the German Christians proves that this movement holds a promise for the future. Zealots only emerge where forces with a promising future are at work. This is most clearly shown in the time of the Reformation under Luther, who had to fight not only against the corruption of the Gospel in the Catholic Church but also against the zealots who exploited and abused his work.

Since the questions in our Volk, prompted by this Sportpalast assembly and its consequences, have now grown large and loud and have taken the form: Church leadership, what do you actually want?, it became necessary to formulate the well-known Saxon course in 28 short, sharply honed Theses, which were to be placed into the struggle of our time. The storm over these Theses, which has also led far and wide to a division of spirits, has shown how necessary this was.

The theses were initially worked out by the theologians of the Saxon Regional Church Office and were then further refined in joint discussions with jurists. The ultimate intent was to express what we want in a manner as clear as possible and in a language that does not rely on the secret terminology of theological scholarship and the expressions of common Christian preaching, which have largely become incomprehensible, but rather in a language that is as generally understandable as possible.

For this reason, the 28 Theses could and should only address those questions that are currently contested and about which clarity had to be established at this moment. That many questions of the overall discussion of the Christian faith heritage are left out, though they hold an important place, is self-explanatory. The silence on these matters does not mean that we have nothing to say about them, but rather that these questions are not presently the subject of religious struggle and ecclesiastical conflict.

Thus, these 28 Theses are intended to serve as a guideline for the church Volk, a directive by which it recognizes what the Church leadership wants.

With this declaration, a number of misunderstandings that have been expressed regarding these 28 Theses become obsolete. As stated, these 28 Theses are by no means a new confession. Pastors remain obligated to the confessions of the Reformation. These Theses also do not constitute a doctrinal obligation imposed upon the pastors; rather, they serve as a guideline and a marching direction according to which we are to proceed. And along this path, the Saxon Church leadership sought to come to an agreement with the church Volk, to obtain, so to speak, the approval of the church Volk for this course.

For this reason, the Church leadership convened the regional synod as the representative body of the church Volk and submitted these 28 Theses to the synod with the question: "Does the Brown Synod approve the 28 Theses of the Saxon Volkskirche, communicated to it by the Church government with submission No. 3 of December 9, 1933, for the internal structure of the German Evangelical Church, and is it willing to declare them as the expression of its own convictions and its own will and to solemnly affirm them?"

In the confusion triggered by the Sportpalast assembly, we had raised the demand that the Saxon course should become the Reich course. A step toward realizing this demand was the submission of the 28 Theses to the Synod. The Synod enthusiastically approved these 28 Theses and declared them to be the expression of its own convictions and its own will. Several other German regional churches, the German Christians throughout the Reich, as well as individual groups and movements, likewise adopted these 28 Theses and placed themselves upon the foundation they established.

However, a storm and a struggle soon arose around the Theses themselves. Misunderstandings spread, statements were attributed to us that we never made, parts were taken out of context, misinterpreted, and then denounced as heresy. As National Socialists, we experienced the same thing we once encountered in political struggle: just as we were denounced as traitors to the nation while we had only one intention—to restore freedom to our Volk—just as we were labeled as servants of capitalism while we carried within us only the one will—to bring the German worker back into the national (völkisch) community —so now we are being branded as heretics and false teachers, while we desire only one thing: to proclaim the Gospel to our National Socialist Volk in a language it understands.

Since it is self-evident that nothing can ever be expressed entirely unambiguously, especially in the form of theses, this small booklet is intended to provide clarification on the specific meaning of these 28 Theses, to explain them, to refute misunderstandings and distortions, and to show those who have recognized in the 28 Theses a path they can follow what this path looks like in detail and how it is to be pursued.

I. Church and State

The National Socialist Revolution, which has placed our German Volk on an entirely new foundation, also brings with it a profound movement and transformation in church life. The position of the German Evangelical Church within the State and Volk is the burning question that weighs first and foremost on the heart of every Christian and National Socialist.

For this reason, the 28 Theses begin with this question and address it first. Many of the criticisms directed at the structure of the 28 Theses have failed to understand this—namely, the claim that a church declaration should have first spoken of proclamation, etc., before addressing its position toward the State. On the contrary, the fact that the most pressing question is placed at the forefront proves that these Theses are truly a word suited to the present situation.

For this reason, there was no extensive theological discussion about the general nature of the Church or the general nature of the State—these are things the Theses assume to be known by every theologian. Instead, they speak concretely about the present National Socialist State and the present German Evangelical Church. Therefore, it was necessary to begin with the point that most clearly demonstrates the present situation: with Point 24 of the Party Program.

Thesis 1:
The German Evangelical Church stands **within** the State. It cannot lead a secluded existence alongside the State, as is desired by currents hostile to Christianity. It cannot persist in a neutral stance toward the State, as those circles wish that approach the National Socialist State with distrust. It cannot be a Church **above** the State, as is characteristic of the Catholic position. Nor can it be a Church **beneath** the State, as was the case in the old state-church system. Only as a Church **within** the State is it a People's Church (Volkskirche). In this way, Luther's original ideas about State and Church become reality.

Point 24 of the Party Program states: "We demand the freedom of all religious confessions in the State, as long as they do not endanger its existence or offend the morality and moral sensibilities of the Germanic race. The Party, as such, represents the standpoint of Positive Christianity, without binding itself to a specific confession . . ."

This clearly expresses that the National Socialist State does not seek a state-church system in which a single Church is granted exclusive state recognition. The National Socialist State grants and proclaims religious freedom. In doing so, it rejects any coercion or compulsion in the most profound matters of faith. This principle is also reflected in the well-known decree of the Führer's Deputy, Rudolf Hess, from October 13, 1933.

This stance is by no means anti-Christian, for the path of a Christian Church can never be one of coercion into Christian faith, but only one of proclamation and struggle to convince others. A Christian Church understands that the fruitfulness of its preaching depends on the work of God, who brings forth the fruit of the Word. Any compulsion toward Christian faith is a misguided path.

At the same time, however, this Point 24 of the Party Program signifies something else: The National Socialist Party, in its programmatic declaration, aligns itself with its Führer on the standpoint of Positive Christianity. Defining what Positive Christianity is—that is the task of the Church. This has also been demanded by leading National Socialists.

The Catholic Church, due to its international bond with the Pope, is only indirectly affected by this reordering of political affairs, whereas the Evangelical Church is directly affected. Throughout the history of the German Evangelical Churches runs the guiding principle that the fate of the State and Volk is directly connected to the fate of the Church. For this reason, the National Socialist Revolution had to intervene in the German Evangelical Churches in an entirely different way and have a transformative effect on their life, unlike in the case of the Catholic Church.

Thus, an Evangelical Church cannot structure its relationship with the State in the same manner as the Catholic Church does. Nothing is more un-Evangelical than to hide behind the Catholic Church and to hope that the treatment of the Catholic Church and the Evangelical Church must be the same. This contradicts both the history and the nature of the Evangelical Church. Therefore, it is essential to clearly recognize the situation created for the Evangelical Church by the Revolution of 1933.

In contrast to a State that degraded the churches to mere religious associations and was utterly indifferent to their existence

—that is, a State that ultimately aimed to be religionless—the National Socialist State, whose sole legal bearer is the NSDAP, stands upon the foundation of Positive Christianity. This does not mean the revival of the false notion of a "Christian State." Rather, it signifies that, because Christianity is esteemed as the religion of the German Volk, statesmen assign the Christian churches an important role in shaping Volk life and education and affirm and expect them to fulfill this role.

This has created an entirely new situation for the Evangelical Church. It must reflect on what stance it wishes to take toward the State. For this reason, Thesis 1 sets clear boundaries: The Evangelical Church does not wish to be a Church *alongside* the State—that is, it is not willing to lead an isolated existence, untouched by the great events shaping Volk and State, where the stream of life flows past the Church, where Sunday is separated from everyday life, where the churchgoer, in attending worship, enters an entirely different world that is disconnected from the world that engages him in daily affairs. The ultimate goal of circles hostile to Christianity is to isolate the Church in this way and to strip the Evangelical Church of its influence over the shaping of Volk life.

Likewise, the Evangelical Church does not wish to persist in a neutral or oppositional stance toward the National Socialist State. In National Socialism, neutrality always means opposition. We, as men of the Church, did not stand in the political struggle of National Socialism only to now be given a Church that remains neutral or opposed to this State. The task of the Church is not criticism, reservation, or hostility toward the National Socialist State. Rather, the Church's task is to proclaim the Word of God, which is simultaneously a word addressing the great events of our time, in which we hear God's step through history.

However, the Evangelical Church also does not wish, like the Catholic Church, to stand *above* the State in a superior position, so that the State must ultimately conform to the Church. Nor does it seek to revive the old state-church system, in which the State commanded the Church. The fate of the German working class and its path through Marxism and godlessness is a sobering testament against the state-church system.

Thus, we are dealing with an entirely new position for the Church, which we have described with the words: *Church within the State.* Only this truly makes the Church a People's Church (Volkskirche). This seems to us to be the Reformation demand of the hour, through which we reconnect with specific ideas that Luther himself expressed in 1520.

Thesis 2:
For the sake of its bond with the Volk, the Lutheran Church cannot adopt a concordat-based stance toward the National Socialist State. As a People's Church (Volkskirche), it stands in trust toward this State; only one who has the trust of the State leadership can be a Church leader. The State grants the Church support and freedom of activity because State and Church belong together as the two great ordering forces of a Volk. Their relationship is one of trust, not of contractual agreement.

Thesis 2 further elaborates on this point. A Church within the State means a relationship of trust. With Thesis 2, the Church leadership extends its hand to the State with the expectation that, under these given conditions, the State will take hold of this outstretched hand. The relationship of trust must be mutual. It is, of course, inconceivable for a Church to speak of trust while the State rejects this trust.

This mutual relationship of trust is made possible by the fact that the Church acknowledges the State as a divine order for our Volk and sees in the National Socialist State the restoration of this divine order—an order that comes from God's holy creative will —after a time when these orders had disintegrated to the misfortune of our Volk. The task of the State is to recognize the mission of the Church by seeing in it the place where, through weak, struggling human words, the living God speaks through His Law and His Gospel. The mission of the Church is to proclaim the Word of God.

We agree with the Fathers of the Reformation when they say that the Church exists wherever the Word of God is preached purely and clearly and the sacraments are rightly administered. Because the State is a divine order and stands by God's will, it can and must recognize the mission of the Church. In this mission, the State does not interfere. Here, the Church is free. But the Church also has an external, human side and order.

From our position, a clear regulation follows for the external order of church affairs. The existing relationships and mutual arrangements must be structured in trust. Therefore, only a National Socialist can be a Church leader, for to be German today means to be National Socialist. And whoever is a National Socialist also has the trust of the State leadership. This excludes any concordat-based stance.

A concordat-based stance means that the two partners, Church and State, stand opposite one another in a relationship of mistrust, each attempting to extract from the other whatever it can. It also means that, within a particular sphere of Volk life, a foreign, independent church law—such as canon law in the case of the Catholic Church—holds authority, thereby excluding state law.

However, the rejection of a concordat-based stance does not mean that agreements should not be reached regarding specific issues in regulating the relationship between State and Church. Matters such as youth education, religious instruction, theological faculties at universities, finances, church buildings, and various other aspects of the mutual relationship between State and Church require regulation. We are realists, not vague romantics; we recognize that such matters must be arranged in a spirit of trust. But this is something entirely different from a concordat-based stance or a state-church treaty.

Only on the foundation of mutual trust can State and Church fulfill their shared task within the Volk. The State is the life order of the Volk according to God's ordering will. The Church, in proclaiming God's Word in Law and Gospel, is likewise an ordering force in Volk life. Therefore, State and Church belong together as ordering forces in a relationship of trust.

Thesis 3:
The People's Church (Volkskirche) affirms blood and race because the Volk is a community of shared blood and essence. Therefore, only one who is recognized by the State as a national comrade (Volksgenosse) can be a member of the People's Church. Likewise, only one who, according to State law, is eligible to be a civil servant (as per the so-called Aryan Paragraph) can hold office within the People's Church.

The inner prerequisite for the renewal of the Church as a People's Church is established by the fact that the German people have experienced national unity and have come together in the national (völkisch) community. National Socialism has given us the experience of the national (völkisch) community. From class antagonisms and social divisions, from economic groupings and ideological factions, a Volk has emerged. But the foundation of this Volk-formation lies in the experience of race.

As National Socialists, we understand the Volk as a community of people of the same blood and the same kind—not merely as a community of those who speak the same language. Blood and race are therefore the foundations of the new experience of Volk and the new national (völkisch) community. In this, we once again grasp the true meaning of Volk. From the natural givens of blood and race, history shapes a Volk.

Every Church has its basis of existence in the Volk to which it belongs. What happens within a Volk cannot be indifferent to a Church that is truly bound to that Volk; rather, it directly affects church life. This new understanding of the concept of Volk leads us to a new understanding of the idea of a People's Church (Volkskirche).

There have been repeated efforts to create a truly living People's Church. We must remember with gratitude the men who have devoted themselves to this noble goal and its realization. However, this goal has not yet been fully achieved. Only the Volk-formation brought about by National Socialism creates the necessary conditions for a People's Church. Where there is no real Volk, there can be no People's Church. But where a Volk comes into being, a People's Church can also arise.

For us as National Socialists, this Volk-formation represents the fulfillment of a divine creative word: Let there be a Volk! And there was a Volk. If we recognize God's hand in this entire process of Volk-formation, then we cannot shirk the duty of actively participating in it. This means that we must create a People's Church that affirms blood and race as God's creative gifts, through which Volk continually comes into being.[49]

---

49 Note: It has repeatedly been criticized that in Thesis 3 we state that the People's Church (Volkskirche) affirms blood and race, with the claim that

This has significant implications for the structure of the People's Church (Volkskirche). As members, it includes all those who are truly national comrades (Volksgenossen). The criteria for belonging to the national community (Volksgenossentum) are determined by state law.

This raises the question of what happens to those who are not national comrades (Volksgenossen) but reside in German lands as guests. If they are baptized Evangelical Christians, they must be granted unconditional guest rights within the German Evangelical Church, just as in the German State. However, guest rights (Gastrecht) are different from the rights of a national comrade (Volksgenosse). Guest rights allow participation in the proclamation of the Word and the reception of the sacraments, but they do not grant access to church office or participation in church governance, such as in church councils and synods.

This restriction is by no means un-Lutheran. In a letter to Justus Jonas, Luther once referred to a baptized Jew as "a guest in the People's Church (Volkskirche) and a housemate in the Church of the Jews." This distinction is the same as the one we seek to establish.

Alongside this decision comes another: that only one who, according to State law, is eligible to be a civil servant (Beamter) can hold spiritual office within the People's Church (Volkskirche). If this were not the case, there would be a great danger that those who, by law, cannot hold public office in the State would turn to church offices instead, thus opening a gateway for foreign blood into the German national body.

---

the term *affirm* (bekennen) as a church expression should not be used in such a context. These critics have completely overlooked the fact that there is a distinction—not merely a linguistic one, but a substantive one—between the expressions: *I confess the Christian faith, I confess the Lord Jesus Christ*, and *I affirm* (bekenne mich zu) *something*, such as blood and race, but also my own guilt or a statement I have made. With this, all criticisms based on the term *affirm* (bekennen) become obsolete.

However, the reasoning for this requirement goes even deeper: The German man, who has rediscovered his German nature (deutsche Art) through his race, does not entrust his legal affairs to a Jewish lawyer or his sick body to a Jewish doctor because the fundamental basis for the deepest resonance and trust of hearts is lacking. Should he then entrust the most intimate and sacred matters of his spiritual life to a man of different blood?

In this pastoral service (seelsorgerlichen Dienst), which the Church owes to the German man, lies the deepest justification for the requirement that officeholders in a German Church must belong to the Aryan race.

Thesis 4:

A People's Church (Volkskirche) does not mean the exclusion of Christians of other races from the Word and Sacrament or from the great Christian community of faith. A Christian of another race is not an inferior Christian, but a Christian of a different kind (Art). In this way, the People's Church (Volkskirche) takes seriously the fact that the Christian Church does not yet exist in the perfection of divine eternity but is bound to the orders that God has given to this life.

Does this understanding of the People's Church (Volkskirche) negate the Third Article of Faith, which states: "I believe in the Holy Spirit, one holy Christian Church, the communion of saints"? The experiences of German missions in heathen lands have shown that the primordial bonds of clan, tribe, and Volk contain something that finds its fulfillment in the Church. They have demonstrated that the racial health and unity of a tribe or a

Volk are not indifferent to church life and Christian piety but are, in fact, of great and significant importance. The experiences of the mission have taught us to see the concept of the People's Church (Volkskirche) in a new light.

We apply to our German Volk only what German missions fully acknowledge for the native tribes of Africa. However, in doing so, mission work in no way seeks to abolish the Third Article of Faith. The living People's Churches (Volkskirchen) are members of the one holy Christian Church, the communion of saints, which we confess in the Christian creed. The People's Churches (Volkskirchen) are the earthly manifestation of the new humanity, gathered according to nations (Völkern) within the People's Churches (Volkskirchen). Their founder and completer is Jesus Christ.

This also means that there can be no talk of Christians of other blood being Christians of lesser rank or lesser worth. The distinction being made is not one of value or rank but one of kind (Art). And it cannot be denied that an Indian, an African, or a Jewish Christian has a different nature (Art)—even in his Christianity and Christian life—than a German Christian.

When the Apostle Paul writes in Galatians 3:28, *"There is neither Jew nor Greek, there is neither slave nor free, there is neither male nor female; for you are all one in Christ Jesus,"* he does not mean that within the Christian community, gender differences or social distinctions cease to exist—that there are no longer men and women, no longer free and slaves. Likewise, he does not mean that racial differences cease to exist—that there are no longer Jews and Greeks. The reality of the world contradicts such an interpretation. Rather, he seeks to express one central truth: There exists a unity in the need for salvation that transcends all other human distinctions, and there is one salvation given in Jesus Christ for all people.

We will speak on this matter more extensively elsewhere. For now, we see in the People's Churches (Volkskirchen) the earthly manifestations of the one holy Christian Church. We confess the one Christian Church in faith and await its fulfillment through God's perfecting act.

Thesis 5:

Because the German People's Church (Volkskirche) honors race as a creation of God, it recognizes the duty to preserve the purity and health of race as a divine commandment. It regards marriage between individuals of different races as a violation of God's will.

From the experience of Volk (Volkserleben), the Church derives the obligation to act in order to preserve the purity and health of race. Race is a part of God's creation. It is one of the gifts He has given us. Therefore, its preservation is among God's commandments. If the German government takes measures to protect and safeguard the purity and health of race in every respect, then a People's Church (Volkskirche)—one that truly understands Volk (Volk)—cannot oppose this government; on the contrary, it must support such governmental action in every way.

Likewise, it must emphasize the fundamental requirement of every healthy marriage, which is that both spouses belong to the same race. Marriage between individuals of different races is contrary to the order that God has given to this life, and for this reason, a People's Church (Volkskirche) recognizes it as a violation of God's will.

It is precisely on this point that a People's Church (Volkskirche) can—and must—demonstrate that it truly takes its faith in God the Creator seriously, and that from this faith arise forces that preserve and shape Volk (Volk). Ultimately, a Volk (Volk) can only be preserved by submitting itself to God's will. Achieving this is the goal of the Church's proclamation.

II. Proclamation of the Church

Thesis 6:
God demands the whole person. The proclamation of the Church has the goal of placing man under the will of God.

Due to the development of our Volk (Volk) and its history over the past hundred years, countless people within our Volk (Volk) have become unable to relate to the Christian proclamation simply because it speaks of God. It is not only the progress of natural science and the technological advancement of the world that have destroyed faith in God for many, but above all, the bitter experiences of the last three decades. These experiences have led countless German people, who entered life with a living and joyful childlike faith, to lose that faith. Many had their childlike faith shattered by the storms of the World War and the hardships of the postwar period. Many, in the face of the terrifying realities of life—in the drumfire of the World War, in the fate of postwar inflation—asked: Where is God now?

This presents an unmistakable and decisive challenge to the Christian proclamation. This question has become even more pressing now that the collapse of the worldview from which free-thought emerged has led to a new search for God. Countless people, who were once free-thinkers, are beginning to realize that human reason alone is incapable of deciphering the ultimate mysteries of the world—that a worldview without God cannot answer the fundamental questions of life: Where does all life come from? Where is all life going? How was the world created? What sustains the world? What is the mystery of life itself? These are questions that a free-thinker cannot answer. Yet they repeatedly confront the thinking and reflective person, ultimately driving him toward the search for God. Thus, in our time, shattered faith in God and a renewed search for God stand in direct opposition to one another.

The decisive question now is: What kind of faith in God has been broken within our German Volk? Was it truly faith in the real, living God, or was it faith in an idol? Could it be that we had all surrendered ourselves to an idolatrous faith and that the living God had to destroy this idol and annihilate this false faith through the storms of history—so that a new search for God could finally find its way to the real, living God?

To this question, there can be only one answer: Yes. We all surrendered ourselves to idolatrous belief, and this idol was called "the dear God" (der liebe Gott). The "dear God", as conceived, was that old, indulgent father about whom one did not need to concern oneself, who let things be, who was the God of bourgeois life, who did not disturb bourgeois comfort and convenience, and whom the worker—who had been cast out of bourgeois life—had no use for and could not relate to. This was the God who was treated much like a health insurance certificate—something one needs and uses only when in distress. In this attitude toward the "dear God", only one Bible verse remained—but even then, only half of it: "Call upon me in trouble, and I will deliver you." What was forgotten, however, was: "And you shall glorify me."

The living God has shattered this idol called the "dear God" in the storm of a great era, through the suffering of terrible events, thereby clearing the way to Himself—the real God. We must seriously ask ourselves: Was the faith that was broken within us true faith in God or idolatry? Every doubt in God should lead us to self-examination—whether, once again, we have not clung to a self-conceived idol.

In contrast, the Christian Church proclaims the real, living God, who makes a claim upon man—indeed, upon the whole person. God demands the whole person. Thus, we do not see God merely as the primal ground of the world, from which the world constantly emerges anew; we do not see God merely as the deepest essence dwelling within the human soul, making man and God one in every person. Rather, we see God as a living Thou, who wishes to encounter us and calls us into His service. To believe means: To have a living encounter and a living relationship with God. The task of the Church, then, is to proclaim, through its preaching, the will of God—who calls man into His service—and to bring this will to recognition. That man continually evades this will is his sin. That God, despite all sin, continually allows His will to be proclaimed—that is what sustains the Church.

Thesis 7:
As the Church of Jesus Christ, it has the primary task of proclaiming the Gospel of Jesus Christ to the German man, who has been created by God as a German.

The proclamation of the Church has a prerequisite—it is not addressed to timeless, abstract human beings. Rather, the proclamation of the Church is directed toward people of a specific flesh and blood, of a particular nature (Art) and way of life. When the German man enters his Church, he wants to be addressed in his experiences and sufferings, in what moves him, in what troubles him, in what causes him to ask questions. He does not want to be transported into another world where he can make no connection between his daily struggles and the message being preached.

This demand is entirely Evangelical. The Apostle Paul spoke of his willingness to become a Jew to the Jews and a Greek to the Greeks. For one who must proclaim God's Word in this time, this means that he must approach the German of National Socialist Germany as a truly National Socialist German, for to be German and to be National Socialist is the same.

The German man who comes to his Church must feel that the pastor in the pulpit has the same heart beating in his chest that beats in his own. He must experience the great bond of shared suffering and shared experience. Then, the language that the Volk understands will naturally arise.

We should not be surprised when, in many cases, the proclamation of the Church remains fruitless. Often, this is not because God refuses to bless the proclamation, but because this simple prerequisite has not been fulfilled.

Thesis 8:
The Gospel of Jesus Christ means that God is our Lord and Father, that this God has revealed Himself in Jesus Christ, and that we humans can find the way to the Father only through Jesus Christ. The Church is bound to this proclamation.

What does the proclamation of the Church mean? We sum it up with the word Gospel—in German, Frohbotschaft, a joyful message, good news that is brought to people. The preaching of the Church must reflect that it has a joyful message to bring. The content of this joyful message is expressed in Thesis 8 with words taken from the larger context of Jesus' farewell discourses in John 14.

The proclamation of the Church today encounters within our Volk both a shattered faith in God and a new search for God. From this arises the urgent question: Where is God to be found? The search for God [which men make] follows many different paths and creates a variety of images and conceptions of God in the attempt to find Him. This search for God is answered by Jesus Christ with His well-known words: "I am the way, the truth, and the life; no one comes to the Father except through me."

With these words, Jesus makes one thing absolutely clear: All the paths that people take in their search for God will not lead to their goal unless they walk the path that is called Jesus Christ. He wants them to allow Him to take them by the hand and to lead them home to the Father. "No one comes to the Father except through me." The joyful message that the Church is called to proclaim is, therefore, that we humans can find the way to the Father only through Jesus Christ.

How does Jesus Christ have the authority to make this claim? This becomes clear when we consider the larger context of John 14. There, the disciple Philip asks the fundamental question of all those searching for God: "Lord, show us the Father!" This is the meaning of the search for God—that people desire a clear understanding, a clear image, and thereby a clear experience of God. Throughout the world's religions, there are profound efforts to see God, to make Him visible: from the idols created by primitive peoples to the highly developed conceptions of God formed by philosophers and poets, all of which express this longing in different ways.

To the pleading disciple, Jesus gives this answer: "Whoever has seen me has seen the Father." He directs all of humanity's longing for God toward Himself. With this, Jesus declares that He is the one who makes God visible. If a person wishes to see God, he can find and see Him only by looking at Jesus Christ. Here, God becomes visible. This is one part of the miracle of Christ.

But the search for God does not stop with the desire to see Him; throughout the world's religions, there is also the longing to hear God—to receive a word from Him. People have made various attempts, from necromancy to magic to the ecstatic speeches of prophetic figures. In His final hour with His disciples, Jesus prays: "The words that You have given me, I have given to them." With this, it becomes clear that in Jesus Christ, God also becomes audible. Here, He speaks to mankind. This is the other part of the miracle of Christ. The miracle of Christ consists in the fact that God reveals Himself in Jesus Christ. The joyful message that the Church is called to proclaim is that we find in Jesus Christ the revelation of God. We see Him revealed as Lord, who demands man's full and unwavering obedience, calling him entirely into His service. At the same time, we find Him revealed as Father, who pours out His love upon mankind, draws them into His love, and gives them the assurance and joy of being children of God. In Jesus Christ, God reveals Himself—making Himself visible and making Himself heard. The Church is bound to this joyful message. It would cease to be the Church if it sought to proclaim anything other than this message.

Later, we will discuss in greater detail what this means in practice and how it truly comes to life. It is part of the religious situation of our Volk that, in the past decades, the Church and Christianity—though not without their own fault—have fallen into discredit and have thus been swept up in the broader religious crisis.

The Church and Christianity can repeatedly be brought into discredit by their representatives and are not exempt from the breaking judgment of history.

But one thing can never fall into discredit—this is evident even from the deep respect that even anti-Christian and free-thinking circles hold for the person of Jesus: the Lord Christ Himself. From His power, which contains both life and truth, the Church must be renewed!

Thesis 9:
God places man within the life orders of family, Volk, and State. Therefore, the People's Church (Volkskirche) recognizes in the total claim of the National Socialist State the call of God to family, Volk, and State.

However, God does not reach man with His will only through the Gospel, but already through the life orders in which man exists. The German distress of the past 14 years is primarily due to the fact that the German man had detached himself from the life orders of marriage, family, Volk, State, and law. These life orders were given for the preservation of life. Their destruction means the destruction of life.

We know exactly how these life orders were destroyed. Marriage and family life disintegrated. Woman was degraded into an object of unrestrained male impulses. The number of unborn children in Germany in recent years exceeds the number of those who fell in the World War. As a result, Volk life declined ever further. We know the picture our Volk presented—division into classes, ideological conflicts, hatred, malice, persecution, murder of political opponents: this was the image of German life. And alongside it, a State that simply watched it all happen and broke the law. Thus, man detached himself from the life orders that were given for life itself. In doing so, he also detached himself from God.

The man who sought freedom from the bonds of God used this freedom to sever himself from the life orders into which God has placed mankind. This led to decay. It was as if God had said to us Germans: Go your own way apart from me, and see where you end up. And we ended up in a terrible collapse. That was His judgment—that He allowed us to follow our own path.

The National Socialism of our Führer is to us a miracle of God's grace: He pulled our Volk back from this collapse and restored us once again to the life orders of marriage and family, Volk and State, leading us into the experience of national (völkisch) unity and national community (Volksgemeinschaft). This cannot and must not be indifferent to a Church. A Church would already have become godless if it refused to recognize how God has visibly acted with our Volk—by giving us the Führer, by saving us from collapse, by leading us once again to fulfill His will in marriage and family, in Church and State.

It is the task of Church proclamation to recognize and proclaim the will of God in these events. The total claim of the National Socialist movement as the bearer of the National Socialist State means that the German man is claimed entirely for the national community (Volksgemeinschaft). There is no sphere of life in which he can move freely apart from it. In every respect, he is claimed by and obligated to the national community (Volksgemeinschaft).

In this claim, after a time of decay and disorder, we recognize a part of God's will. For in acknowledging this total claim as God's will, we show the German man that in his selfishness and self-centeredness, he becomes guilty—not only before the law of the State and the community of the Volk, but ultimately before the will of God.

By recognizing and proclaiming God's call to Volk, State, and family in the total claim of National Socialism, the German Evangelical Church proclaims the will of God, which has been revealed at all times in the Law of God. But where man knows something of God's Law, there he begins once again to ask about the Gospel.

III. The Foundations of the Church

Thesis 10:
The foundations of the Church remain the Bible and the Confession. The Bible contains the message of Christ, and the Confession bears witness to the message of Christ.

From what does the Church draw its proclamation? It is impossible for the message entrusted to it—the message that is to speak of Jesus Christ—to come from human reason and human thought alone. If that were the case, the Church would be no different from any ideological association or philosophical circle. It would never be able to give man the certainty of peace in his search for God if it merely proclaimed human opinions and human ideas.

The decline of our Church has its roots in the fact that, more and more, human opinions and human thoughts were preached in place of the divinely commissioned message of Christ. In contrast, the Church—even in the Third Reich—holds fast to its unshakable and inalienable foundations: the Bible and the Confession.

Its message is the message of Christ—the joyful news of God to the world. This message of Christ is found in the Bible. It is also found in the Confession, for in the Confession, the Church —seized by the message of Christ—has borne witness to this message in the great moments of history.

Thesis 11:

The decisive revelation of God is Jesus Christ; the document of this revelation is the New Testament. Therefore, it has a norm-setting significance for all Church proclamation.

The essential word of the Church is the message of Christ. Through its proclamation, the Church seeks to bring people into an encounter with the Lord Christ. We have already recognized Jesus Christ as the image of God and the Word of God—that is, as the one who makes God visible and audible, in whom God reveals Himself. Jesus Christ is the decisive revelation of God, concerning all of humanity. In His person appears the holiest that the world has ever seen and known. The New Testament speaks of this revelation.

In the New Testament, we have the testimony of Christ as given by the disciples and apostles; we have their preaching, through which the Church was founded. Therefore, the New Testament has norm-setting significance for all Church proclamation. Every sermon of the Church must continually prove itself by the message of Christ as given in the New Testament and must be subject to examination by it.

This does not mean that we are simply to repeat New Testament terminology word for word. When Luther translated the Bible, he did not merely parrot the text; rather, as he put it, he listened to the common people's speech in order to express what the New Testament says in a language that people could understand and speak. Today, we have the same task. We must translate anew. Even Luther's terms are not always readily understood.

However, every translation must be a true translation of the New Testament and of the message of Christ contained within it. It is not permissible to divide the New Testament—accepting some parts while rejecting others. The message of Christ in the New Testament is a unified whole. The differences between the various New Testament authors merely show how the message of Christ is received differently by different people, but they also demonstrate that it is a single message that all of them have received.

This is particularly true of the Apostle Paul. It is incorrect to label Paul's preaching as "Jewish." As certain as it is that Paul came from Jewish theology, it is just as certain that through faith in Jesus Christ, Judaism is overcome in the deepest sense. The very foundations of Judaism—descent from Abraham and adherence to the Law—are destroyed in Paul's teaching. Neither being a child of Abraham nor observing the Law grants any special privilege.

Thus, through the message of Christ, the religious substance of Judaism is inwardly overcome in Paul's writings. Whatever hope and longing for a Messiah lived within Judaism is fulfilled in Jesus Christ—but in a way that destroys and eliminates the political and world-dominating aspirations.

Paul's testimony is a living, direct witness to Christ, through which the Church was established—particularly in the non-

Jewish world. The Church, therefore, cannot in any way distance itself from the Church-founding preaching of the Apostle Paul; to do so would be to abandon and relinquish part of its own foundation.

Thesis 12:
The Old Testament does not have the same value. The specifically Jewish national morality and national religion have been overcome. The Old Testament remains important because it transmits the history and decline of a nation that, despite God's revelation, repeatedly separated itself from Him. The God-bound prophets demonstrate through this nation a lesson for all of us: A nation's relationship to God is decisive for its fate in history.

Thesis 13:
We recognize in the Old Testament the apostasy of the Jews from God and, in this, their sin. This sin is made manifest before the whole world in the crucifixion of Jesus. From that moment onward, the curse of God has weighed upon this people to this very day. At the same time, however, we also recognize in the Old Testament the first rays of God's love, which is fully revealed in Jesus Christ. For the sake of these insights, the People's Church (Volkskirche) cannot discard the Old Testament.

But what purpose does the Old Testament serve? The Old Testament is significant for the Christian Church because it contains a special preparation for the coming of Christ. Luther insisted that we should retain from the Old Testament "whatever drives toward Christ". However, the Old Testament does not hold the same value as the New Testament. Jesus Himself speaks of this, pointing to His own person. He says of Himself that "here is something greater than Jonah," "here is something greater than Solomon," and that "the least in the Kingdom of Heaven is greater than John the Baptist," who represents the highest point reached within the Old Testament. With His "But I say to you", as He begins interpreting the Ten Commandments in the Sermon on the Mount, Jesus places Himself above the Old Testament. He speaks with divine authority. He sees Himself as the fulfillment of the prophetic line that runs through the Old Testament, reaching its climax in John the Baptist. This is the prophetic line, whose proclamation pervades the entire Old Testament. The prophets have one great concern—the concern expressed in the First Commandment: "I am the Lord your God; you shall have no other gods before me!" They proclaim that God is the Lord of the world, the Lord of history, the Lord of the nations, the Lord of mankind. This is evident in the Old Testament Law, but also in the promises that speak of God's coming act of grace. The Law seeks to establish God's rule among men, while these promises foreshadow something of God's love, which is ultimately revealed in Jesus Christ. Faithful men who placed themselves under God's rule bear witness to this love in the Old Testament—such as in Psalm 23, Psalm 73, and Psalm 103. However, another line also runs through the Old Testament. It shows how the Jewish people resisted God, who sought to establish His rule among them, how they went their own way, how their nature (Art) rebelled against God's nature (Art) and, in doing so, committed dreadful sin. This line also runs throughout the Old Testament. Much of the criticism directed against the Old Testament today points specifically to this aspect.

This line reaches its fulfillment in the Pharisees. Jesus calls them hypocrites. They incited the people to demand the crucifixion of Jesus. And in that moment, the fate of the Jewish people was sealed. Having always rejected the prophets, they now rejected the one who uniquely revealed God. Jesus vividly describes this in the parable of the wicked tenants, concluding it with the declaration that now the curse of God will come upon the Jewish people. The history of the Jews up to the present day is revealed in this. This people has been under the special curse of God since the day it crucified Jesus. In doing so, it lost both its homeland and its state and became a curse upon all nations. What we experience in the Jewish Question is rooted in God's curse upon this people. Luther spoke of how he saw God's wrath uniquely revealed in this people. And this brings us to the final significance of the Old Testament: It shows us how the history of a people is determined by its relationship to God and how a people's fate in history is decided by that relationship.

Therefore, when considering the Old Testament, we must be fully aware of all that is Jewish within it. Jewish sin and Jewish history no longer concern us. In fact, it is a pedagogical necessity that a school Bible be created for our children, one that omits precisely these passages. However, we must not "throw out the baby with the bathwater" and dismiss the question of the Old Testament with mere slogans. On the other hand, the Old Testament also shows us how God establishes His rule in the history of a people, how He prepares the coming of Jesus, and how the decisive question of God and Volk finds its resolution. For the sake of these insights, the Church cannot abandon the Old Testament. But it must be emphasized that in all of this, the Old Testament has only a preparatory, not a decisive, significance. Regarding the Old Testament, we must ultimately embrace Luther's understanding of Christian freedom:

"Just as when the sun rises and makes the moon appear pale, so that it loses its light, and the stars also fade and are no longer seen during the day because the sunlight is too bright, so it is with the word of Jesus. The prophets are the stars and the moon, but Jesus is the sun. Wherever He appears, preaches, and shines, His word is so great that the others fade into nothingness before Him. Moses and the prophets are indeed learned and refined preachers, but compared to the preaching of Christ, they are nothing."

Thesis 14:

In the Augsburg Confession and the other confessional writings of the German Reformation, the content of the Christian proclamation is testified. Through these confessions, we are bound to our fathers in the faith. A Church without a confession would be like a State without a constitution and law.

Thesis 15:

A confession is always tied to a specific time and its particular questions. Certain questions, which the confessions of the fathers addressed, no longer exist for us today. At the same time, new questions arise that the confessions of the fathers could not yet answer. Therefore, we strive to find a confessional response from the People's Church (Volkskirche) to the questions of our time, drawing from the confessions of the fathers: Not backward to the faith of the fathers, but forward in the faith of the fathers!

The confession of a Church seeks to summarize the Christian faith in clear, unmistakable statements and, in doing so, bear witness to the content of that faith. In this, we distinguish between faith and confession. The first is always the living, fresh faith, which is bound to the Lord Jesus Christ and which arises from a personal encounter with Him. A Christian is one who, in his life, has experienced something of the liberating power of Jesus Christ. Thus, the decisive element in Christianity is the living faith in the Lord Christ. The confession always comes second, never first. The confession bears witness to this Christian faith. The confession is formed and expressed by the community of believers within the Church.

The confessions of the Evangelical Lutheran Church are the confessions of the Reformation. When the Evangelical Church emerged from Luther's Reformation, it was questioned—not only by Emperor and Empire, not only by the Catholic Church, but also by the German Volk—about what its faith was and what it preached. This led to the Reformation confessions, the first and most decisive of which was the Augsburg Confession, which was publicly read before the representatives of the Empire and the Church in 1530 with the participation of the Church Volk (Kirchenvolk). Alongside the Augsburg Confession, there are additional confessional writings that define and articulate the Evangelical Lutheran faith. The most widely known and accessible of these confessions, later included in the collection of confessional writings completed in 1580, is Luther's Small Catechism.

The confessions of the Reformation seek to bear witness to and confess the rediscovered New Testament Gospel in the midst of their time, with its particular questions and struggles. These Reformation confessions were examined in light of the confessions of the early Christian Church. Within the confessional writings of the Evangelical Lutheran Church, they are placed before the Reformation confessions.

In the present time, which has been prepared by more than a hundred years of development, we are confronted with entirely new questions and challenges. A new way of thinking and feeling has arisen, and from within our Volk, the question is being asked once again: Church, what do you have to say to us? Above all, what does the Church have to say about the questions of blood and race, Volk and State? What is its inalienable, eternal message for the man of National Socialist Germany? These pressing questions demand an answer. It is not enough to respond to them simply with the time-bound formulations of the Reformation era.

Emerging from the historical development of our Volk, our Church—if it wishes to remain connected to the Volk—is called and obligated to a new confession. However, this new confession cannot be formed by simply disregarding the confessions of the fathers. Just as the Reformers tested their confession against the confession of the early Church and sought only to proclaim the rediscovered Gospel of the New Testament to their time, so too must it be with us.

The past decades of theological and ecclesiastical work have once again made the ancient New Testament Gospel understandable to us. Now, it is necessary to state clearly what, from this Gospel, must be proclaimed to the people of National Socialist Germany as the word of the Church. However, this new confession must prove itself and be tested against the confession of the fathers. If our Church fails to do this, it would betray its history and the legacy entrusted to it. And no one transgresses against history without consequence.

Just as the Reformers found their confession upon the foundation of the early Church's teaching, so we now strive to find, upon the foundation of the confession of the fathers, a new confessional word for the questions of our time—a word of the

Church for the people of the National Socialist Volk. The German Evangelical People's Church (Deutsche Evangelische Volkskirche) will not truly become a unified Evangelical People's Church (evangelische Volkskirche) within National Socialist Germany until it has found unity in its confession and through its confession.

Many in our time have asked whether a confession is even necessary. This question is foolish. Every person must express and articulate what he carries within him as faith and conviction. Every community of people that pursues a specific goal must declare and state that goal. This can only be done through firm, clear statements that contain the convictions of faith. And every statement that expresses a conviction of faith in some way is a dogma—a confession. There is no community of religious people without dogma and confession.

We see this clearly in the German Faith Movement, which claims to be pagan and must not be confused with the German Christians (Deutsche Christen). This German Faith Movement seeks a religion without dogma. Yet within its ranks, creeds, guiding principles, and theses continue to emerge—meaning that, in the end, it too has dogmas and confessions.

Just as a State cannot exist without a constitution and laws, which express the will of the State, so too can a Church not exist without dogma and confession. The confession is the fundamental law of the Church's existence.

We are therefore determined to preserve the faith of the fathers and to bind ourselves to it. More than that—the faith of the fathers is our faith because it is the faith of the Church. But we do not seek to lead the German man simply back to the faith of the fathers; rather, we seek to lead him forward into his new time, into the Third Reich, in the faith of the fathers.

Therefore: Not backward to the faith of the fathers, but forward in the faith of the fathers!

IV. The Path of the Church

Thesis 16:
The People's Church (Volkskirche) opposes liberalism. Liberalism dissolves faith in Jesus Christ because it sees in Him only a man. It knows Jesus only as the proclaimer of a high morality or as a heroic figure. It places human reason above God. But to us, Jesus Christ is the Son of God, and His appearance is the miracle of human history.

The entire worldview of the 19th century was shaped by liberalism. From liberalism grew Marxism and Bolshevism—both of which are nothing more than variants of liberalism. But what exactly is liberalism? We can best understand it by recalling an event from the French Revolution, which led to the political victory of the bourgeoisie. During this revolution, a mob in Paris paraded through the streets with a wagon carrying a young woman—a street prostitute—who was worshiped as the Goddess of Reason. They declared that God had been dethroned and instead worshiped human reason.

That is liberalism: Man places his reason above all else. He arrives at the conclusion: What I can comprehend is real; what I cannot comprehend is not real. In this, all reverence for the mysteries of life is lost. The rise of science and technology, which seemed to unlock all the secrets of life—so much so that Ernst

Haeckel could proclaim the solution to the world's mysteries—further strengthened this faith in reason. It seemed that there were no mysteries left.

This faith in reason, characteristic of liberalism, proved especially destructive when applied to the person of Jesus. The person of Jesus is and remains a mystery. Liberalism tries to unravel this mystery. It presents Jesus in a way that it can comprehend: as the preacher of a high morality, as a model of virtuous living, as the proclaimer of a rationally purified faith in God, or as a heroic figure. Everything about Jesus that was surrounded by mystery—everything expressed in terms like Son of God, everything found in His miracles and in His resurrection, which defied rational comprehension—was dismissed and rejected.

Through National Socialist experience, we have overcome liberalism. We stand once more in reverence before the mysteries of life. This transformation is occurring everywhere. Scientists now recognize that the great mysteries—life and power, the origin and destiny of the world—are beyond human explanation. No man can say what life truly is or how life arises, and no one can say where the world has come from.

As National Socialists, we have directly experienced the great mysteries of all existence in the very thing we call Volk. Sixty million people speaking the same language do not yet constitute a Volk—at most, they are a mass. What transforms this mass of people into a Volk—the great mystery of Volk-formation (Volkwerdung), which we have witnessed—is something that remains unfathomable.

From this changed perspective—one that has also led to the collapse of free-thought (Freidenkertum)—we now stand once again in reverence before the mystery of Jesus and confess above all that He is the miraculous mystery of God in human history.

Thesis 17:
The People's Church (Volkskirche) likewise opposes a new
orthodoxy. This orthodoxy, through its rigid adherence to dogma,
obstructs the path to Christ for the struggling and searching
individual and hinders the living proclamation of the Gospel.

Within the Church, liberalism posed a severe threat to the
message of Christ. Because believers knew the saving power of
this message, they sought to protect and defend it. This led to a
restoration of orthodoxy. Orthodoxy, through its doctrinal
formulations, sought to safeguard the message of Christ by
surrounding it with the protective barrier of dogma.

However, this orthodoxy is itself a child of liberalism. Through
its dogmas, it also attempts to make the message of Christ
comprehensible and rationally accessible. It, too, seeks to unravel
the mystery of Christ. It failed to understand dogma as a pointer
toward the miracle—something that is not meant to be explained
but rather pointed toward. Instead, it used dogma as a means to
explain the miracle.

Thus arose the well-known orthodox formula: You must
believe this and this and this, whether you understand it or not,
and then you will be saved. This rigid dogmatic stance, which
may have once sought to protect and defend the message of
Christ, has now—at a time when liberalism has been overcome
and its counterpart no longer holds credibility—become an
obstacle to the Christian proclamation.

A living faith in Christ breaks through all dogmatic rigidity
and seeks to bear witness anew. And this is a serious concern. We
think, for example, of our youth and their religious questions.
They do not want the proclamation of abstract dogmas; they seek

a livingly testified faith in Christ. Any rigid dogmatism blocks the way to faith in Christ.

The servants of the Church are called to the love of the Savior —one that understands people in their questioning, seeks them out, and wrestles for them in order to lead them to faith.

Thesis 18:
The People's Church (Volkskirche) also opposes attempts to replace faith in Christ with a religion shaped by the experience of race. All religion, as the search and questioning for God, is racially distinct. However, Jesus Christ, in His miraculous person, is the fulfillment of all that is alive in the human soul as longing, questioning, and intuition. The debate over whether Jesus was a Jew or an Aryan does not touch upon the essence of Jesus at all. Jesus is not the bearer of human nature (Art), but in His person, He reveals to us the nature (Art) of God.

Yet today, faith in Christ is once again being called into question. From the experience of race, of which we have already spoken, comes the attempt to create a distinct racial religion. The accusation is made against faith in Christ that it is the product of a foreign race and therefore does not correspond to the German nature (deutsche Art). It is demanded that, beyond Christianity, we should arrive at a German faith that may acknowledge Jesus as a religious figure from another world but has nothing more to do with Him. It is absolutely true that religious searching, questioning, and discovery are conditioned by race. Just as race asserts its influence in art and culture, in law and custom, so too does it shape religion. But all religion is only the questioning, searching, and intuition of the human soul as it reaches out toward the eternal, the divine, and the holy. In all religions, attempts are made to provide fulfillment to this questioning, searching, and intuition. The images of God in the various religions, which arise from racial differences, are made by men and are idols. We human beings, in our religions, can arrive only at an intuition of God and a search for Him. We can only create for ourselves an image of God, shaped by our intuition. We do not arrive at the certainty of God.

As Christians, we know that the miracle of Christ, the miracle of the person of Jesus Christ, consists in the fact that in Him, God becomes visible and audible. Jesus Christ is the image of God, the Word of God (see Thesis 8 above). Thus, He enters this world, into the sphere of humanity. He appears in Palestine, within the world of Judaism, [which is to Germans] a foreign racial and cultural environment. But what is decisive about Him is not that He appeared in the Jewish sphere, but that He appeared as the bearer of the nature (Art) of God. That is why the debate over whether Jesus was a Jew or an Aryan is a fruitless one, because it concerns only the human nature (Art) of Jesus while overlooking what is essential and important—namely, that in His human nature (Art), Jesus is the bearer of God's nature (Art). He is this as the image and the Word of the living God. In this way, He is the fulfillment of all religious questioning, all religious searching, and all religious intuition. He lifts us out of the mere intuition of God into the certainty of God by leading us to the true God and bringing fulfillment to our intuition.

However, this fulfillment that Jesus brings is not a straightforward one, for He shatters all idols. Man's religious striving and religious possessions break before Him. He takes this man by the hand and leads him to His Father, the true God. At the same time, He reveals to man his own nature (Art) and shows him how distant he is from God. This is the offense that Christ brings. And that is why He Himself says: Blessed is he who is not offended by me!

It is difficult for us as human beings to allow Him to shatter our religious possessions and simply stretch out our hands for Him to take hold of and lead us to the Father. But if we surrender ourselves to Him, then we experience His liberating power, then we recognize that His claim is justified, and then He grants us the highest nobility that exists for us as human beings—that we may become children of God.

Thesis 19:
The German People's Religion (Volksreligion) can therefore only be a Christian one. Christianity takes on different forms according to race and national character. For this reason, we strive for the realization of a German Christianity.

We cannot abandon the message of Christ because it alone gives us communion with God and certainty in God. A Christian Church can do nothing other than confess and proclaim this message of Christ. Because we do not want our Volk to once again surrender itself to an idol, and because we do not want our Volk to be thrown back into mere searching, questioning, and intuition when it could have certainty, clarity, and communion with God, we hold fast to Christ. Therefore, we say: The new German folk religion, which must arise for our newly reborn Volk, can be no other than a Christian one.

Thus, we strive for a German Christianity. The eternal element in Christianity is the message of Christ. Christianity is faith in the message of Christ and life lived from the message of Christ. This Christianity takes on different forms according to Volk and race.

There is a German Christianity alongside an Indian Christianity, a Chinese Christianity alongside an African Christianity, a Roman Christianity alongside a Nordic-Germanic Christianity.

Christianity can be brought into discredit by its representatives. And in our Volk, it has fallen into discredit. But the figure of Christ remains exalted above this. We want our Volk —newly awakened in race and national character—to encounter the holiest thing in the world: Christ. From this, a rebirth of Christianity arises.

Out of faith in the message of Christ, we struggle for the realization of a German Christianity, one that corresponds to the Nordic-Germanic nature (nordisch-germanischer Art).

Thesis 20:

We find this German Christianity embodied in Martin Luther. In Luther's Reformation, we see the breakthrough of a German faith in Christ. German Christianity means Lutheranism. As German Lutherans, we are fully German and fully Christian.

If we are asked for the name of this German Christianity, then we give its name: Martin Luther. Martin Luther is the German Christian. We know exactly that Luther's decisive act was that he rediscovered the pure, unadulterated Gospel of Christ, freeing it from all foreign Roman Catholic influence. The Reformation first and foremost means the restoration of the pure, unadulterated Gospel.

But we also know that Martin Luther, with this rediscovered Gospel, united it with the German nature (deutsche Art). Thus, he embodies in his person, in his faith, and in his life a German Christianity. It is no coincidence that the nations to which the

Reformation spread are, for the most part, nations of Germanic race. They found in Luther's Christianity the form of Christianity that corresponded to their own nature. For this reason, we see in Luther the German prophet, who gives the German Volk its faith. Lutheran Christianity is German Christianity. As German Lutherans, we are entirely people who carry and fulfill the German nature (deutsche Art). As Lutherans, we are also entirely people who receive, believe, and live the message of Christ in its purity. As German Lutherans, we are German Christians.

Thesis 21:

At present, many claims are being made about man that are deceptive. It is a deception to claim that man has no responsibility before God and therefore no guilt before Him. It is a deception to claim that man can, by his own strength, overcome fate and death. It is a deception to claim that man is capable of redeeming himself.

With the three words—guilt, fate, and death—the boundaries are marked that are set for all human life. No matter how appealing the deception may be that attributes all kinds of possibilities to man, it cannot remove the seriousness and reality of these limits. Human possibilities fail in the face of the reality of guilt, fate, and death.

When we speak of guilt, we do not mean merely what is commonly referred to as human imperfection, of which every person has a share. Rather, we mean the power of evil, which repeatedly takes hold of man and destroys communal life. This power of evil seizes the human heart and poisons his will and actions. Let us look into our lives as we truly live them! Let us look into the small circle of life in which we stand—into our homes and neighborhoods, among colleagues and wherever we interact with others—can we not see how selfishness, envy, hatred, and malice embitter life and diminish joy? And we ourselves are not without guilt in this!

Whoever stands seriously before his own life and does not shy away from a hard self-examination knows that life is not merely a matter of imperfection but of the power of evil that makes a person guilty. This guilt manifests toward other people in selfishness. It manifests toward God in the fact that we do not fear, love, and trust Him above all things, but instead love, fear, and trust in all things more than Him. This fact of guilt is not removed by a man forcing himself toward goodness through sheer willpower and discipline. The moral will of man can accomplish much, but in the end, it cannot overcome the power of evil, nor can it erase guilt once it has occurred. It is not the case that through moral striving we can undo what we have done wrong. Whoever has truly stood still before God in a moment of quiet and decisive self-examination feels that it is a deception to deny guilt or to believe he can remove guilt by his own means. Here, man encounters one of his limits.

The same is true of fate. A dark, unknown fate governs our lives. It is already evident in the way we come into the world. We had no part in it. No one can choose in which land, in which Volk, or in which family he is born. No one can choose the talents with which he enters life. Even our birth shows us the inescapability of fate. And when we look into life itself, when we consider all that we sum up with the single word chance, it becomes clear how we, as individuals and as a community—even as a national community (Volksgemeinschaft)—are subject to fate. The last twenty years have shown us this with unmistakable clarity. The shaping of life according to one's own will is met with insurmountable limits by the power of fate.

And the same is ultimately true of the reality of death. No man can overcome death. We, by our own means, have no possibility of immortality. What happens to us after death is, at first, entirely dark and uncertain. At most, we can speak of living on through our children. And no man can determine his own death. One person, with his head full of plans and his heart full of desires, has the thread of life cut short. Another, weary of life, stumbles through his days, wishing to cast it away, yet he must continue living. But the power of death compels us all, and we have no way against it. And even if we were able to push back the limits of life, we would not achieve a paradise populated by joyful people, but only a place where weary old men linger in exhaustion.

It is therefore a disastrous deception when it is claimed in our time that man is naturally good and that, for him, there is no real guilt, or that he can overcome this guilt on his own. It is a disastrous deception when it is promised—as is done by various representatives of the German Faith Movement—that, as a good man, he has the potential to overcome fate and death and transform the earth into a paradise. And it is a deception to claim that man can redeem himself from all the limitations that confine him. Even the most heroic shaping of life meets its limits in the realities of guilt, fate, and death.

Thesis 22:
The bondage of sin, the compulsion of fate, and the power of death are overcome only through faith in Jesus Christ. Through Him, we receive the forgiveness of guilt, communion with God, and eternal life.

With the three words—bondage of sin, compulsion of fate, and power of death—the boundary of human reality is marked, whether we wish to acknowledge it or not. Jesus Christ teaches us to recognize this. Our own conscience testifies to this truth. It is part of the joyful message (Frohbotschaft) that Jesus Christ brings us, that His life is the place in the world where the struggle began and where victory was won over sin, fate, and death.

We look into the life of Jesus as the Evangelists portray it. We see this Jesus engaged in battle against the power of evil and guilt, against the burden of fate and death. We see how He teaches people to recognize their guilt, how He speaks the word of forgiveness to them, and how He frees them from every compulsion of guilt. This is what Luther called justification by faith alone. It means that we receive liberation from guilt only through Jesus Christ.

We see how He takes up the struggle against dark and oppressive fate, how He brings help and deliverance to people, and how He leads them through all the power of fate to the Father. In the communion with God and the divine sonship that we receive through Jesus Christ, we recognize that, in the end, we are not ruled by blind chance or oppressive fate, but that the Fatherly goodness of God guides us. He has determined eternal and mysterious purposes for mankind and leads man along his rightful path. In this communion with God and this divine sonship, we become certain of God's help, and we find joy in walking our path, even through dark hours. We know ourselves to be secure in God's hand.

And we see how Jesus Christ takes up the battle against the power of death, and how before Him, death is shattered. What we see in the life of Jesus is not a one-time event. Rather, the word applies: I am with you always, to the end of the world. The Jesus Christ who is invisibly present with us continues this struggle—

for us and with us—to give us, through His word and His Spirit, the forgiveness of guilt, communion with God, and eternal life.

Thus, we are entirely dependent on Him, who reconciles us with God and delivers us from all the power of guilt, fate, and death. This is what it means when we confess, even in the Third Reich: There is salvation in no one else.

Thesis 23:
This is not a degradation of man but a sober assessment of him. His nobility is the communion with God that is newly granted to him through Jesus Christ.

Against this Christian proclamation, it is often objected that it degrades man. It has been said that Christian preaching speaks of fallen man, while others attempt to contrast this with an exalted man—one who is good and possesses all possibilities within himself. However, Christian preaching does not degrade man— whoever claims this is lying—but rather presents a completely sober view of reality. It is not acceptable for us to indulge in any illusions about the reality of man.

Man, as a creature of God, has been endowed with the greatest potential in his reason, in his will, and in his spirit. Man is God's creature and, as God's creature, the crown of creation. As the crown of creation, he has been given the promise to subdue the earth and rule over it. That is why the Bible says of man: "You have made him a little lower than God."

But man misuses these potentials, and they are therefore limited by guilt, fate, and death. His final and true nobility is given to him through Jesus Christ. This final and true nobility of man consists in the fact that he may be called a child of God—a son or daughter of God. In this, Jesus Christ completes God's work in us, in that He shares with us His own unique name: Son of God. That is why John says: "See what love the Father has given us, that we should be called children of God."

In divine sonship, we receive a special communion with God and security in God, which leads us into eternal life. This nobility of communion with God, this nobility of the calling to eternity, does not come from man himself. He receives this nobility solely through Jesus Christ.

Thesis 24:
This is the Christian message of salvation, which all people of all times and nations need. Salvation is firmly founded in the cross and resurrection of Jesus.

It is self-evident that all people of all times and nations need this message of salvation. For what we have designated as guilt, fate, and death are the boundaries set for all human life. This is why this Christian message of salvation is a message to the entire world. The decisive element of this Christian message of salvation, however, is the word of the cross and resurrection. Without this word of the cross and resurrection of Jesus, the entire message of salvation would hang in the air without a firm foundation. Only the cross and resurrection together constitute the true victory over guilt, fate, and death.

In our time, we are once again gaining a new understanding of this. As National Socialists, we bear the hooked-cross (hakenkreuz)[50]. The hooked-cross is a sign of sacrifice, which

---

50 Commonly called the "swastika" today.—Editor.

makes the cross of Christ shine before us in a new light. Under the hooked-cross, we have learned that all true, new, and powerful life exists only through sacrifice and can only arise from sacrifice. We think of the two million fallen of the World War. Through their blood, our fallen brothers protected our land, our homeland, and our lives. Through their sacrifice, it was possible for German women to remain unviolated, to become mothers, and to bring children into the world. The greatest distress of the postwar period was that these sacrifices seemed to have been in vain.

We understand Adolf Hitler best when we grasp his will as driven by a fanatical determination to strike out the word in vain that seemed to be written over the sacrifice of the two million. This was the meaning of the sacrificial struggle led by Horst Wessel and his brown battalions. The Third Reich of our Führer stands on sacrifice and lives from the sacrifice of our fallen brothers. In this, we have come to recognize the law of sacrifice that pervades the entire reality of life: new life can only arise from the sacrifice of the best life. This law of sacrifice applies even to the beginning of life itself. No child is brought into the world unless its mother is willing to risk her life for it. All sacrifice carries within it the idea of substitution. The meaning of sacrifice is substitution.

Our fallen brothers of the war and postwar period died for their Volk, for their women, children, and parents. A mother risks her life for her child so that she may give it life.

This law of sacrifice finds its ultimate and greatest fulfillment in the cross of Christ. The cross of Christ, together with the resurrection, completes Christ's victory over sin, Satan, and death. At His cross, all the power of the most terrible human guilt rises up. Johann Sebastian Bach expresses this beautifully in his St. Matthew Passion, where a gentle voice answers Pilate's question, What evil has He done? with the words: "He has done us all good." The One who did good to all suffers the most terrible suffering. But this rising guilt collapses under His words: "Father, forgive them, for they know not what they do." At His cross, all the power of the most terrible, darkest fate is revealed. Seemingly meaningless suffering befalls Him, who desired only good. And yet, even this power of fate is broken, as He reaches through it and entrusts Himself into the hands of God: "Father, into Your hands I commit my spirit." And at this cross, the final and terrible power of death rages, seeking to take life from Christ, who came from God's eternity. But death itself is shattered beneath His sovereign word, in which the dawn of Easter already shines: "It is finished." The meaning of this sacrifice of Christ is substitution. For us, He overcame guilt. For us, He broke fate. For us, He crushed death. What is impossible for any man, He made possible.

Just as we have received new national life from the sacrifice of our fallen, and just as we owe our earthly lives to the willingness of our mothers to give themselves for us, so too do we receive from the sacrifice of Christ on the cross our calling to eternal life —and with it, eternal meaning and purpose for our lives. We are secure in God's hands and, through this sacrifice of the cross, receive bold and steadfast trust in God's guidance and Fatherly goodness. Christian faith in the cross is not a matter for superficial people, but only reveals its full depth to those who know the dark sides of life, who know suffering, who know guilt, fate, and death. Christian faith in the cross is a matter for mature people. For them, it also makes possible a truly heroic shaping of life—one that draws its strength from Christ's victory over guilt, fate, and death. The image of the Crucified One does not, as some have claimed, show the collapse of all human strength, rendering man incapable of life. Rather, it shows us Christ, who deliberately takes upon Himself suffering, who actively shapes His suffering, and who willingly submits to the will of God. It shows us Christ, who in His suffering steps onto the battlefield against the powers of guilt, fate, and death. "This was a strange battle, where death and life struggled." It shows us Christ, who allows these powers to rage against Him and, through suffering—this is the meaning of the much-maligned image of the Lamb—becomes Lord over them, as Easter reveals. Thus, the message of the cross forms the firm foundation of Christian faith, for over this event stands the word: For us!

Thesis 25:
This proclamation, which takes both the true God and the true man seriously in equal measure, prevents the return of materialism and liberalism by way of religion.

For the national and state-building efforts of the Third Reich, the resolution of the religious question of the German Volk cannot be a matter of indifference. The resolution of the religious question shapes and determines human action. What a person wills, what a person thinks, and how a person acts depend decisively on how he responds to the questions of guilt, fate, and death.

Only true liberation from the power of guilt, fate, and death gives man the ability to truly dedicate his life to service and sacrifice for others. Fear of fate and dread of death on one side, and indulgence and selfishness on the other, are inseparably linked. For this reason, the Christian proclamation renders a great service to the moral forces of duty and willpower, as well as to the national and state-building efforts, because it binds man to the will of God, who desires his salvation and frees him from the bondage of guilt, the fear of fate, and the terror of death.

Liberalism and materialism were the forces that threatened to destroy our German Volk. Liberalism and materialism arise wherever people separate themselves from God. Only in Christian faith in God is there a true overcoming of liberalism and materialism.

Thesis 26:
Faith in Christ that does not lead to action is worthless in a People's Church (Volkskirche). The action of faith in Christ is the resolute struggle against all evil and the courageous determination for service and sacrifice.

Only faith in Christ that becomes action is true and living faith in Christ. The action that arises from faith in Christ consists in awakening moral strength for service and sacrifice. On one side, Christian action turns against all evil in the world—against godlessness and hypocrisy, against injustice and falsehood, against disloyalty and impurity. On the other side, it is the power of love, which dedicates life and sacrifices comfort in service to one's neighbor.

And the neighbor who is given to us, particularly in the experience of National Socialism, is above all the German national comrade (Volksgenosse), regardless of class or education. Christian action within the Volk means resistance to all nation-destroying forces and the awakening of the deepest strength of every true national community (Volksgenossenschaft) —through service, sacrifice, and love.

It is the particular task of German Christians to live out a truly active Christianity (Tatchristentum) from a living faith in Christ. Certainly, this active Christianity does not create salvation for us. We receive salvation solely as a gift from Jesus Christ. But it is just as certain that the gift of Jesus Christ is worthless and fruitless for us—and is therefore taken from us—if it does not compel us to action.

Thesis 27:

For this reason, the People's Church (Volkskirche) understands positive Christianity (positives Christentum)—as referenced in Point 24 of the Party Program—to mean: Faith in Christ, Redemption through Christ, and Action from Christ.

The National Socialist movement declares that it stands on the foundation of positive Christianity. It now asks the churches, as the representatives of positive Christianity, what this positive Christianity actually is. Our 28 Theses seek to provide an answer to this question. The German Evangelical People's Church (Volkskirche) confesses: Positive Christianity means faith in the Lord Christ, who, as the image of God and the Word of God, reveals the true God to us. It means redemption through the Lord Christ, who frees us from the burden of guilt, leads us from the power of fate into security in God's Fatherly goodness, and calls us from the destiny of death into eternal life. It means action from the Lord Christ, who awakens in us the militant strength to resist all forces of evil and gives us the spirit of love and service, just as He Himself carried it within Him.

Thesis 28:

This German Christianity forms the only foundation upon which German people can also find unity in faith.

Our German Volk has achieved unity—across classes, ranks, and interests—through the experience of blood and national character. A common goal stands before all Germans: Germany's freedom and honor. And a common will stirs in all German hearts: to be one Volk, in which every single national comrade (Volksgenosse) is given work and bread, and in which all the good forces that the Creator has placed within our Volk are awakened.

Thus, we have become united in the struggle for freedom and honor, for work and bread, for national community (Volksgenossenschaft) and for the prestige of the German name. Yet unity in faith—the final and deepest unity—remains unrealized. The religious question of the Third Reich is still unresolved. Religious groups and sects, different interpretations of Christianity, struggle and contend with one another. Before us stands a radiant goal, which alone will complete Germany's unity: the goal of a German Christian Church, in which even confessional differences are overcome. This goal is only attainable by establishing a foundation on which German people can also find unity in faith. There is no resolution to the religious question of the Third Reich without the living, eternally present Christ. The resolution of this question can therefore only take place on the basis of Christianity—specifically, a German Christianity.

The 28 Theses seek to contribute to establishing this foundation for the unity of faith within the German Volk. They are a beginning. Before us stands the radiant goal: One Volk, one Reich, one Faith, one Church.

For the birth of a new faith in Christ, for the birth of the People's Church (Volkskirche), for the birth of a German community of faith, we pray—knowing that without this prayer, all church work and all struggle would be in vain: Come, Creator Spirit!

Addendum: The Struggling Church

The unity of the German Volk has been achieved. In his time, Bismarck created the Reich across the various lands and tribes, but from the very beginning, it carried within it the seed of dissolution—liberalism and Marxism. In contrast, the Chancellor of the Volk has now given this Reich its Volk. He is in the process of raising up the Third Reich with this new Volk. Through race and national character, the German Volk has renewed and united itself in the miracle of becoming a Volk, as it heard the voice of the Führer given by God and stood unanimously behind this Führer. If the construction of the Third Reich is to succeed and if the German Volk is to have a historical future, then this unity of the Volk must be preserved at all costs. It was first forged within the National Socialist Movement and has now been extended to the Volk as a whole. As the bearer of the awakened and united Volk, our National Socialist Movement has the single task of preserving, strengthening, and realizing the unity of the Volk. This is made unmistakably clear in Alfred Rosenberg's speech of February 22, 1934, which is of decisive and far-reaching significance for the entire spiritual and religious condition of the German Volk. In this speech, we first recognize the earnest will to preserve the unity of the German Volk at all costs. But at the same time, another realization speaks from it: The future task is to reshape the inner disposition of the German person—his character—toward the goal of national unity. From this renewed national character, a new cultural and national life is meant to arise.

There is no doubt that this shaping of the German character will be the final step toward the complete unity of the German Volk. This brings us to the religious question. The German Volk is religiously divided as never before. Alongside the two major confessions, which themselves are filled with internal disputes and struggles, there arises a movement that explicitly calls itself un-Christian and pagan—the German Faith Movement, which has been consolidated into a single working group. Yet even this movement is united only in its rejection of Christianity and is otherwise fragmented into various factions. Those who observe these movements closely know how they even fight against each other. Added to this are numerous domestic and foreign sects, each of which claims to offer a different path to salvation. This religious division poses a great danger to the hard-won unity of the Volk. As Alfred Rosenberg explained, the formation of a new German character is linked to a struggle over values. Whatever the German person comes to recognize in the future as the highest value of life will ultimately prevail, drawing the new German person like a magnet, thus bringing about the final unity of the German Volk. However, this struggle over values—this struggle for the final unity of faith within the Volk—cannot and must not take place in the Third Reich on any other foundation than that of a Volk united by blood and soil, national character, and race. Only those who stand on this foundation have the right to struggle for the soul of the German Volk, which has been awakened to life.

For us National Socialists, who earnestly wish to be Christians, this sets our path for the future. We must unite into a struggling community, into a fighting church. Anyone who believed that a new church could be created cheaply on the back of a political movement and on the foundation of a political revolution has deceived himself. These vain hopes have been shattered by the Lord of History. The unity of faith within the German Volk must develop according to its own laws. Our goal stands firm before us as a great and shining vision: The Volk united by blood and soil must become a praying community— meaning a Volk united in faith. This unity can only be realized on the foundation of a German Christianity. We German Christians are the bearers of German Christianity.

As German people, we are deeply overcome by the mystery of God revealed in Jesus Christ. We know that within man, there exists a longing for the fulfillment of life, for connection with God. We know that this longing, driven by a sense of God, takes various forms. But we have just as surely experienced that there is no certainty of the true, living God unless He encounters us and overcomes us. Every thought of God that we create for ourselves gives us no certainty. Jesus Christ, who says of Himself: "I am with you always, to the end of the world,"—is the One in whom God once met mankind—and in whom He still meets us today and forever. Thus, through faith in Jesus Christ, we receive certainty of God, and at the same time, we receive eternal security in God's hand. Whoever has encountered the Lord Christ knows that He bestows a peace and a joy in which all guilt is dissolved—a peace and a joy that no blow of fate and no power of death can take from us. This Jesus Christ alone is the victor over guilt, over fate, over death, and He has won this victory for us as well. In faith, we stand on the side of the victor.

We also know that faith in Jesus Christ takes on different forms according to national character and race. German Christianity is different from the Christianity of the Englishman, the Frenchman, the African, or the Chinese. They all share the same message of Christ, but they live out this message in accordance with their own nature. Thus, it is justified to speak of a faith in Christ appropriate to one's nature. What German nature is, we see symbolically before us in the figure of Siegfried. In Siegfried, as in the other heroic figures of the German Volk, we have before us the warrior-heroic man with a childlike spirit. It was from this nature that Luther's piety was shaped. It embodies both the defiant strength of a man, as it lives in the hymn A Mighty Fortress Is Our God and as it is alive in his entire character. And it embodies the childlike nature of trusting devotion to the Father, as he expresses it in his explanation of the Lord's Prayer: "God wants to entice us with this, so that we believe that He is our true Father and we are His true children, so that we may ask Him with complete confidence and certainty, just as dear children ask their dear father." German Christianity is thus built upon the encounter of German nature with the Savior Jesus Christ. With this, the goal of the struggling church is also defined. In this encounter, the final decision over the destiny of Germany is made.

It is now a question of aligning this struggling church in the right way. We German Christians are the bearers of the struggling church. We first need congregations that gather around the most sacred, so that there may be an encounter between the Lord Christ and the German nature from which we live. We German Christians are establishing in our church congregations a piece of Christian community order. The ceremonial gatherings that we have begun throughout our land and wish to expand further are meant to serve this purpose. The attendance of church services, to which we commit ourselves regularly, is meant to serve this purpose. Luther identified the essential element of worship as the interaction between man and God, in which man speaks to God through prayer and hymn, and God speaks to man through His Word and the sermon. Likewise, however, we also need instructive deepening. Our study evenings are meant to lead us into the struggles, questions, and seeking of our time. We want to gain clarity through them and find the ways to bear witness to the Lord Christ in the right way for our German nature. We establish a firm order of service, knowing that through it we are united as a fighting company. The German Christians have the great task that will decide the destiny of Germany: to struggle so that Christ encounters the soul of the German Volk. This struggle concerns every single German national comrade (Volksgenosse). Only those who submit to this order of service are truly German Christians.

A real Christian community order, in which the struggling church aligns itself for its battle, must be built on a Christian household order. The Christian home is, in a sense, the cell that must be formed and from which new strength flows into the struggling church. We German Christians commit ourselves to a Christian household order. A Christian household order means that the father of the family gathers his household—including servants, farmhands, and maids—for regular daily devotions. This household devotion must connect us daily with the most sacred —with the Lord Christ—so that we may live daily from His Word, from His strength, from His joy, from His peace. A Christian household order also requires that we do not begin the day without looking up to Him, thanking Him for protection through the night, and asking Him for blessing over the day. It requires that we do not end the day without bringing everything that the day has brought us before His holy presence. It requires that we receive our daily bread as His gift from His hand, knowing that it is He who provides it. We German Christians commit ourselves to such a Christian household order. This Christian household order does not stand apart from the community order, but rather it is the cell from which the community order is formed. That is why the Christian home must always participate in the celebrations and service of the congregation.

Only from such a Christian household and community order can a true German Christian national order grow. That order will exist when the nation understands that our German nature is God's gift, and when the nation places itself under God's command: We shall fear and love God so that we gratefully receive our German nature from His hand, preserve it in purity and authenticity, and live from it. That order will exist when the German Volk, in its sacred celebrations, remembers the eternal God, who gives us our nature and gathers us into His eternal community through Jesus Christ, calling us into His eternal Kingdom. Only in this German Christian national order, which emerges from a German Christianity, can the German Volk truly unite as a Christian Volk. Thus, the struggling church aligns itself. Thus, it struggles toward its goal.

We summarize what has been said:

1. The renewal of the German Volk and its unity through race and national character has been achieved. The struggle for the formation of the German character now begins.

2. The German Church of Jesus Christ, whose bearers we German Christians will be in the future, is called to be a struggling church. As a struggling church, it strives for the

encounter between the soul of the German Volk and the Lord Christ.

3. Only a German Christianity can form the foundation for a unity of faith within the German Volk. This Christianity knows of Jesus Christ, who reveals the eternal Father to our search for God and secures us in God's hand through His coming into the world, through His life, suffering, and resurrection. As German people, we encounter this Christ in a German way.

4. The destiny of Germany depends on this encounter between the soul of the German Volk and the Lord Christ.

5. We German Christians commit ourselves to a Christian community order. We seek to deepen our connection with the Lord Christ, who desires to meet our German nature, through regular church attendance, sacred gatherings, and study efforts. We commit ourselves to a Christian order of service, as followers of Jesus Christ, by helping our German national comrades encounter Christ.

6. We German Christians commit ourselves to a Christian household order, building it upon house devotions and regular prayers in the morning, evening, and at mealtimes.

7. We struggle for the formation of a German Christian national order, through which our Volk finds its path into God's eternal community and becomes a Volk that sets its eyes upon God.

Other books currently available from Sacra Press:

A Treatise of Christian Religion
by Thomas Cartwright
Father of the Puritans & of Presbyterianism displays the full jewels of a systematic theology in a catechetical format. Newly republished for the first time in centuries.

The Old Faith
by Henry Bullinger
Titanic Swiss Reformer weaves a mixed work of biblical & covenant theology, born of pastoral concerns, to prove the antiquity of the Christian Faith.

Lectures On Human Nature
by Samuel Doak
18th century American Presbyterian, church-planter, and school teacher keenly pens an introductory philosophy of human nature. Includes his sermon to the Overmountain Men just before their victory at King's Mountain.

A Precept for the Baptism of Infants
by Nathaniel Stephens
17th century non-conformist Minister proves the precept of paedobaptism from the New Testament in response to the objection of anti-paedobaptists.

The Cambridge & Saybrook Platforms
by Miscellaneous Ministers
New England Congregationalists inscribe their polity.

Books now or soon-to-be-published by Sacra Press:

Christian Race Realism
by Michael Spangler
Drawing on nature, Scripture, history, and experience, Spangler defines, defends, and applies race realism from a Christian perspective.

On the First Sin of Adam
by Franciscus Junius
French Protestant Reformer and theologian explores Adam's first sin and its relation to God's foreknowledge and decree, necessity, and free will.

On the Establishment of the Republic
by Francesco Patrizi
Roman Catholic bishop and key Renaissance philosopher of the 15th century marshals myriad classical sources to construct a timeless treatise of virtue-politics.

The Christian Obligations of Citizenship
by John G. Sheppard
19th century Anglican academic exploits logic, rhetoric, history, classical sources, and Scripture to construct his Christian political theory.

The Concept of Economic and Political Doctrine
by Franco Burgersdijk
17th century Dutch Reformed scholar and philosopher parses through economics (household life) and politics with clarity, brevity, and precision. Classic intro to reformed political theory.

With many more books to come—Lord willing.

Visit www.sacrapress.com/armory to purchase available books, to stay updated on releases, to become a sponsor, to donate, and more.

www.ingramcontent.com/pod-product-compliance
Lightning Source LLC
Chambersburg PA
CBHW022042020426
42335CB00012B/507